CHICANO Manifesto

CHICANO
Manifesto

Armando B. Rendon

The Macmillan Company, New York, New York

Collier-Macmillan Ltd., London

The Macmillan Company
866 Third Avenue, New York, N.Y. 10022
Collier-Macmillan Canada Ltd., Toronto, Ontario

Library of Congress Catalog Card Number: 76-143782

First Printing

Printed in the United States of America

To Helen, Mark, Gabrielene, Paul, John
and
In memory of Ruben Salazar,
friend and colleague

Contents

CHICANO
Manifesto

Introduction

Exactly when the Mexican American people became a revolutionary force in this country will be fixed at various times by different observers:

The rally protesting the ouster of VISTA workers in Del Rio, March 1969;

The student walkouts in East Los Angeles, March 1968;

The La Raza Unida conference in El Paso, October 1967;

The courthouse raid by the Alianza Federal de Pueblos Libres in northern New Mexico, June 1967;

The founding of the Crusade for Justice, growing out of a protest against the tactics of the administration of the city of Denver, April 1966;

The "guarache-out" by fifty Chicanos at the Equal Employment Opportunity Commission workshop in Albuquerque, March 1966; and

The strike of grape pickers in Delano, California, which began in September 1965—

All are landmark events.

The violence that occurred in East Los Angeles on August 29, 1970, communicated on a national level and in no uncertain terms that the Chicano was nei-

1

ther docile nor subservient. That short-lived eruption against police oppression was only a prologue to future conflicts.

In retrospect the Delano strike ranks first. It had a specific objective, and it continues to grow in importance as a starting date. The other events had their own purposes, and each was different in nature and methods from the others. No connection between the events is apparent—they were seemingly spontaneous and unrelated. Yet all of these historic moments had certain goals in common. Their diversity indicates only that the Chicano revolt is being acted out on many levels. In that each incident involved its own particular leaders, the various kinds and numbers of leadership within the Chicano community become apparent.

The August 29 incident, however, was not a positive, premeditated effort. It was, essentially, an outburst of anger and frustration, a reaction to a police riot. It was the largest and most destructive of any police-barrio confrontation to date. It was probably not the last. But because of its ultimately self-destructive nature, such an act, however justified, must be considered outside of constructive, sane Chicano activism. It was a symptom rather than a problem or a remedy. Because death intervened tragically for three Chicanos, the outrage becomes even more futile. We Chicanos know the police and sheriff's deputies are the murderers of raza and that they merely use "riot" situations to harass and destroy our people. We have made every effort to withhold such occasions for genocide from the agents of the law, yet they make it increasingly difficult for Chicanos to work peacefully; they make rioting almost inevitable.

Some Chicanos, as well as the nonraza public, may think that the Chicano's course toward revolution was begun on August 29, 1970. That would be a betrayal of history and of our forefathers' memory. It is closer to the truth to say that there has always been a Chicano revolt. That is, the Mexican American, the Chicano, as he calls himself and his carnales, brother and sister Chicanos, has never ceased to be a revolutionary all the while he has suffered repression. Even though our bodies have been in bondage, our expectations of a better life, if only for our children, have enabled us to survive in spite of the gringo tyranny.

That ingrained rebelliousness has been prefigured by the Mexican rebels who fought against a repressive Mexican Government in the early 1800s shortly after Father Hidalgo had raised el Grito de Dolores (the Cry for Independence); by Joaquín Murieta and Tiburcio Vasquez, who sought to avenge the mexicanos driven off their claims by gold rush gringos; by Governor José Martínez and Elfego Baca of New Mexico's early history; by Juan Cortina's attempt to liberate the Rio Grande Valley between 1860 and 1875; and by the hundreds of farm-labor and mining strikes in which Chicanos have played a major role for many decades.

The Mexican American, it should be recalled, is a fusion of two revolutionary wellsprings (the United States and Mexico, both born in rebellion against Old World despotism), with a Mexican Indian people who had developed one of the most highly civilized and complex cultures of the Western Hemisphere.

It should surprise no one that Chicanos have become increasingly aggressive in asserting their rights and an identity symbolized by cries of Viva la raza! Viva la causa! and by the concepts of Chicanismo, el Quinto Sol, and by the psychological as well as the seminal birthplace of Aztlán.

The assigning of a specific starting date for this phenomenon is not particularly essential and leads only to needless haranguing, with which later historians can fill their books, if they wish. What is essential to recognize and understand is that a revolution is now in progress in the Southwest. It has a Spanish accent, it oper-

ates through some unique methods. and it poses some
rather new problems for the Anglo-dominant society. The
revolution reaches into many states outside the Southwest, involving the lives and futures of perhaps six
million Mexican American people today, and some fifteen million by the year 2000.

The Chicano revolt strikes at the myths of Anglo
supremacy, discards the Anglo-or-nothing value system,
and seeks the creation of a meaningful and sensitive balance between the dominant Anglo way of existence and
the Chicano way of life.

Unlike the efforts of the Negro people in America
—who in past decades sought equality of treatment
and opportunity in an Anglo-dominated world on the
Anglo's terms and only recently sought anew a black
identity and cultural separateness—the Chicano from
the earliest phases of his uprising in the 1960s has
sought equality and respect for his way of life, for his
culture, and for his language.

The Chicano perceives that he cannot be a whole
man if he forfeits these birthrights for the Anglo pot
of atole (porridge) euphemistically called equality. He
knows that the dominant society has sought to castrate
him (cortarle los huevos) culturally and psychologically
by offering him social and economic success if he only
eschews his heritage, his Chicanismo. This the true Chicano refuses to do; the price is too high.

The Chicano believes that he can contribute something extra to the society. Despite Anglo attempts at destroying the Chicano culture, the Chicano believes that
society must meet him at least halfway and acknowledge
the peculiar value and depth of heritage that is his. The
Anglo should be aware of the Chicano's unique ties to the
land and of his living language and cultural dimension,
which date back centuries, unbroken. The Anglo should
realize that the Mexican American recalls firsthand or
from his elders a bloody revolution within this cen-

tury by which the dictatorship of landholders, industrialists, and militarists was overthrown.

The Anglo should realize that the loyalty the Chicano nurtures for a language, a culture, and a history
that on the surface seem to pertain to a foreign land
is not disloyalty to this nation but rather a special
bond to the land, another source of inspiration and a
channel of communication with the brown peoples of
the world. It is this mixed heritage that has thrust the
Chicano into a nationwide movement, a national search,
individual by individual, to reassess our role as Mexican
Americans and to achieve fully the guarantees of the
United States Constitution and the Treaty of Guadalupe
Hidalgo. By and large, this thrust is being carried forward by the people who have profited the least from the
rights, benefits, and responsibilities of citizenship.

There has been some physical violence by Chicanos; there have been many displays of anger and
frustration in demonstrations and walkouts. The Chicano has been accused of being Communist, of moving too fast, of not representing the real Mexican Americans, and of practicing racism in reverse. If more demonstrations do occur, if greater violence does erupt—or
worse, planned insurrection—if a people becomes alien-
ated to the point of seeking by force a separate state,
Anglo America will have only herself to blame and the
most to lose from the conflict that will ensue.

The current revolt of Chicanos against the Anglo
system of life and thought is essentially a prophetic
statement of purpose. We Chicanos are convinced that
it is our destiny to carry out a major role in the coming
decades, not only in the United States but in all the
Americas. Los Chicanos hope to participate in the creation of a new world. Few, if any, Chicanos hope personally to enjoy that future. Nevertheless, with the promise
of a new day for our children in mind and heart, we
strive to bring the tomorrows of social and economic

equality, of creative and intellectual opportunity, closer to today.

The making of a new world of the Americas—that is the essence of the living manifesto which los Chicanos are writing in action and word everyday. It is my hope that this book may add to that document of my people.

—Armando B. Rendon

1

THE PEOPLE OF AZTLÁN

WE ARE the people of Aztlán, true descendants of the Fifth Sun, el Quinto Sol.

In the early morning light of a day thousands of years old now, my forebears set out from Aztlán, a region of deserts, mountains, rivers, and forests, to seek a new home. Where they came from originally is hidden in the sands and riverbeds and only hinted at by the cast of eye and skin which we, their sons, now bear.

Driven by drought, or enemies, or by the vision of a new motherland, my people began walking toward the south in the hope of founding a new world. Among the earliest of my ancestors were the Nahúas, from whom sprang the most advanced and sophisticated peoples of the North American continent. They made their own wandering journey to Anáhuac, as the region of the Valley of Mexico was then known. From about the time that the Christ Passion was unfolding on the other side of the world, and for perhaps a thousand years afterward, a way of life and thought was evolving which the man-god Quetzalcoatl had forged and which the Nahúas, the Toltecs, the Chichimecas, and then the Aztecs nurtured through the centuries.

7

The Toltecs forged Teotihuacán, the City of the Gods and the center of the Nahuatl religion. Their influence continued for fifteen hundred years, until the arrival of Hernando Cortez, the final inroad of a searching people that was to spell the end of a great, involuted civilization.

The Chichimeca, nomadic tribes who, tradition tells us came from the North, from Aztlán, or what is now the southwestern part of the United States, began moving down by ancient trails into the Valley of Mexico in about the eleventh century A.D. The Aztecs, who derive their name from Aztlán, were the last significant group to arrive in Anáhuac. Those that survived this exodus came among shallow marshes by a lake and in 1325 founded the city of Tenochtitlán. It was there in the marsh waters that they saw a sign, an eagle grasping a serpent in its claw as it perched upon a cactus sprouting from a rock. Tenochtitlán means cactus upon a stone.

Quetzalcoatl gave birth in his people to the Fifth Sun. Four Suns prefigured the coming of el Quinto Sol, which was to destroy and subsume the rest. The Fifth Sun was the epoch of the Aztec civilization. Huitzilopochtli, who led the Aztecs out of Aztlán, personifies this Fifth Sun, but Quetzalcoatl (historically identified with Topiltzin, the last Toltec king, who reigned in the late tenth century) is the creator of the epoch and its spirit. Earth, air, fire, and water preceded the fifth epoch; the Fifth Sun was movement, progress, life vibrant. The people of the Fifth Sun developed a complex system of religion in a region that was to be New Spain, Mexico, and much of present Central America. They developed an elaborate symbolic language to depict their beliefs. To convey the concept of the Fifth Sun a basic pattern was used of five circles, one circle at each of four corners, with the fifth in the center. An intricate refinement is seen in a circular network of human features incorporating the five-circle mode; the great Aztec calendar stone is a huge representation of this principle. (Laurette Séjourné in her book *Burning Water* provides an invaluable description and interpretation of the religion and language of our ancient forebears.)

Discovering the spiritual sensitivity and depth of the people of the Fifth Sun, the Chicano begins to fathom what must be one of the most psychologically important elements in the make-up of the Mexican. Octavio Paz, the Mexican poet and former ambassador to India, comments in *The Labyrinth of Solitude* that the Aztec religion was notable for its generally being a "superimposition" on older beliefs (the Nahuatl religion was so infused with various primitive ideas and superstitions that the Aztec version suggested a predisposition to Catholicism and its ally, Spanish rule). Paz says unequivocally, "The Mexican is a religious being and his experience of the divine is completely genuine. . . . Nothing has been able to destroy the filial relationship of our people with the divine."

The spiritual experience of the Chicano, in turn, is profound. From the standpoint of the people of Ollin Tonatiuh, the Nahuatl name for the Fifth Sun, the Chicano's religious experience embodies all of nature. The epic of the Four Suns begins with the Sun of Night or Earth, depicted by a tiger, a period that by itself is sterile; then the Sun of Air, or God of Wind, pure spirit whose indwellers became monkeys; the Sun of Rain or Fire, in which only birds survive; and finally the Sun of Water, friendly only to fish.

The Fifth Sun is born out of man's sacrifice. At its center is the spirit; its mode is movement. It is the unity, cohesion, synthesis of all that has come before, bound into the human soul. Thus, the Fifth Sun is the very foundation of life, of spirituality, not in the re-stricted sense of an organized religion but in the nature of a common bond among all soul creatures. We can speak, therefore, of a union with the cosmos, of a cosmic sense of spirit, of an alma Chicana (a Chicano soul). The concept of La Raza Unida is a further reassertion and profession of that principle of a cosmic Chicano existence. We can think of ourselves as a community of the future and of the past seeking its destiny in the present.

My people have come in fulfillment of a cosmic cycle from ancient Aztlán, the seed ground of the great civilizations of Anáhuac, to modern Aztlán, characterized by the progeny of our Indian, Mexican, and Spanish ancestors. We have rediscovered Aztlán in ourselves. This knowledge provides the dynamic principle upon which to build a deep unity and brotherhood among Chicanos. Ties much more profound than even language, birthplace, or culture bind us together—Aztlán represents that unifying force of our nonmaterial heritage. This is not meant to revive long-dead religions, but rather to resurrect still-living principles of brotherhood (carnalismo), of spiritual union, which we have come so close to losing.

A statement composed in March 1969 in Denver, Colorado, during a Chicano youth conference sponsored by the Crusade for Justice, elaborated for the first time the concept of Aztlán. Notably, a young Chicano writer and poet, Alberto Alurista, proposed Aztlán as the fundamental theme, and this inspired a new awareness of self-concept and intent among Chicanos. In brief, the Spiritual Plan of Aztlán (see p. 336) asserts:

In the spirit of a new people . . . *we*, the Chicano, inhabitants and civilizers of the northern land of Aztlán, from whence came our forefathers, reclaiming the land of their birth and consecrating the determination of our people of the sun, *declare* that the call of our blood is our power, our responsibility, and our inevitable destiny. . . .

With our heart in our hand and our hands in the soil, we declare the independence of our mestizo Nation. We are a bronze people with a bronze culture. Before the world, before all of North America, before all our brothers in the Bronze Continent, we are a Nation. We are a union of free pueblos. We are *Aztlán*.

References to Aztlán as the place of origin of the Mexican Indian peoples are negligible in North American chronicles. Two of the most easily attainable texts by historians in the United States are William H. Prescott's *History of the Conquest of Mexico* (1843) and Alvin M. Josephy, Jr.'s *The Indian Heritage of America* (1968). Prescott, in reviewing the various histories, compiled for the most part by priest-scholars, noted that "The ingenuity of the chronicler was taxed to find out analogies between the Aztec and Scripture histories, both old and new. The emigration from Aztlan to Anahuac was typical of the Jewish exodus." This suggests the legend that the American peoples were derived from one of the lost tribes of Israel. Commenting on another possible source, Prescott wrote:

The theory of an Asiatic origin for Aztec civilization derives stronger confirmation from the light of *tradition*, which, shining steadily from the far North-west, pierces through the dark shadows that history and mythology have alike thrown around the antiquities of the country. Traditions of a Western, or North-western origin were found among the more barbarous tribes, and by the Mexicans were preserved both orally and in their hieroglyphical maps, where the different stages of their migration are carefully noted. But who at this day shall read them? They are admitted to agree, however, in representing the populous North as the prolific hive of the American races. In this quarter were placed their Aztlan and their Huehuetlapallan, the bright abodes of their ancestors. . . .

In a footnote, he said of the maps: "But as they are all within the boundaries of New Spain, indeed, south of the Rio Gila, they throw little light, of course, on the vexed question of the primitive abodes of the Aztecs."

It so happens that the Rio Gila flows from southwestern New Mexico, starting a few miles west of where the Rio Grande cuts through the center of New Mexico before it forms a border between Texas and Mexico. From there, the Gila connects with the Colorado River at the junction of California, Nevada, Arizona, and Sonora, Mexico, just above the Gulf of California—a convergence of rivers and cultures as significant for the

Americas as the confluence of the Tigris and Euphrates in Mesopotamia! Yet Prescott would have us seek a more distant source.

In a comprehensive study of the Indians of the Americas, Josephy recounts the arrival of the Mexica, a Nahuatl-speaking tribe, "weak and relatively primitive," in the Lake Texcoco area in the early thirteenth century, and their settling on the site of today's Mexico City. The historian says that the Mexica took the name Aztec from Aztlán, whence they had come, "somewhere vaguely to the Northwest and may even have been in the present-day United States Southwest."

An analysis and compendium by Mexican historians of the ancient native peoples, *México a Traves de los Siglos* (1939), relates, according to its editors, "the pilgrimage of the Mexicans from the time they left Aztlán until they founded the City of Mexico." The first of the three volumes in this work presents a detailed account of the Nahuatl religion and of Nahuatl origins, and notes specifically that the region encompassing Nevada, Utah, New Mexico, Arizona, California, and the Mexican States of Sinaloa and Sonora contain artifacts and remains of living facilities closely related to those of the Aztecs in the Valley of Mexico. That region is also given the name Chicomoztoc, literally, las siete cuevas (seven caves), later to become the fabled and much-sought seven cities of Cibola. Huehuetlapállan was the most important of these population centers. But the Mexican scholars clearly identify Aztec and Mexican origins with the southwestern United States. However, aside from the two United States sources cited, further reference to Aztlán is difficult to find in Anglo history; it is obviously of no consequence except to the Chicano. We still know very little about our ancient origins.

The Chicano is unique in America. He is a descendant of the Fifth Sun, bound to the land of Aztlán by his blood, sweat, and flesh, and heir to gifts of language and culture from Spanish conquistadores. But in him, too, is another dimension.

Some observers have said of the Mexican American that he is an in-between, neither Mexican nor American. The truth is that the Mexican American is a fusion of three cultures: a mezcla of Mexican Indian, Spanish, and the North American—yes, even the Anglo-dominated society is his to absorb into himself.

Too many Mexican Americans have invested solely in the Anglo world, cannot see the value in their multiculture, and do not have the courage to reclaim it and fight for it. I refer not to the culture that the gringo has allowed us to retain, of taco chains and fiesta days, but to the culture, which is the indomitable wellspring of our mestizo character, the fusion of Mexican Indian, Spanish, and now even Anglo. In the Southwest, the Chicano, who is the blending of these three elements, personalities, and psychologies, has come to a time of self-assertion. The word Chicano is offered not merely as a term of differentiation (some would say separation or racism) but also as a term of identification with that distinct melding of bloods and cultures. The term Chicano is anything but racist, because it declares the assimilation of bloods and heritage that makes the Chicano a truly multicultured person.

Chicanismo offers a new or renewed adaptation to a reality of life for the Mexican American. Segregated, maligned, despised, subjugated, destroyed for what he is, and barred from becoming what he would be, the Mexican American turns toward a new path. Unleashing the frustrations and emotions of many generations of lifetimes, reviving suppressed memories, and casting off the weighing terrors, he resurrects himself as a Chicano. He can face the onslaught of cultural racism perpetrated by the Anglo, which he has only endured up to now, with new power, new insight, new optimism—if not for himself, at least for his family and the Chicanos that are to come.

By admitting to being Chicano, to being this new person, we lose nothing, we gain a great deal. Any Mexican American afraid to join with the Chicano cause can only be afraid for himself and afraid of the gringo. The black has faced this truth and found that he must make his way as a black or as nothing, certainly not as the white man's "nigger." We can no longer be the Anglo's "Pancho."

The Federal bureaucrat who shies away from being too Chicano or plays down the cause should get out of government and stop being window dressing; he is harming the people he could especially serve por no tener tripas. The Mexican American businessman or professional who disclaims his Chicano roots and will have nothing to do with la causa because it might hurt sales or cut down the size of his Anglo clientele has sold out to the gringo dollar long ago and now betrays the very people who probably put him where he is. The people in the barrio who criticize and decry the Chicano revolt because "it's not how we do things" have forgotten two histories, and they lie to themselves if they believe that the gringo will eventually relent and give them or their children an education, a job, a decent home, or a future.

Any Mexican American who can celebrate the Fourth of July and el dies y seis de septiembre must realize that revolt, action for change, is not a thing of the past. The Chicano revolt is a marriage of awareness and necessity that must be consummated over and over if justice is to be done. The Chicano revolt embodies old values that have been suppressed over generations. It goes a step beyond the black revolution in that Chicanos assert that they have a personal and a group point of view which the dominant "culture," made up of blacks and whites, must accept now or suffer the consequences. The Chicano insists that the Anglo respect his language and grant it equal value in any educational system where Chicano students are dominant. The Chicano insists that his culture, his way of life, and that *he* as a person be taken into account when housing is built, when industry offers jobs, when political parties caucus.

There has been a two-way infusion of Anglo-Saxon and African elements within the dominant "culture" to the extent that the color of one's skin, unfortunately for both sides, is the sole measure of acceptance or rejection of one's fellow man in American society. If it were not for color there would be little to distinguish black from white. Black people display a cultural perspective and philosophy little different from what the Anglo desires and demands. We Chicanos see the Negro as a black Anglo. But we Chicanos, as we must admit sooner or later, are different from the Anglo and the black in more ways than merely color. Our people range widely from light-skinned güeros to da k-skinned Indios. Certainly, we have our share of black blood from the Negroes who escaped into Mexico, a free country, from the southern slave states, and even Arab-Semitic traces from the Moors. The güeros remain Chicano by force of cultural attraction; they would rather be Chicano than Anglo, although they could easily pass as a white gringo.

But besides color, the Chicano may be discr mi-nated against because of his Spanish surname, which he may change; or by his Spanish accent, which he may hide by calling himself "Spanish"; or by the effects of past discrimination, which restrict the kinds of jobs or social encounters he will seek; or even by the family structure which, if strong enough, could effectively thwart the desire to break away from the Chicano com-munity. Add to this list of barriers, dark, "swarthy," or "Indian" skin, and economic and social stability may be an impossible objective. Yet there are still too many Mexican Americans who not only refuse to accept who and what they are, but reject the fact that however com-fortable and secure they may be in their present situa-tion, they evolved out of days of discrimination. Nor should they be blind to the jeopardy in which they re-main, because they will always be different from the gringo.

The impact of discrimination on the Mexican Ameri-can has been somewhat obscured by our lack of numbers, our generally passive resistance in past years, our depend-ence on the white man's justice, even our own blind acceptance of the white man's way as *the* way. Time and again I have questioned Chicanos about the discrimination they have experienced. Invariably, every one who began the conversation with the approach that he had never been discriminated against soon reversed his view. Racism, cultural discrimination, has affected every Chicano. Any of us who at some time has denied his heritage by changing his name or birthplace or by purifying his English of any accent, any who has been forced to leave his home alone or with his family for lack of opportunity, and has felt shame in his language, accent, or skin color, or in the food he eats—that Chicano has tasted the Anglo's kiss of death.

The Anglo-American society is a bastard issued from the promiscuous concubinage of several hundreds of ethnic and racial peoples who have cast their cultural identities into the American melting pot. While it may have been easy and necessary for some ethnic, non-Anglo-Saxon people to do, it is not necessary—nor easy—for Mexican Americans to throw away their birthrights. The need is exactly the opposite. We Chicanos, the people of el Quinto Sol, must realize Aztlán in ourselves, individually and as a group. We are part of the land, but we need not seek a geographic center for our Aztlán; it lies within ourselves, and it is boundless, immeasurable, and limited only by our lack of vision, by our lack of courage, by our hesitancy to grasp the truth of our being.

We are Aztlán and Aztlán is us.

Our ancestors also foresaw that after the Fifth Sun another epoch would ensue, but what form it would take they did not know or say. We Chicanos face the same unknown future. We do not know where the Chicano revolt will lead. It must lead somewhere. Will Chicanos have a say in what eventually happens? Was the Aztecs' Sixth Sun the coming of Cortez, of the white man, and the advent of his destruction? Is this also to be the Chicano's Sixth Sun—destruction at the hands of the white man, the Anglo, the gringo?

2

THE CHICANO NATION

FOR more than a century, the Mexican American
has journeyed on an unrecorded pilgrimage to every
section of the United States searching on many
roads and at many doors for opportunity. He has
desired the comforts of life: a home of his own, financial
security for his family, and schooling for his children. To
achieve these goals he has undertaken work that other
men would not do—in the harvest fields, on the railroad
crews, in the silver, zinc, and copper mines, and in the
steel mills; he has risked his life and often forfeited it
in the armed services. His strivings have taken him to
every part of the land and to foreign countries; and he
has either returned to his ancestral home in the Southwest or settled in fringe or core city-barrios of the large
and small urban areas in the North and East.

His struggle for survival is an unappreciated saga in
the making of the nation, but it has made him a national
person. Colonias, small settlements of Chicanos, can be
found in nearly every state. Apart from the largest con-
centrations in Arizona, California, Colorado, New Mexico,
and Texas, the states that generally describe Aztlán, Chicanos may be found in fair-sized groups in Florida, Illinois, Indiana, Kansas, Michigan, Missouri, New York,

17

Ohio, Utah, Washington, and Wisconsin. Agricultural interests and industrial centers have attracted the Mexican American to these states. In the early part of the century and through the 1930s, he was often used as a strikebreaker, a fact which did little to ease his adaptation and acceptance in these regions.

But because the Chicano people have been concentrated in the five southwestern states and their collective contribution ignored by the nation, they have been readily dismissed as a regional problem to be solved on a regional basis. This notion, that Mexican Americans reside only in the Southwest, so they need not be the concern of anyone beyond this region, is completely erroneous and has proved nearly fatal to the Chicano. The fortunes of the United States are closely tied in to the misfortunes of the Chicano. Neglected as an alien even in his own land and even more crudely deprived of first-class consideration outside of the Southwest, the Chicano has poured more than his share of toil and blood into the development of the nation. Yet it is the Chicano who has profited the least from the progress he has helped to force out of the land with the raw energy of his labor.

Mexican Americans have increased in numbers steadily in the Southwest since 1848, the year of the annexation (the land grab) of what are now seven states under the Treaty of Guadalupe Hidalgo. This growth in itself tended to push out many families and individuals, since the chances for employment did not also increase and the potential for better, uncrowded housing and adequate educational facilities did not improve. There have been periods of fluctuation of the Chicano population, but because of a birth rate second only to the American Indian, and because of the continual influx of Mexican immigrants, there has probably been only one serious time of reduction in our population. That occurred during the Depression thirties, when mexicanos were repatriated to Mexico in significant numbers. In fact, the United States Government and local municipalities encouraged repatriation, offering free bus rides to rid cities and counties of Mexican families who were burdening welfare rolls when there were no jobs available for anyone. A Mexican Government source counted more than three hundred thousand official repatriations during that period. With manpower at a premium during the Second World War, however, the Chicano community recouped its 1930s losses. Immigration was accelerated legally via Public Law 78, the bracero program, which brought many mexicanos to the United States as farm workers. Many never returned to Mexico or went back only to gather their families and recross the border for life; many other mexicanos contrived illegal methods of entering the United States.

Prior to these North-American-made disruptions of the Mexican American community, a psychological upheaval occurred during and for a few years following the 1910–17 revolution in Mexico. Many, if not the majority of Mexican Americans today, can recall or have heard firsthand stories of that revolutionary period and the social convulsions it created. An untold number of Mexicans fled to the United States for political, economic, and sometimes psychological reasons. No one, however, left Mexico without incurring psychic shocks from the precipitate flight that usually characterized the departure from Mexico—the severing of ancestral roots, the sudden destitution, and the disruption of a way of life that refugees had no assurance they could later recapture either in the United States or in Mexico. Chicanos experienced some fallout, too, for the effects of the revolution were nearly as upsetting on this side of the border. The accounts by friends and relatives of atrocities committed by participants in the many-sided affair; the prejudices against any established government and politicians, which served to confirm longstanding distrust; and the sacrifices required of them when refugees turned to them for help—all left vivid mental impressions that can still be traced today.

Nevertheless, the thought of return someday persisted in most, if not all, of the refugees. In spite of the mental and physical anguish, the economic reversals, and the political alienation that had driven them from Mexico, mexicanos still hoped for repatriation. This attitude, typical of refugees (the tendency is also strong among the Cuban exiles I've met), along with the proximity of the border, has much to do with the aversion among many Mexican people to assimilating North American ways, learning English well, and becoming citizens. The nearness of the border plays a persistent role in the lives of mexicanos and in the development of survival skills against the Anglo world. Families from as far away as Chicago, Detroit, Boston, New York, Sacramento, and quite likely from Seattle and Montreal as well, visit their Mexican hometowns at least once and sometimes twice a year, traveling by plane, bus, or automobile to spend a few days, but often weeks at a time, on vacation.

A couple of years ago, a Hollywood film company was shooting a Western in Parras, a small wine-making town in the northern state of Coahuila, Mexico. The director searched among the spectators for a "typical Mexican family." The family he selected turned out to be on vacation from East Chicago, Indiana. Nevertheless, they landed the part. While for this family the trip to Mexico, an annual one most likely, was particularly profitable and memorable, this reverse migration still affects the kind of job a man can hold, his children's education, whether he buys a house or rents an apartment, and his ability to become financially secure when a year's savings end up financing a few days' trip.

The psycho-cultural reactions may also be quite serious, since the annual pilgrimage tends to foster a cultural ambivalence rather than create a cultural equilibrium. The mexicano will more readily continue to identify with his traditional heritage and upbringing, not a bad thing in itself, but be hampered in coping with an alien way of life that requires the capacity to balance the best, and worst, of the two modes, Mexican and Anglo, for survival. If we can understand these psychological and geographical forces at work on the Chicano and his Mexican-born brother, we can more easily understand the total Chicano personality.

Chicanos empathize with the perennial pilgrimage to Mexico; any of us would treasure a more personal and deep association with that cultural homeland which is most distinctively ours. But the true Chicano, while he always feels an affinity to Mexico, also must face the reality of the time and place in which he lives, and establish an internal reality of himself that can be independent of the need for the physical surroundings of the Mexican culture, traditions, and language. In talking to Mexicans about the Chicano movement, it has been this independence, or new awareness, that is least understood, because for him, the Mexican way of life and thought has been a very real and pervasive element in the formation of his mind set. He cannot understand what the Chicano is talking about or how he has a Mexican personality and at the same time a different personality as well, independent of the usual Mexican circumstances. I always have the feeling that my Mexican brother will diagnose my case as acute schizophrenia. Yet, the Chicano can rather easily identify with hot dogs or tacos, jazz or mariachis, Spanish or English, Lincoln or Juarez. The mexicano would rather not break the ties of birthplace or accept the new consciousness of the Chicano that thrives on a personal, interior reality which is different from the Anglo's and the Mexican's, and yet partakes of both.

For our part, we Mexican Americans have been ignorant by and large of our brown brothers in the northern states (al norte). We knew they were there but until recently had little idea of their numbers, their problems, their progress in completely alien surroundings, their views on Chicanismo, and their role as norteño Chicanos

in relation to la causa. Distance may partly explain our
lack of knowledge of our norteño brother; for many decades the early immigrant settlements in the Midwest and
other regions developed in virtual isolation from the
Southwest. Many Mexicans went directly from Mexico to
the Midwest, the Great Lakes area, or other northern
states, with hardly a pause in the Southwest. To our
present chagrin and fault, not until the past decade
has much effort been made to draw the regions together—but that is changing rapidly. Every so often
I hear that, tucked away in some state, is a colonia of
Chicanos I had never imagined existed, or I'll be shocked
to learn that several thousand Chicanos live in cities
such as Milwaukee, Wisconsin; Kansas City, Missouri;
or Seattle, Washington. The Mexican American's presence across the continent is a basic fact about the Chicano. For us Chicanos, the breadth of our presence and
our own lack of real knowledge of its extent suggest that
we face a larger problem in regard to communications
and organization than we realized. But it is a problem
that we, as a Chicano people, must resolve.

A Mexican American more than fifty years old, a
native of Chicago, tells a revealing story of the norteño Chicano. The story of his family represents a many-
times-told tale of migration, sacrifice, and discrimination
for the Chicano who traveled al norte.

Eligio Fernandez, as I shall call him here, remembers
the evolution of the Pilsen area of Chicago from its early
days as a predominantly Dutch quarter to its present
status as the largest Chicano concentration in a city outside the southwestern states, with perhaps a quarter of
a million Mexican Americans. His father and uncle came
from Mexico in 1917 to work on the railroads, laying ties
and rails. Their intention had been to make a bundle of
money and return to Mexico, where they could then live
royally. But perhaps the specter of the revolution that
still ravaged Mexico discouraged them; or, quite as likely,
the young mexicana that Eligio's father met and married in Chicago encouraged him to settle there.

Manpower needs in Minnesota during the early twenties caused a considerable increase in the recruiting of Mexican Americans to the farms and factories, a 1953 report to the Governor's Interracial Commission recounted. The Minnesota Sugar Company, since renamed American Crystal, offered guaranteed wages, transportation, and credit and welfare programs, but these ended in 1933 when the Depression put Minnesotans of every background out of work. Signs went up where Mexicans once were the only non-Anglo workers: Only White Labor Employed. In 1935, 328 Mexicans were deported to Mexico by relief authorities, creating "confusion and misunderstanding among Mexican American communities in Minneapolis and St. Paul," the report stated. But the Chicanos understood full well what had happened and why. Through the late thirties and war years, when employment picked up again, Mexican Americans generally chose to take a passive role; many feared the threat of deportation if they were to openly assert their rights either individually or as a group; some joined labor unions, or, through church associations, formed credit unions and developed educational programs.

Not until after World War II did a major organization develop on an issues-program base. At the prompting and support of the Cardinal's Committee for the Spanish Speaking, the Spanish-speaking people in the city formed the Illinois Federation of Mexican Americans, ILFOMA. The group prospered for about seven years, with social events the chief source of revenue. Since that time, a number of groups have been established, including old-line clubs such as American G.I. Forum posts and League of United Latin American Citizens clubs which have roots in the Southwest. More recently, new entities have arisen, born out of problems and needs in the North. The War on Poverty spawned a variety of program-oriented groups. Aspiring activist youth elements have adopted the militant style and dress of the Brown Berets and the Mexican American Youth Organizations of the Southwest. A recent collaboration has sprung up between Puerto Ricans and

Chicanos through the Latin American Defense Organization (LADO), whose forces are directed primarily at the educational and welfare problems of the two communities in Chicago. The co-operative movement seems more viable than earlier efforts, which may have bogged down in money-making social affairs: the chief aim is to solve problems of the community by meeting issues head-on and together.

Because politics is controlled by city hall, Chicano involvement in political activities is limited to a few individuals, but there is potential for Chicanos to have an impact on local government. The potential, however, is diluted at this time by many factors. Chicago is famous for its stockyards and its Saul Alinsky, for its Marina Towers and the black West Side ghetto, but its brand of politics and its mayor invest it with its most notorious features. Chicago's First Ward, one commentator in the barrio estimated, incorporates some of the city's richest real estate and also the largest Chicano barrio—and Chicanos could hold, theoretically, the decisive edge in the ward. However, of some twenty-five thousand Mexican Americans of voting age and eligible to vote, only about two thousand are registered. But the percentage of naturalized immigrants of the total Chicano population is incredibly low, so that the political influence the Chicano could have is almost nil. The traditional answer to such political impoverishment would be a large-scale naturalization campaign and registration drive. However, there are complications. It seems that the Chicanos in Illinois are waiting for something to happen that will fuse the many forces in the Chicano community. The catalyst to move more Chicanos into active politics has not yet erupted. It seems that Chicago's Mexican Americans may not realize the power potential they possess collectively. Among the reasons, as indicated by the statistics, is an aversion to becoming citizens or committing themselves permanently to the city. In that way they betray the dream of eventual return to Mexico

or the Southwest. Like Eligio's father, the dream over-
rules the reality, and time passes. The Chicano ends
up passing the years in a limbo of expectation.

The repatriation syndrome extends to housing and
education as well as to citizenship. A young Mexican
American, still wary about the term Chicano, has been
active for about five years as a community worker in the
Pilsen neighborhood around Eighteenth Street and South
Blue Island Avenue, perhaps the largest of several Chicago districts where Mexicans predominate. He has
found that few mexicanos will buy a house, because most
believe they are going to return soon to Mexico and don't
want to tie themselves down, even though buying would
be more economical in the long run than renting. Older
mexicanos shy away from adult-education courses provided by all kinds of agencies to teach them English.
But then, why should they bother when they won't be
here that long anyway? So politics is also out of the question, for politics is for those with a stake in a country,
and besides, you know how those políticos promise you
everything but never fulfill anything. Meanwhile, for
many Chicanos, the future never comes as they wait for
a dream to come true.

While the sentiment for an eventual return to their
former home is an important and revealing element in
the northern Chicano's make-up, another significant, and
to me the most disheartening, factor among the norteño
communities is the factionalism that exists among
brothers caught together in the trap of a Chicago. The
most crucial barrier retarding the evolution of barrio
groups into issue-solving, politically influential, economically impactful forces is a regionalist split of the Mexican pueblo, which, unfortunately, is keenly reflected in
the Midwest. Roughly, the Chicano community breaks
down into three general groupings: the mexicanos, recent and older immigrants still strongly identifying with
the Mexican fatherland and in great part still Mexican
citizens; the native-born Mexican Americans, politically

aware, conscious of the social problems surrounding them, seeking outlets for their frustration, some young, some old activists; and the Tejanos (Texans), highly independent and proud of it, aloof from involvement in overall community affairs, just freed from the migrant stream. These categories are not absolute but generally portray the irrational fissions that have occurred in Chicago as well as in other large-city barrios.

Only recently, an antipoverty program in the Pilsen area went down the drain because of a rift over the directorship. During the first part of 1969 several leaders in the community had sought the ouster of the program director, but disunity reigned supreme, and the main objective couldn't be achieved. Finally, when the director quit, the competing factions could not decide on a director or on programs, so that in the end the entire CAP (Community Action Program) agency was scrapped by Washington. Perhaps this was a good thing. With the dependence on federal money broken and intervention from city administrators and federal rules-keepers cut to a minimum, the Mexican American community is forced to handle its problems by itself.

As a first step to concrete progress for norteño Chicanos, realization and acceptance of a universal Chicanismo must be consciously sought and promoted by the activist Chicanos. A young native Chicagoan, commenting on his hometown scene, mentioned something about "brazers."

Brazer? What's a brazer?

Don't you know what a brazer is? He's a guy coming here from Mexico to work, farm work, maybe in one of the factories or mills. You know, a bracero.

You're kidding. You call them "brazers." Who do you think they are? They're your brothers, brown like you. Your father came here the same way probably. What's this brazer jazz?

Well, man, they try to make their movidas (time) with the girls with that fancy Spanish, you know, like real Latin lovers. . . .

Are you serious? How can any mexicano call his brother

something like that? Don't you know that's the kind of stuff
the white man pulls when he calls a black man, "nigger," or
me or you, "Pancho"?

We commit a gross injustice, brother against brother,
when words like brazer crop up in our vocabulary. Although technically the bracero no longer exists as a
legal entity since Public Law 78 was terminated six
years ago, Mexican nationals still enter the United States
under other kinds of permits such as the infamous "green
card." The word brazer creates artificial and needless barriers among brown brothers; blood has been spilled over
the use of the term. When so much has to be done to pull
the Chicano community together, to forge a strong union
against Anglo deceit and prejudice, the existence of such
internal trigger words is anti-Chicano and could be
fatal to la causa.

Although our linguistic heritage should be one of our
most forceful bonds, Chicanos still ape the Anglo in his
penchant for words that divide. Of course, some traces
remain also from the class-color consciousness that strati-
fied Mexico from the early days of the peninsulares (the
Spanish-born who came to colonize and govern Mexico).
These were eventually replaced by the criollos (creoles,
the Mexicans born of Spanish parents). Then came the
mestizos (of mixed Indian and Spanish blood), and
finally the indio, lowest man on the social-racial strata.
For a period of time, in the early 1800s, the zambo (of
mixed Negro and Indian lines) developed as a small,
distinct group, but it was soon absorbed. This class-
culture categorizing has been fortified by Anglo American
racism. The Chicano, falling into the racist trap, creates
verbal barriers between himself and his brothers.

As counterpoint, Dr. Sabine Ulibarri, a professor
of Spanish at the University of New Mexico, has said
so beautifully: "In the beginning was the Word, and
the Word was made flesh. It was so in the beginning,
and it is so today. The language, the Word, carries

within it the history, the culture, the traditions, the very life of a people, the flesh. We cannot even conceive of a people without a language, or a language without a people. The two are one and the same. To know one is to know the other."

Yet Mexican immigrants often speak fluent Spanish but disdain learning English or speaking it. Native Chicanos may not speak Spanish well at all, or know only a few swear words or enough Spanish to eat in a Mexican restaurant. The Tejano has introduced the Spanglish style of speech using phrases such as, Ay te watcho, for See you later.

Caló, slang sprung from the pachuco complex, universally used among Chicano youth, and visible as graffiti on barrio walls, provides another view of the subtle differences between norteño Chicanos and their southwestern brothers:

C/S, one of the most widely used caló symbols, means Con Safos in the Southwest barrios but has become, in Chicago, Can't Score, a term somewhat diluted in the translation. Literally, the words apparently derive from a Spanish naval term, zafo, meaning free and clear, or out of danger. Evolving through the bato loco (crazy guy) complex and pachuco cant, con safos came to signify defiance, marking a place, an area, or a wall that must remain untouched and the sole property of the gang named in vivid lettering above the C/S. A still more subtle connotation is being given con safos by young Chicanos who are seriously attempting to communicate the meaning of the Chicano revolt to their own communities: a new literary magazine has been named Con Safos because, its editors explain, the phrase "symbolizes the rejection of the 'American identity'; and the beginning of a Chicano literary genre, a definition of the Chicano identity, and an assertion of the moral and aesthetic values of the barrio experience."

A commentary must be added at this point concerning the element of pachuquismo in the Chicano frame of mind. The pachuco, whom the Mexican poet and essayist Octavio Paz found to be "a group for whom the fact that they are Mexicans is a truly vital problem, a problem of life or death," has embellished the Chicano experience with his life style and his language. The existence of the pachuco, in fact, the creation of him out of the Mexican American community, has been denigrated in polite circles among the Spanish-speaking people. But taking into account the essential nature of alienation and self-rejection that embody the pachuco, he represents a strong tendency among Chicanos and provides an example of the ability of the Mexican American to create a new identity and to endure the alien and destructive pressures of Anglo society. Army, marine, and navy servicemen made the pachuco the target of a week-long series of assaults on the East Los Angeles barrio in June 1943 in what the news media termed "zoot-suit riots" (after the stylized dress worn at the time by many youths), but which were in actuality military riots. Pachucos rejected much of both Anglo and Mexican styles of life and demonstrated an innate creativity by formulating an extensive vocabulary and pattern of relationships among themselves.

Dr. Jorge Alvarez of the University of California at Santa Cruz has compiled some of the pachuquismos: calcos (shoes); lima (shirt); jefito (father); cohuetes (guns); borlotear (dance); vacilar (fool around); aguila (sharp, as in sharp dresser); ojáles (eyes); escamado (afraid); chanates (Negroes); la melena (long hair); ruca (girl); tando (hat); chuchuluco (candy; garas (clothes); mono (movies); rolar (to sleep); chante, cantón (home); tacuchi (dressed up). In response to persons who criticize the use of the word Chicano on the basis that it derives from a pachuco word meaning to double-cross, Dr. Alvarez explains that cachuquear is pachuco for double-cross, and Chicano is an acceptable term, derived from within the Mexican Ameri-

can community itself. In short, the pachuco has contributed to our Chicanismo, or, to put it another way, there
is a little of the pachuco in every Chicano: the sense of
alienation, a confirmed distrust of the non-Chicano society, a passion for self-fulfillment, and a clear vision of
what it means to be a carnal, a brother in flesh and
spirit.

As a Chicano I can understand why a monolith
Chicano community does not exist, and even why di-
visions appear among us. We speak of ourselves as a
people, but at the same time we are richly diverse
among ourselves. No Chicano would have it any
other way. From the early days when Chicanos first
began to spread out all over the nation, they took
with them certain traits: an innate individualism, a
tough and thorough stoicism, a spiritual integrity, a
keen grasp of the essence of human dignity, a dependence on family structures and internal resources,
and an independence from alien social forms or services. We also tend to be tolerant of those who seem
outlandish to us in their dress and speech; we often
bear with them for no other reason than not to em-
barrass anyone. Our elders feel a revulsion toward
the aggressive actions of the militants, young or old;
they do not wish to offend, and even feel shame for
those who seem not to feel shame for themselves.
Such attitudes and principles can work to fortify us
against the vicissitudes of living in unfamiliar and
hostile environments, but they can also create barriers
within ourselves.

The norteño barrio people are no different from the
southwestern Chicanos. In the Midwestern barrios, the
Chicano life style may be even stronger, since its roots
are derived so directly yet are so severely isolated from
the Mexican sources. Chicago boasts a Little Mexico as
a result of this definite isolation. Around South Blue
Island Avenue and Eighteenth Street, for example, tortil-
lerias, panaderias, peluquerias, librerias, and every kind

of shop that would be found in a Mexican urban center is there for the norteño Chicano. For many blocks, the non-Spanish-speaking person would find it difficult to' know where to eat or have his shoes repaired or his hair cut unless he looked in storefronts or found some symbol of the service offered.

Most exciting of all is that Chicago's barrio is a fluid microcosm of what is happening or has happened in many other Mexican American barrios. Old battles are being fought anew, old ways are being re-evaluated, new paths to a better life are being sought, and always with the hope that as much as possible of the old way will be preserved in the new. There is every indication that the norteño Chicano is at the fringe, not merely geographically, but philosophically and organizationally, of the Chicano revolt. I don't mean to say that they are any less Chicano, just as I don't mean that there aren't sections of the Southwest where Mexican Americans still have a long way to travel toward Chicanismo. But the truth of the matter is that fragmentation exists among us along fictitious regional lines and that there is a lack of communication regarding Chicano activities in the rest of the country. The Mexican American is most attuned to the circumstances of his status in the United States, but many Mexican-born persons are also becoming excited by la causa; they see their futures tied in with the evolution of a more forceful Chicano identity. Mexican-born brothers I've spoken with about the Chicano movement have distrusted our motives in seeking their co-operation and collaboration in organizational efforts, but I hope to see this distrust fade away, along with the anachronistic words of demarcation that have always bothered me. Words such as cholo for the Mexican living in the United States and pocho for the Mexican American are old verbal fences thrown up in years past to distinguish between regional backgrounds.

Communication lines need to be established between the Southwest, the Midwest, the Northwest, the Great

Lakes, and other regions. The huelga, the farmworkers' strike, remains the major national issue drawing together Chicano forces everywhere, but the strike itself is limited in its appeal. Very often it is carried on by a Delano boycott organizer and Anglo sympathizers. To some degree, a kind of brown pantherism imitative of black organizations is extant in norteño barrios, but it reflects only a surface understanding of Chicanismo, and needs a deepening of cultural and ideological roots to move closer to the true Chicano revolt. Increased intelligence has been shown at dozens of Chicano conferences, including the Crusade for Justice's annual conferences in Denver since the summer of 1968; conferences in Albuquerque, New Mexico, Kansas City, Missouri, and McAllen, Texas, in the fall of 1969; and a Midwest convention in South Bend, Indiana, in April 1970, a first for the region. Missionary sorties have been organized by MAYO and Brown Beret youths to northern cities and throughout the migrant stream. Chicano Press newspapers have multiplied rapidly in the last three years. And even the Inter-Agency Committee on Mexican American Affairs (now the Cabinet Committee on Opportunity for the Spanish Speaking) has tried to establish liaison with norteño organizations, stretching out a Chicano network over the country. But much more needs to be done.

Everywhere—in Chicago, Detroit, Gary, East Saint Louis, Salt Lake City, Kansas City, Seattle, as well as in the Southwest—there is a groping for identity, for communion as well as communication, and for nationhood as well as for nationality. Young Chicanos naturally tend to gang together, unconsciously forming into opposition forces, pachuco style. Although misdirected, disorganized, and competing against each other, they represent the raw material to be converted into the aggressive, dynamic Chicanos who are the future of Chicanismo. They are most adaptable and most in need of an identity—that need has been tangible in the young Chicanos I've met, whether they were in Chicago, East

Los Angeles, or McAllen. Where they now live is irrelevant; they and their elders need to know that what counts are the inherent birthrights of Aztlán, of la raza, of Chicanismo.

The Chicano is everywhere. Each one is a reservoir of multicultural depths, bilingual comprehension, and human sensitivities. Factory owners, growers, and industrialists have found him a natural resource in building their empires and their cities. It is the Chicano's turn to gather his own energies so that he can have an impact on his own personal desires and on the fundamental wants of the nation, benefiting not only himself but all other Americans as well. The Chicano is not a regional phenomenon or quirk of fate. He is a built-in foundation stone of this country. Anyone who persists in writing him off as only a southwestern personality and not a person of national significance is denying history and refusing the Chicano his rightful place in history.

In spite of the efforts of the government to persist in ignoring him, the Chicanos, Mexican Americans, have been counted in the 1970 census, not by surname or by place of birth or language spoken, but as a specific people.

The resistance of the Census Bureau over the past two or three years against changing the make-up of the 1970 questionnaire was a cause célèbre among some Chicano community spokesmen. At the root of the bureau's and other official government agencies' refusal to include Mexican Americans as such in the census has been the gringo myth that Mexican Americans are Caucasian, white, and invisible; that they live mostly in the Southwest; and that they should be kept there; therefore the "problem" can be ignored. The Mexican American is not a national person, nor does he have a distinct personality, Washington would have us believe. But that viewpoint was not to prevail. There is an interesting lesson to be learned about the fantasy land in which the Anglo-American government exists, as the story behind the great census reversal of 1969 will bear out. Of course, everyone takes credit for what finally occurred.

This most recent change in the census-taking approach to Mexican Americans has a long history of vacillation as to how we wanted ourselves to be called. Of course, our having a choice at all has developed only in recent decades. When the first census was taken in 1790, only an estimate was provided of the number of Spanish-speaking persons, about twenty-three thousand, in the area of Arizona, California, New Mexico, and Texas. Not until 140 years later were we counted with any accuracy, this time as a separate Mexican race numbering some 1.3 million. Under the label of "persons of Spanish mother tongue," 1.6 million were counted in 1940. Reclassified as "white persons of Spanish surname" after some strenuous maneuvering by well-meaning groups such as LULAC and G.I. Forum, we totaled 2.3 million in 1950. In the last census using the same category, the Spanish-surname population in the Southwest had risen to 3.8 million.

It is crucial to understand that these latest figures represent only the Southwest. The 1970 census, for the first time since 1930, permitted the Chicano to say specifically that he is Mexican American. It is a landmark in establishing our identity and deriving some of the benefits that accrue to being accurately counted in reference to the allocation of programs and funds, and in political representation. Because the census-taking did not start until April 1970 and results are not fully processed for a year to a year and a half, concrete data will not be available until mid-1971.

Suspense, excitement, and apprehension have been expressed by Mexican Americans at the thought of the outcome of the census. How many Mexican Americans really are there in the nation? Are there more than any of us have guessed? More than six million? Less than five million? Will fewer Chicanos identify themselves as Mexican Americans than we who have actively sought specific representation in the census expect? Has all the struggle been in vain? And struggle it has been for a number of Mexican Americans keenly interested in the numbers game. Early in the spring of 1969, Robert Aragon, who then headed the Los Angeles County Urban Coalition, brought a little bit of drama into the seeming stalemate persisting in Washington, D.C., with an eleventh-hour sortie to pressure the Bureau of the Census into revising the census questionnaire. At that time, bureau officials insisted the issue was closed. "Over the period of the last two or three years, and particularly in the last several months," Aragon argued, "a variety of individuals, organizations, and institutions from the Mexican American community have voiced serious reservations over the adequacy of the 1970 census questionnaire. They have made it clear that the questionnaire, as it now stands, will fall far short of servicing the strategic data collection needs of the Mexican American community and of other population groups of Spanish heritage."

Aragon was one of many Chicanos who personally involved themselves in the effort to unlock the census questionnaire. It was at this point of impasse in April that Aragon conferred with the newly appointed chairman of the then Inter-Agency Committee on Mexican American Affairs, Martin Castillo of Los Angeles. Brand new on the national scene, Castillo lost little time in exploring Washington's fabled labyrinth. He enlisted the aid of high-level compatriots such as Robert Finch, then Secretary of the Department of Health, Education, and Welfare and former Lieutenant Governor of California (where Castillo had chalked up a few items in the credit column), and Secretary of Commerce Maurice Stans, to whom Castillo spoke directly about the Census Bureau's recalcitrance.

Suddenly, the attitude of Bureau of the Census officials changed, became even solicitous, some observers remarked. Inter-Agency staff and Mexican Americans from other agencies reconvened with census personnel to establish the exact needs for the revised questionnaire. The usual questions about names, relationships, sex, age, marital status, and race or color were asked of everyone. Mexican Americans should have written "Mexican American" in the box provided for the purpose. In addition, a special form of the basic questionnaire was mailed on a random basis to 5 percent of the households, or every twentieth residence in the United States, to elicit specific information about people of Spanish descent. The special questionnaire contained questions on housing, utilities, furnishings, appliances, other property, employment status, education, and health. Persons were also asked for place of birth, national origin, whether naturalized, and for how long a resident of the United States.

A preliminary sample survey in November 1969 disclosed that about 9.2 million persons in the United States claim Spanish descent, that is, 4.7 percent of the population (excluding persons in military service or in penal or other institutions). Statistically, the Census Bureau estimated, half of that population was under 20.5 years of age, 7.5 years younger than the national average. Nearly three-quarters of the 9.2 million were native born; the rest were immigrants, with half coming from Mexico. The language spoken was Spanish for 4.6 million persons.

Preliminary work by the Inter-Agency under its first chairman, Vicente T. Ximenes of Texas, a member of the Equal Employment Opportunity Commission, had finally borne fruit. In a memorandum dated April 1, 1969, Dr. Michael B. Hernandez, of the University of Texas at Austin, had summarized for Ximenes the findings and recommendations of a panel of Mexican American authorities, including Dr. George I. Sanchez, also of the University of Texas at Austin; Dr. Julian Samora,

head of the Department of Sociology, University of
Notre Dame, Indiana; and Dr. Julius Rivera, Department of Anthropology and Sociology, University of
Houston, Texas. The memorandum sharply criticized
the indirect means of obtaining data on persons of Spanish background. Hand coding by Spanish surname was
limited to the Southwest and would miss those persons
of Spanish descent who did not have Spanish last
names; counting by place of birth would miss persons of
Spanish ancestry native to the country but living in
other states; speaking a language other than English in
the home as a determinant would tend to pass over families of Spanish descent where only English was spoken.
Dr. Hernandez pointed out that a Mexican American
should have as a constitutional right the opportunity to
identify himself rather than have an enumerator do so
for him.

Perhaps 10 percent of the Negro population was
overlooked in the 1960 census because of inefficient
practices, and it is not unreasonable to assume that as
many if not more Mexican Americans and Puerto
Ricans, to cite one other Spanish-descent group, were
also missed. Consequently, it would follow that people
of Spanish background were unjustly overlooked and
denied a fair share in the country's programs and services. Equally as important, the 1970 census will effectively wipe out the myopic myth perpetuated by the
Anglo that the Chicano is restricted to the Southwest in
point of residence and importance, and will prove con-
clusively that the Chicano is a national personality.

The Bureau of the Census came under some pressure from Mexican American and Puerto Rican groups
at the time of the census, beginning in late March. Bert
Corona, a long-time spokesman for the Mexican American Political Organization in California, led in the filing
of a suit seeking an injunction against the Census Bureau to delay the census until there was greater assurance that it would be adequate. The suit was turned

down by a federal court. However, the basis of the suit remained valid: a 5 percent random sample was inadequate, and the census would inevitably miss tens of thousands of people of Spanish origin. Puerto Rican organizations were aroused by the Census Bureau's grossly insufficient effort to communicate the importance of the census to latino barrios. For a fact, the bureau set aside a mere ten thousand dollars to launch a national promotional campaign in the final month prior to the delivery of the questionnaires!

For the statistically minded, here are some specific figures gleaned from what data the Bureau of the Census and other federal agencies have provided. They will change radically when the 1970 returns are converted into hard information.

The Mexican American population ranks as the second largest minority group in the nation, with about five million persons. The number of Mexican Americans in the Southwest increased by 51 percent between 1950 and 1960, as compared to an overall increase in the same region of 39 percent. As of 1960 the Chicano community in the Southwest amounted to about 12 percent of the total number of residents; of this 12 percent, the native-born population numbered nearly 85 percent. Population increases are based on a higher birth rate among Mexican Americans (compared with Anglos or Negroes) and unlimited migration from Mexico, which takes place at a rate of approximately 3,500 persons per month. In the first eight years of the sixties about 387-000 people of Mexican birth emigrated to the United States, according to the Immigration and Naturalization Service.

We are an urban people; more than 80 percent of us live in cities. Sometimes the cities surrounded or grew out to meet us where we lived, in what had been semi-urban or rural colonias. Also, in line with a national pattern of movement, many of us have left the farms for the cities. As a consequence, our jobs are urban ori-

ented; farm work involves only a small percentage of
our people.

Estimates of Chicano populations in non-Southwest
locales include: Seattle, 8,000; the state of Utah, 40,000;
Kansas City, 20,000; Milwaukee, 18,000; Gary, 25,000;
Detroit, 40,000; Chicago, 250,000. As of 1960, the
largest Mexican American populations in the Southwest
included: Albuquerque, 68,000; Corpus Christi, 84,000;
Denver, 60,000; El Paso, 137,000; Fresno, 61,000; Houston, 75,000; Laredo, 50,000; Phoenix, 79,000; San Antonio, 257,000; San Diego, 64,000; San Francisco-Oakland, 177,000; San Jose, 77,000. Because of the factors
of increase, it is quite probable that these populations
will have climbed by half or two to three times the 1960
figures. If all the Chicanos in Los Angeles County were
to incorporate into a single city, that metropolis would
rank as the tenth largest in the United States, with
nearly one million people. Not a bad idea.

3

THROUGH GRINGO-COLORED GLASSES

THOSE familiar with the modern Mexicans will find it difficult to conceive that the nation should ever have been capable of devising the enlightened polity which we have been considering. But they should remember that in the Mexicans of our day they see only a conquered race. . . . Under the Spanish domination, their numbers have silently melted away. Their energies are broken. In their faltering step, and meek and melancholy aspect, we read the sad characters of the conquered race. . . . His outward form, his complexion, his lineaments are substantially all the same, but the moral characteristics of the nation, all that constituted its individuality as a race, are effaced for ever.

Who could write such distortions about the Mexican people? How could anyone condemn a whole nation as devoid of all moral fiber, purged of values, and damned forever as an abject people? The initial reaction might be that the words came from a bigoted mind, a carpetbagger of racist hate.

No. Worse than that. The words are quoted directly from William H. Prescott in *History of the Conquest of Mexico*, which was published in 1843. The author's fame and scholarship as a historian lend weight to his prejudice; the words in themselves damage the people they describe; but the date, 1843, is most telling of all. Communication between the Mexicans and Anglo-Americans probably had been minimal even up to the time of the United States attack on Mexico in 1847, although diplomatic relations had existed for many years. Prescott's sociological foray against the Mexican people came much sooner and must have been the first written by a historian of his caliber. There may be earlier but none so timely and portentous a stereotyping of the mexicano as contained in Prescott's massive study of Cortez' rape of the Aztec Empire.

This historical work, which included several other racial slurs, was issued at the same time that slavers' appetites and gringo greed were mounting to annex Texas and anything else the Anglo states could grab. Mexico had abolished slavery in 1831. Texas, where Anglo settlers as well as Mexican military officers and landholders lived, rebelled against the Mexican government in 1836. In that year Texas declared itself a republic and made the declaration concrete by defeating General Santa Anna's forces at San Jacinto. The republic then legalized slavery and sought annexation by the United States or recognition as an independent republic.

It was a time of caution, however. President John Tyler and Secretary of State John C. Calhoun had it in their minds to annex Texas, but everyone had to proceed carefully because it was feared that admitting Texas with its slave policy would throw out of balance the equilibrium between slave and free states. America's "manifest destiny," however, was becoming an obsession, and Mexico stood in the way of a sweep toward the western shores of the continent.

James K. Polk succeeded Tyler as President in 1845 on a platform that promised to add Oregon and Texas to the Union. Since Mexico had twice refused to sell Texas during Tyler's Administration, by the time Polk came into power a money deal seemed out of the question.

Although Texas' status as a sovereign country was dubious, Polk offered to annex Texas in 1845, an offer that was quickly accepted by the Lone Star government. But California, tempting the Anglo, still lay beyond Mexican territory. When Mexico rejected Polk's offer to redeem unpaid claims Mexico held against United States citizens in Texas in exchange for recognition of the Rio Grande as Texas' southern border and refused to negotiate the purchase of New Mexico and California, Polk sent General Zachary Taylor across the Nueces River. This unprovoked action against Mexico was an act of war. When Mexican troops engaged American forces at Matamoros, within Mexican territory, Polk announced that American soil had been invaded and promptly declared war on Mexico for defending its own land.

The Polk Administration acted dishonorably against a neighboring sovereign nation, and one is led to ask to what extent the ideas of men like Prescott influenced the ideals and avariciousness of the policy of the warmakers. Mexico's boundaries were found to be barriers to westward expansion, so, rudely and calculatedly, Anglo supremacist doctrine had its way, and those boundaries were callously ignored. Americans were already inbred with an intoxicating sense of supremacy over other peoples on the continent, a feeling fostered by a history of oppressing the Indian and the Negro. And they could read in Prescott's book that Mexicans were pushovers, a conquered race is as a conquered race does, so to hell with the critics or any principles of justice.

Critics there were, but only a few. A freshman member of the House of Representatives, Abraham Lincoln, called Polk's war unjust, unconstitutional, and unnecessary; James Russell Lowell, in *The Biglow Papers*, condemned the war as a plot to create more slave states; Henry Thoreau withheld payment of his state poll tax in protest, was put in jail and later wrote the famous essay, "Civil Disobedience," first published in 1849, to set out his reasoning. "When . . . a whole country is unjustly overrun and conquered by a foreign army, and subjected to military law," Thoreau wrote, "I think it is not too soon for honest men to rebel and revolutionize. What makes this duty the more urgent is the fact, that the country so overrun is not our own, but ours is the invading army." Although economics, constitutionality, and human rights were cited by those opposed to the war against Mexico, the more fundamental element was the inherent disdain Americans exhibited toward people who were different. While Americans justified slavery on the basis of economics, they absolved themselves of any guilt in sacking Mexico on the basis of a pseudodivine calling to lap up all the land that could be bought or taken by deceit or force. What Prescott had said as a historian was implemented as if it were reality, and it soon did become the accepted way of treating mexicanos—a conquered people.

Latter-day observers, for all their good will, have perpetuated the stereotype inaugurated by Prescott. Even Carey McWilliams, author of *North from Mexico* (1948), and Jack Forbes, also a California historian, have detailed the evolution of the conquered-people syndrome to explain why Chicanos today get inferior educations, the worst jobs, and lowest pay. I've heard the phrase coming from otherwise proud and militant Chicano leaders who must not realize what they are saying. I dispute that the Mexican American has ever been or will ever be conquered.

The Anglo has done his best to act the role of conqueror. Possessing the law, the guns, and the will to bend these elements to his purpose, the Anglo has subdued the Chicano, as he has other peoples, and not only subdued him but punished him for his subservience, beaten him, murdered him. But, as Chilean Pablo Neruda put it in one of his poems, "Amador Cea," A nosotros no nos rompen sino matandonos (Us, they cannot break us unless they kill us). The Mexican American has suffered through generations of torment, prejudice, subjugation, and outright murder. He is still alive and fighting back in Delano, Tierra Amarilla, Phoenix, Chicago, Gary, San Antonio, El Paso, Denver —all over America.

A concomitant lie about the Chicano that has grown into a stereotype in the Anglo mythology is the image of the "sleeping giant," which conjures up the old scene of the mexicanito squatting with his sombrero pulled over his eyes for his siesta as his humble little burro dutifully waits nearby. We have never been a conquered people and we have not been sleeping: our history in the farm labor organizing movement; the crops we have harvested all along the migrant stream; the railroads we have built; the steel we've helped to forge; the silver, copper, and coal we've dug out of the Southwest; and the blood that Chicanos have spilled in the gringos' wars demonstrate full well that we have not been sleeping.

Our ideals, our way of looking at life, our traditions, our sense of brotherhood and human dignity, and the deep love and trust among our own are truths and principles which have prevailed in spite of the gringo, who would rather have us remade in his image and likeness: materialistic, cultureless, colorless, monolingual, and racist. Some Mexican Americans have sold out and become agringados (Anglicized—assimilated, in sociologists' jargon), like the Anglo in almost every respect. Perhaps that has been their way of survival, but it has been at the expense of their self-respect and of their people's dignity. They assure their Anglo patrónes that the Chicanos who are speaking out are but a vocal, loco few. Ironically, these vendidos (sellouts) are often the same ones who accept the educational, economic, and prestige opportunities that activists have opened up,

and then turn their backs on la raza. In the end they
convince the Anglo that the mexicano is still submissive
and happy with his lot and that the Anglo need only
throw out a few crumbs: jobs, programs, or appointments to placate the rabble. That kind of Mexican
American is one example of the stereotype in reverse.
Aware of how Anglos look upon the Mexican American,
they do everything in their power to divest themselves
of any such appearance and by so doing, they fortify
the Anglo's sense of superiority.

Chicanos suffer from a kind of inverted discrimination; our own people become traitors to themselves to
avoid being stigmatized by the stoop-labor myth, the
lazy "meskin" scene, and the greaser-wetback image.
This represents one of our most serious internal problems because very often these people could be our best
leaders—artists, writers, professionals, and politicians.
But having surrendered to the white man's doctrine of
white makes right, and profit, there has been a strong
tendency among many Mexican Americans to dissolve;
not just to assimilate or to acculturate, but to vanish
into the Anglo milieu. After all, having become Anglicized, success in school, at work, and in the social
sphere comes more easily for the mexicano than if he
had kept faith with la raza. They seem to prove that the
white man's way is the only way to success. The effects
of such losses to the Chicano community have wreaked
havoc among us in efforts to organize politically and
economically.

This problem is virtually unknown to other minority
groups. The Negro people in particular have built-in
assurances that few blacks will simply disappear into
white suburbs. Even though the black community has
its Uncle Toms, it can still identify them readily. Our
Uncle Toms become dropouts, and our pueblo that
much weaker against oppression. The Anglo world says
that if you're light-skinned enough, if you are willing to

pass as some other ethnic person, change your name, or lose your accent, that is, if you can deny your parents, your people, and your own self, then you're on your way in the Anglo world. How much self-respect can a man have living in hypocrisy? Unfortunately there are many who have refused to fight the stereotype. To those Chicanos who did not have these "opportunities" or were unwilling to take them, it meant that doors would remain closed, that our heritage was a curse, and that our mother language was useless—if they swallowed the gringo lie.

While the stereotype in the sense I've just discussed has been self-fulfilling to some degree, the Anglo has had tremendous opportunity to exploit and perpetuate the caricature Chicano. With control over the media, the Anglo has been able to keep alive the false front of the lazy mexicano, the bandito mexicano, the good-for-nothing mexicano.

Dr. Thomas M. Martinez, a professor at Stanford University in California, has documented the methods used by the communications media to degrade the Mexican American. It seems that the mass media (radio, television, magazines, and newspapers) have had to resort to us to pick up the slack in their propaganda left by the demise of Step'n Fetchit. Nowadays (when the media aren't destroying the American Indian) we Chicanos and our children can see the Frito Bandito, lazy Paco smoking an L&M, and the masked bandit "El Marko" marking everything in sight with his Flair pen. Dr. Martinez points out:

TV commercials and magazine advertisements of the type referred to, symbolically reaffirm the inferior status of Mexicans and Mexican Americans in the eyes of the audience. Exaggerated Mexican racial and cultural characteristics, together with some outright misconceptions concerning their way of life, symbolically suggest to the audience that such people are comical, lazy, and thieving, who want what the

Anglos can have by virtue of their superior taste and culture. The advertisements suggest to the audience that one ought to buy the product, because it is the duty of a member of a superior culture and race.

As director of seminars on Mexican Americans at Stanford University, Dr. Martinez had his students send letters to the corporations that have aired stereotyped commercial versions of Mexicans. A pair of letters went to Liggett and Myers, makers of L&M cigarettes, one letter objecting to the stereotyping of Mexican Americans, the other to the belittling of gypsies. Here are the two responses:

First:
This acknowledges your letter of February 25 about an L&M TV commercial. We sincerely regret your reaction to this commercial because we did not intend to be derogatory to any ethnic group. "Paco" is a warm, sympathetic and lovable character with whom most of us can identify because he has a little of all of us in him, that is, our tendency to procrastinate at times.

Second:
The gypsies are warm, sympathetic and lovable characters with whom most of us can identify because he has a little of all of us in him; that is, our tendency to procrastinate at times.

Dr. Martinez contends that the Anglo projects his worst traits upon unsuspecting and defenseless minority groups to avoid any suspicion that he himself might have these same characteristics. Paco and the Frito Bandito become scapegoats that the Anglo can burden with his own bad traits at the expense of someone else.

A list of derogatory commercials to be seen on television or in newspaper and magazine ads has been compiled by Dr. Martinez, and for the sake of making the public and other Mexican Americans aware, a sampling of the list follows:

The Advertiser	The Medium	The Message
		Mexicans are:
Granny Goose	*Fat Mexican toting guns, ammunition	Overweight, carry deadly weapons
Frito-Lay	#*Frito Bandito	Sneaky, thieves
Liggett & Meyers	*"Paco" never "feenishes" anything, not even a revolution	Too lazy to improve selves
A. J. Reynolds	*Mexican bandito	Bandits
Camel Cigarettes	*"Typical" Mexican village, all sleeping or bored	Do-nothings, irresponsible
General Motors	#*White, rustic man holds Mexicans at gunpoint	Should be and can be arrested by superior white man
Lark (L&M)	#Mexican housepainter covered with paint	Sloppy workers, undependable
Arrid	*Mexican bandito sprays underarm, voice says, "If it works for him, it will work for you."	Stink the most

*—TV Commercial
#—Newspaper or magazine ad

Of course, some of our best friends are Mexican American stereotypes, such as José Jiménez, created by Bill Dana, who for so long parlayed an exaggerated Spanish accent into television, radio, billboard, and other media advertisements and into an hour-long special on television as well. Somewhere, no doubt, reruns of the Cisco Kid are still played on television stations that need some innocuous program to fill in a half-hour a day; so there rides again the Robin Hood of the West, the romantic, articulate, suave Cisco, strongly Spanish-looking, and at his side his not-so-suave Mexican companion, the paunchy, always-smiling, broken-English-speaking Pancho, playing the stereotype to the hilt.

Beyond the electronics and printed news media are the textbooks, the novels romanticizing the Southwest, and the so-called social scientists who have created scientifically tested stereotypes. In 1925, Harcourt, Brace and Company published a textbook called *North America*, by J. Russell Smith, a Columbia University professor. In its last pages, the author quotes an Anglo mine superintendent from deep in the Southwest who says of his Mexican workers:

It is physically impossible for the Mexican to worry.
. . . [They] are children. It is childish not to worry.
. . . . [They] have an inclination to be lazy.

Nevertheless, the Mexican, native-born or immigrant, formed the backbone for the silver, copper, and zinc industry in the Southwest for decades prior to and after 1925. In fact it was Mexican miners, experienced in Spanish-operated mines in Mexico, who instructed the ignorant prospectors in the rudiments of mining for the gold rush bonanza.

A map depicting the diversity of ethnic origins of people comprising the nation was published in 1956 by Friendship Press for distribution as a social sciences aid. The chart displayed dozens of immigrant groups, but only one tasteless word appeared for the group being depicted: "wetbacks." The small caricature of the Mexican campesino (field worker) next to the word, by the way, is shown straddling the Rio Grande.

A *Time* magazine article dealing with the grape strike, published, significantly, on July 4, 1969 (the issue with Cesar Chavez on the cover), contained this statement: "One major impediment to the Mexican American is his Spanish language because it holds him back in U. S. schools."

How could anyone view the Spanish language as an

impediment? The Anglo authors of the article were repeating a stereotype and reinforcing on a national scale
the erroneous concept that Chicanos fail in school because they speak Spanish. They fail in school because
the teachers and the administrators don't speak Spanish.
The impediment Chicano students face is the gringo,
not their mother tongue. It seems impossible for the
Anglo to understand that he is the impediment. I say
"seems" only because I assume that there are some
Anglos who are only unconsciously cultural suprema-
cists or culturally myopic.

In the September 1969 issue of *Music Educators
Journal*, the Artley Company of Elkhart, Indiana, ad-
vertises its bass flute by displaying a full-page photograph of a mexicano-bandito type in full revolutionary
regalia—rifle, bandoleros, and a sidekick burro to boot
—playing a flute! Now why did they have to pick on the
Mexican bandito stereotype? The ad did say something
about a revolution in flutes, but why us?

I've had many encounters with the reverse effects of
the stereotype, too many in fact. But one of the most
interesting, because it is within my own family, has to
do with the macho, or male, side of my people in San
Antonio. Anyone raised in the West Side barrio of San
Antonio knows full well what a man has to overcome to
keep a good job, establish a small business, educate
himself or his children, and raise a family. Having
scratched his way out of deprivation, taking jobs sometimes without pay just to learn a trade and prove himself, he and his offspring condemn Chicanos who won't
accept menial, low-paying jobs today: "First, they ask if
you'll give them lunch; will you take them out to the
job, and bring them back; and how much will you pay;
if they find out the job is a little physical, they'll tell you
to forget it. They won't work; maybe they'll take a job
for a couple of weeks and quit, or they'll stay home
when they feel like it." My rebuttal, time and again, is:
be specific. Who are you talking about when you say
"they"? It sounds as if you're talking about the whole

Chicano world, but you really mean the fellows down in the plaza, tomando el sol, basking in the sun every day.

My own people, mi familia, are living proof that the stereotype is just that, a lie. Besides, who built the railroads in most of the Southwest and helped put down the rails in the Midwest? Who mined the silver and copper in New Mexico? Who harvested the crops from the redwood forests to the Gulf Stream waters? The Chicano.

How many people travel thousands of miles a year each year for work in the Northwest, in the Rocky Mountain region, in the Midwest, the Great Lakes area, and in Florida? The Chicano does it because he wants work, income, a home, and comforts for his family—everything we Chicanos who are better off take for granted but that he's forced to migrate for, taking to the road in spite of the suffering and humiliation he has to endure.

The Anglo has forced the Chicano into stoop-labor jobs by denying him education and withholding decent, well-paying jobs, and then has turned the situation into an image of the Chicano that says: "They're built close to the ground." "Give 'em beans and tortillas and a bottle of tequila, and they're happy."

No Chicano should get trapped into playing that insidious Anglo game. If Mexican American men, young or old, refuse a job or fail in a job, blame the gringo society that deprives a man of his manhood, that disgraces the womanhood in our women, and deprives so many of our youths of an image worthy of following.

In the eyes of Chicanos, the most tragic effect of stereotyping is the deprivation of a true, positive image of the Mexican American for Chicano youths to imitate. How do you undo the harm of one Frito Bandito commercial or the adverse effects of an ad showing a single Anglo, gun in hand, in control of three swarthy-looking Mexican Americans?

Then how do you crack the cement-block mentalities of the advertising agencies and their clients, who share equally the responsibility for such damaging commercials? Isn't it enough to tell a major corporation executive that you find his idea of a good commercial offensive and insulting to yourself and your people? Is it asking too much of advertising executives to turn their talents, as they have done in regard to the black American, to presenting a positive view of the Chicano and of Spanish-speaking people in general (and while they're at it, of the American Indian)?

Advertising that uses false images of Mexican Americans to sell a product is racist, the Chicano insists. The corporations that pay for the commercials, the advertising firms that write them, and the media that make them public cannot consider themselves free of prejudice merely because they no longer exclude Negroes from the ads and programs. As long as they portray the Chicano and other Americans as inferior, or in a false and belittling light, they are prejudiced. It is another form of exploitation and degradation based on race and color which the Anglo has devised, and he continues to do nothing to remedy the situation.

For the time being, it seems that only continuous publicity by Chicano groups and public pressure may force the agencies and advertisers to stop maligning the Chicano. At present there are a few Chicano groups intent on ending the discriminatory portrayal of Mexican Americans in the media, including the Mexican American Anti-Defamation Committee, in Washington, D.C.; the Involvement of Mexican Americans in Gainful Endeavors, in San Antonio, Texas; and the Council to Advance and Restore the Image of the Spanish Speaking and Mexican American, in Los Angeles, California. These groups are hampered by lack of funds and manpower to field the necessary forces in an assault against the networks, the studios, the unions, the advertising agencies, and the corporations. Their efforts have resulted in the exposé of the Frito Bandito, although his sweetly leering, dark-brown face was still appearing in various parts of the country well after the official deadline that Frito-Lay had set for August 1970. However, while one version of the stereotype may fade, others spring up as if from its ashes to continue the defamation of the Chicano character. Recent creations for television include an ad for Valencia oranges, grown in Florida, depicting a conquistador in cartoon form (alias the Frito Bandito) who says: "Buenos dias, you all"; another for Gwaltney meat products showing a Ché-looking, mustachioed, heavily Spanish-accented man on an airplane, apparently being dissuaded from hijacking the plane by being served tasty bacon for breakfast; Flair's variation, with El Marko riding through a sleepy Mexican village marking up everything he can reach; and Crest toothpaste's special offer of hand puppets that included Speedy Gonzalez as the only ethnic-related puppet among some half-dozen cartoon characters. Kellogg's offered a collection of Little People that included stereotypes not only of the mexicano, "the Mexican caballero," which again looked like the well-known bandito, but also of a Chinese philosopher and the American Indian princess Pocahontas. These were in contrast to other characters based on fictional or fairy tale personalities.

An almost incredibly blatant example of media insensitivity to the feelings of raza occurred in May 1970 when Elgin National Industries published in more than seventy Sunday supplements across the country an ad which declared: "Your new Elgin is better than the Elgins Zapata was willing to kill for in 1914." Terming Zapata "the Mexican Robin Hood and revolutionary," the ad concluded, "It's a good thing Emiliano Zapata's gone. He'd be stealing Elgins as fast as we could make them." To complete the entire insulting affair, Elgin offered a "Handsome Zapata poster" for one dollar to what it must consider a thoroughly gullible and equally insensitive public. Anti-defamation groups in Washington, San Antonio, Chicago, and Los Angeles initiated a national protest that startled Elgin executives and their advertising hirelings, and in the end Elgin withdrew any future use of the advertisement.

The most direct economic method of convincing the media, I'm sure, would be a boycott of the offending products, but unless more persons than Chicanos could be convinced to desist from buying certain brands, the Chicano population could not have the necessary impact. And it is quite apparent that many of the kinds of products in question are beyond the means or interests of most Mexican Americans anyway. But a successful boycott has been implemented by the grape strikers; perhaps the same kind of structure and tactics could be implemented, one product at a time, one city or region at a time (as was done in Pueblo, Colorado, in 1970 against Coors Beer) to persuade the communications media to recognize the harm being done in its commercials and to change the image into a positive one. Eventually, Chicanos must bring to task the media purveyors of prejudice.

Concurrent steps that must be taken include the hiring and training of more Mexican Americans for jobs in the communications industry at every level, from crews to actors and directors. An affirmative approach must be adopted in the depiction of Spanish-speaking people in theaters and on television as well as in commercials. There needs to be a pronounced opening-up of opportunities for Mexican Americans in the theater, in moviemaking, and in other mass media.

The few entertainers of Mexican descent who have made it in show business are far from committing their talents and lives to working from inside the industry and supporting Chicanismo to the extent they should. Individually, some have contributed to la causa at benefits and the like. I know of only one nationally famous personality who openly professes his Chicanismo—Joe Kapp, world champion pro quarterback and a native of

Southern California. Show business personalities apparently hesitate to identify too closely with the Chicano movement. Many of them made a successful career in singing or acting as a result of Anglos buying their records or viewing their films; too close an identification with the Chicano might jeopardize their money-making potential. Consequently, agents have probably counseled against such activist roles; of course, they're right —and probably white.

Very simply stated, the Mexican American is nearly defenseless against the denigration that results from the use of stereotypes in the mass media. From the Chicano's viewpoint, we are being made the communication industry's new "nigger." Since they can no longer denigrate the Negro, they turn to safer prey such as the Chicano and the Indian.

4

GENESIS, ACCORDING TO CHICANO

T is a tale told to us by the viejitos that after forming the earth and the waters, breathing forth the sky, and striking the fires of the sun to heat the world, the Creator decided to make man.

At first he took some earth and water and molded the two elements into the shape we know as man; then he breathed upon it, and to complete its form he placed the figure into a kind of oven where the full rays of the sun would finish the work. When the Creator returned a short while later, he found the man alive and well, but something, the Creator thought, wasn't quite pleasing; his color, yes, too light, that's what it was. Once again he molded a man and set him in the oven for the sun's rays to do their work. Returning much later than before, he saw that this second man had become quite well done; dark of skin he was, but the Creator felt that this still wasn't the right color for man. So one more time he fashioned a figure, breathed upon it and placed it in the oven in the sun's full rays. This time he was gone longer than the first time but not as long as the second, and when he came back to the third man he was pleased to see him a warm shade of brown. He was now satisfied that this brown man pleased him most of all.

This is the creation of man according to the viejitos, the old storytellers of the Mexican people. While the message of the tale seems quite obvious, it presents new subtleties in the light of the current struggle of the Chicano to achieve a strong self-image and a vibrant group identity.

I can remember hearing the legend as a little boy growing up in the barrio on the West Side of San Antonio. The conditions in which the Chicano community existed seemed natural to me, and the fable about our brown skin did not appear at all like what it actually is—a defense against the gringo's avowed racism and cultural supremacy and an undisguised chauvinist effort to put down the white and the black man whom we recognized as the enemy.

The story has much to say about the psychology of the Mexican American. While it's anyone's guess as to when the story originated, it could date back to the invasion of Mexico by Cortez and the first importation into the Western Hemisphere of black slaves soon after by the Spaniards. The powerful impact of color prejudice introduced by Europeans is apparent in the probable antiquity of the fable as much as in its telling. And yet its very form, that of an anthropomorphic god making mud-pie men and baking them to just the right turn, suggests a quality of innocence that contrasts with the vicious and violent racism perpetrated by the gringo and the black.

There is a distinct difference between people with a color consciousness who resort to allegory or fable to make a point and those who depend on science, whether it's anthropology, sociology, psychology, biology, or some other "ology," to establish their superiority over another group of people. One method may only be more sophisticated than the other, but the real difference lies in the nature of the deception. Chicanos can pass off the story simply as allegory, not really meaning race prejudice but indicating personal conviction and

pride in one's own personality. The Anglo-Aryan myth-
odology, however, conjures up every theory, fact, or
fallacy it can to prove to its own satisfaction its supremacy over all non-Anglo-Aryans. The fact that Anglos
have more sophisticated procedures adds no credence
to their claims; rather it demonstrates the abuse man
can make of his intellect.

While I don't mean to deny the existence of racial or
class prejudice in Latin Americans and in Mexican
Americans, I do want to point out that peoples of Spanish descent have more easily intermarried and set aside
race consciousness than some other races, and that the
Mexican American himself is a blend of races as well as
of cultures. Chicanos and most peoples of Spanish-Indian descent honor San Martin de Porres, a Catholic
saint of mixed Spanish, Indian, and African blood; we
have a special love for the Virgen de Guadalupe, who is
the Mexican brown madonna. In Mexico and several
other Latin countries, October 12 is celebrated as el dia
de la raza (the day of the people), not to commemorate
the dubious feat of one man, as is done in the United
States, but to rejoice together in the creation of a new
identity, the blending of Indian, Spanish, Negro, and
Mexican bloods into a bronze people.

The white man has been incapable of accepting the
humanity of other persons regardless of their skin pig-
ment; only he among the immigrants to the Americas
rejected marriage with the native peoples. The Anglo-
Saxons' rejection of native American tribes as mere sav-
ages and nonhuman has much to do with the present
racial conflict in the United States. Even though the
Anglo was willing to have sexual intercourse with Indian "princesses" (of which there must have been thousands, or a prolific few, Vine Deloria, Jr., a Standing
Rock Sioux spokesman relates, judging by the many
Anglos today who claim to be descended from one), a
truly mestizo rendering was not meant to be. In spite of
the search for religious freedom that motivated the

Anglos to come to the New World, they themselves did not choose to grant the Indians religious or cultural freedom.

The Spaniards attempted genocide also, but being fewer in number than their Anglo-Saxon counterparts, they were absorbed more readily by the Mexicans. The Spanish elements that remained unassimilated, specifically under Bourbon rule and European controls, were partly removed in 1810 and again in 1870, until finally the last vestiges were eradicated in 1910, culminating in the present national character of the Mexican Republic. Mexico endured three major revolutions before it achieved its own national consciousness and form of government, although it does appear that further change is still to come.

Americans now have more money and more leisure than ever before in their history, but at the same time greater tensions, less sensitivity toward a positive use of their money and leisure, greater civil conflicts than ever, and social disintegration not only between minority and majority groups but within the majority group itself. America may be preparing for a third revolution which, bloody or not, will be spearheaded by a coalition of Americans no longer satisfied just with time and money and the chance to spend them and those who have lots of time but very little money and for whom opportunity has been a rhetorical all-day sucker offered by one President after another. These Americans will attempt massive surgery to cut out the Puritan Ethic and the Anglo supremacist elements that have no place in the Americas.

The Mexican American, as the Chicano version of creation tells us, does represent the best combination of sun and time, but because he is what he is, he can also embody and bring together the white and the black and the red for their mutual benefit and that of the whole nation. The short fable prefigures the inevitable dissolution of colors and races into one worldwide people for whom only the level of one's humanity toward his fellow man will matter.

Frankly I think that the ancient story about us is actually true, the Bible and scientific knowledge notwithstanding. And if we play our cartas right, carnales, we just might pull the blacks and the whites out of the mess they're in. It's the least we can do for people who are culturally deprived. We need not expect any thanks.

5

THE AMERICAS—BEFORE AND
AFTER COLUMBUS

HISTORY as Chicanos see it began with the peoples who inhabited the North and South American continents at least twenty thousand years ago, perhaps much earlier. The ways of life developed by these peoples ranged from very primitive frameworks to socially complex and sophisticated structures.

About the time of the start of the Christian era in the Mediterranean area, highly evolved societies were emerging in the regions of the southern half of the North American continent, today known as Mexico and Central America, and a portion of the upper half of the South American continent. These regions were diverse in soil, climate, and natural resources and from them there burgeoned elaborately structured and evolved societies.

The Mayas of Central America, the Incas of Peru, the Chibchas of Colombia, and the Aztecs of central Mexico devised systems of irrigation, cultivated food and medicinal plants now taken for granted, and implemented well-formulated governments (particularly the Aztec and Incan), replete with systems of travel and communication. In the sciences, the arts, and religion,

these civilizations demonstrated a remarkable understanding and skill from the most basic points of knowledge to the most precise shadings of speculative
thought. And in the fundamental evolutions of mind
and spirit, the first peoples of the Americas took to
paths that were widely divergent from those of the Europeans.

Each of these dominant kingdoms unified a large
number of different tribes within its area of influence
under a single government, emphasizing a particular
language and religion. By the end of the 1400s, by our
reckoning of time, these civilizations had reached a certain level of organization and quasitheocratic rule (the
Aztec being now the most notorious for its human sacrifices), and it appears that they were at a critical point
of ascent or decline according to each people's abilities
and aspirations. The historian Samuel Eliot Morison, in
The Oxford History of the American People (1965),
estimated that the Aztecs and perhaps the Iroquois in
North America might have evolved sufficiently, given
another century or two of self-development and freedom from Europe, to form "strong native states capable
of adopting European war tactics and maintaining their
independence to this day, as Japan kept her independence from China."

However, that indomitable combination of capital-
istic foresight, adventuresome spirit, and insatiable
avarice, later known as Yankee enterprise, intervened.
In 1492, a Genoese sea captain, Christopher Columbus,
landed on an island which he promptly named San Salvador, undoubtedly because it saved his neck. A few
historians, such as Morison and John Collier, have let
out some secrets about Columbus that school children
probably never hear lest the "discoverer" of the New
World lose his heroic aura. Shortly after making his first
landfall in what is now the Caribbean, Columbus' greed
for gold and other riches that could be gleaned from the
Indies (where he thought he had landed) led him to

institute a system of gold tribute from the "Indians," the Arawaks, and to subdivide the native peoples' land among his own men. In short, Columbus was the first to establish a slave economy which, in fifty years, virtually wiped out a native Caribbean population that had numbered more than three hundred thousand in 1492.

Being the first man to have the opportunity, Columbus readily beat the Anglo-Saxons to the institution of slavery and the initiation of policies of extermination among the "Indian" tribes. He also kept alive the fable of gold cities and Indies riches just around the next cape, thus preparing the path for the inhumanities that Cortéz, Pizarro, and de Quesada would soon inflict on civilizations that had been centuries in the making but were eradicated within a fifteen-year period of conquest.

By the mid-1530s, Spanish adelantados (advancers) had penetrated into the present southwestern United States in their quest for gold. With them were Spanish padres, also avaricious—for converts. In the 100 years following the attacks on the Mexican, Peruvian, and Colombian peoples, the Spanish influence had spread like a fan from the initial Caribbean points of contact to cover South America and the North American continent halfway up the present western United States and into what is now Florida as well.

We believe that the people who civilized Mesoamerica and made the Valley of Mexico the center of their civilization had come from a northwestern region we know as Aztlán. Perhaps this region had been fertile and conducive to developing a great civilizing mentality among its inhabitants, but for whatever reasons—climate, overpopulation, hostilities, or adventure—exodus after exodus took place. A people called the Nahúas (of the Uto-Aztecan family, anthropologists say) found their way into the Valley of Mexico. First came the Toltecs, the great artists, builders, and scientists, evolvers of the Nahuatl religion; then the Chichimecas, a number of barbarous tribes who overwhelmed the Toltecs but absorbed their civilization including the Aztecs, who were the administrators, legatees, and disseminators of Nahuatl thought and culture from the mid-1300s until Cortéz' arrival in 1519.

Most Chicanos who are aware of the history enjoy repeating the fact that eleven years before the Mayflower's Anglo-Saxon cargo disembarked at Plymouth Rock, Spanish, Mexican, and Indian explorers and aides had established a settlement at Sante Fe and had laid much of the framework for the present-day character of the western states. Alvar Nuñez, Cabeza de Vaca, Estevan, an African, and two other Spanish members of an ill-fated expedition that had started out to find a route through Mexico to India in 1527 but were shipwrecked on the Texas coast survived six years of wandering through the Southwest by doing as the Indians did.

Estevan was the first European to sight the fabled cities of Cibola, mud-hut Zuñi villages in reality. Acting as advance scout for an expedition begun in 1539 by Fray Marcos de Niza, Estevan pushed through Sonora up into what would become Arizona and New Mexico in the senseless search for Cibola. The next year Francisco Vasquez de Coronado sought Golden Quivera, another fantasy the Indians dreamed up to keep the foolish Spaniards moving on. He traversed Texas, Kansas, and up as far as Indiana, where he may have been the first Catholic to set foot on land that was to be the University of Notre Dame campus. Along the way, he burned 200 Indians at the stake in a village called Tiguex, near what is now Albuquerque, New Mexico, when he discovered that Cibola did not exist. This insane slaughter touched every white man, Spaniard or otherwise, who later ventured into the area. It was the beginning of the history of racial murder and intimidation which has since haunted the Southwest.

By 1535, the major Mexican and Indian civilizations of the New World had been subsumed by the Span-

iards, and there had been initiated—through intermar-
riage, the interchange of ideas, knowledge, and religion
—the creation of a new raza, a new people. The blending of Indian and Mexican bloodlines with Spanish and
African strains and the merging of culture and tradition
was to become la raza as we know it today. The document, Recopilación de Leyes de los Reinos de las Indias
(the Laws of the Indies), promulgated in 1680 and representing a compilation of nearly two centuries of colonial
cedulas (laws) decreed by the Spanish royal crown, ex-
pressly recognized the existence of a new race, the
mestizo of the Americas. According to the laws, common lands were to be held perpetually; upon these laws
were predicated the land grants that served as the
foundation for the exploration and settlement of the
Southwest.

Before the colonists in the East had begun to establish an independent government based on Anglo tradition and laws, Spanish explorers, padres, and settlers
had assured the future development of the Southwest
and Mexico as a bicultural region and had unknowingly
paved the way for Anglo incursions of the future. Juan
Rodriguez Cabrillo opened the shores of California for
exploration and colonization with his discovery of San
Diego Bay in 1542. Between 1598 and 1630, Juan de
Oñate colonized New Mexico extensively, but Indians
drove out the Spaniards in 1680. Not until 1692 did one
of them, Diego de Vargas, return, make peace with the
Pueblo Indians, and settle many of today's urban sites.
Father Eusebio Kino had charted most of the territory
of southern Arizona by 1700. Juan Bautista de Anza led
an incredible march across the California desert in 1775
and later pushed on to Monterey and San Francisco. By
the 1820s, twenty-one missions were established in California under Father Junipero Serra and other Franciscan friars, four presidial towns were founded (San
Diego, Santa Barbara, Monterey, and San Francisco),
and two pueblos were settled, San Jose and Los Angeles (1781). In Texas, twenty-five missions had been

raised, and the principal towns of San Antonio (1718), Goliad, and Nacogdoches founded. In Arizona, an equal number of missions had been raised, with Tucson founded in 1776.

While personal contacts between Anglo-Americans and Mexican or other Latin countrymen had been limited to diplomatic relations during the formative years of both the colonies and Mexico, there did exist a common bond in the method by which both nations had achieved independence from Old World sovereignties. The United States, Mexico, and Central and South American countries underwent similar periods of social upheaval and revolution between 1776 and 1821, during which most of the New World won independence from Europe. That time bridges a span between the Anglo-American Revolution and the overthrow of the Spanish garrision at Veracruz in 1821, which forced the Spanish viceroy to sign a provisional treaty making Mexico and Central America in effect free nations. In the 1820s both Mexico, which had revolted against Spanish control in 1810, and the United States, which had been kept busy by the aftermath of its revolution and then the War of 1812, suddenly found time to consider their neighbors. Formal diplomatic relations were established between the two countries in 1822 at a time when, for trade purposes, the United States was vying with Britain for the good will of Latin-American countries.

Anglo goods and men began to flow via the Santa Fe Trail from Independence, Missouri, to the New Mexican trade center in the early 1820s. In 1823, the first significant emigration of non-Mexican settlers—a few hundred Anglos—occurred in that part of Mexico which is now Texas. That tiny chink in the Mexican dam grew rapidly; in 1834, the twenty-two thousand non-Mexicans (including two thousand slaves) were four times the number of Mexican Texans. John Quincy Adams named the first United States minister to Mexico in 1825, Joel R. Poinsett (a bright red flower he brought back was named for him), who had the bad luck to

foment a civil war in Mexico between proponents of
Scottish rite Masonic lodges and those of York rite
lodges. Scholastic interest was shown on the part of
William H. Prescott, who, in 1843, wrote a pro-Spanish,
pro-ancient Mexican Indian account of the conquests of
Mexico and Peru; by John Lloyd Stephens, who, in
1828, reported on personal travels in Central America;
and by Washington Irving, who published studies of
Columbus and Spanish history. Two accounts of California and the West appeared in the 1840s, one by
Richard H. Dana and the other by John C. Frémont.

While diplomatic maneuvering for Mexican and
Latin American trade characterized the central interests
of the United States during the 1820s and 1830s, the
growth of the obsession called "manifest destiny" and
the smoldering conflict over slave versus free states
prompted certain interests to turn toward the annexing
of Texas and as much of northwestern Mexico as possible—or of all Mexico if need be.

The battle at the Alamo in 1836 shattered any
chances for a gentlemanly settlement of conflict between Texas-United States and Mexico. The Alamo was
the first major clash of Anglo-Mexican concerns; it convinced Anglo-America that Mexico would fight rather
than be robbed of its land, however feebly adminis-
trated or controlled, and it inflamed feeling on both
sides of the border. Men of good will on both sides
notwithstanding, the pattern was set for the United
States to follow—toward premeditated war.

Following some dubious conciliatory moves by both
the Anglo-American and Mexican governments, the
United States launched a ruthless and calculated attack
on Mexico in 1847 to wrest control of Arizona, California, Colorado, Nevada, New Mexico, Texas, and Utah.
The Anglo overwhelmed a vast region and, along with
the land, a mestizo culture. To this day, the Anglo does
not know or will not admit that he owes everything he
found in the Southwest to the Indian tribes who first
forced an existence out of the land, to the Spanish who

explored, colonized, and unified the character of the
land, and to the Mexican American who contributed his
labor (and, in the process, almost lost his identity), to
transform the land into a new civilization.

The historical evolution of the Americas as seen
through Chicano eyes is drawn in sketch only—a history
text is not intended here. We know that first there was
the presence for thousands of years of tribal peoples
throughout the North and South American continents,
that vital and fascinating civilizations evolved within
the past two thousand years, and that the most relevant
among them for the Chicano was the Mexican. But then
there came the influx of the Spanish, flowing up from
the Caribbean, altering the character of the ancient cultures, not quite replacing them but combining with them
to form a Spanish-Mexican-Indian confluence of civilization. From the beginning of the sixteenth century, a
third thrust of peoples pushed out from the eastern
coast of North America, clashing with the new mestizo
culture in the early nineteenth century, rejecting that
new culture, and so never allowing itself or that culture
to be enhanced by a new fusion of humanity.

In point of fact, there is not much to draw upon for
a detailed history of the Chicano since 1848. From the
Chicano's vantage point, much more is known of the
Southwest's history before 1848 than after the year of
the signing of the Treaty of Guadalupe Hidalgo. The
Chicano's sense of history is only that—a sense—not a
deep knowledge of his contributions in the past or his
role in shaping the present and future of his country.
Thus the Chicano sees his history as a Mexican American as if through the wrong end of a telescope: the scale
of his past seems tiny and very far away. The Chicano
must gain the correct perspective on his own history
and rewrite the textbooks in which we have never been
mentioned except in a role that reassures the Anglo of
his supremacy over all peoples.

6

THE SPIRIT OF '48: THE TREATY OF GUADALUPE HIDALGO

THE Chicano experience with the Anglo-American's sense of justice and honesty has been marked by the continual denial of his rights, a relentless program to purge him of Chicano and non-Anglo values, and the unremitting violation of the most unique treaty—and for the Chicano, the most important—in U.S. history.

The Treaty of Guadalupe Hidalgo climaxed the first of our imperialistic and declared wars against a people outside the boundaries of the United States. Signed by Mexican and American representatives on February 2, 1848 the treaty differed little from the compacts drawn up between the United States Government and American Indian tribes. Full American citizenship and protection were offered to the Mexican people captured behind the new boundary lines established by the treaty. Their culture, language, and religion as well as property and other civil rights were guaranteed them.

What actually ensued after the conclusion of the treaty is remarkably the same as what happened to the American Indians. Lands and property were stolen, rights were denied, language and culture suppressed, opportunities for employment, education, and political

71

representation were thwarted. Many Chicano leaders, particularly Reies Tijerina and Rodolfo "Corky" Gonzales, charge that the United States has violated every provision of the treaty dealing with the Mexican people it subsumed. But whereas retribution in land or money or services has been made to the American Indians, nothing of the kind has been returned to Mexican Americans who were the unsuspecting victims of the Anglo perfidy. We Chicanos contend that the Mexican American's present status as a citizen, the material deprivation, the loss of self-respect and dignity, and the whole aspect of virtual subjugation, all stem from violations of the treaty. Through its Congress, its federal and state agencies, its unscrupulous politicians, agricultural corporations, law-enforcement bodies, and through its courts, American society has stripped away the rights and benefits that all Mexican American people should have enjoyed.

The pertinent paragraphs which follow are taken from the treaty as amended by the United States Congress on March 16, 1848. The original pact was changed —it will soon become apparent why:

ARTICLE VIII. Mexicans now established in territories previously belonging to Mexico, and which remain for the future within the limits of the United States, as defined by the present treaty, shall be free to continue where they now reside, or to remove at any time to the Mexican Republic, retaining the property which they possess in the said territories, or disposing thereof, and removing the proceeds wherever they please, without their being subjected, on this account, to any contribution, tax, or charge whatever.

Those who shall prefer to remain in the said territories may either retain the title and rights of Mexican citizens, or acquire those of citizens of the United States. But they shall be under the obligation to make their election within one year from the date of the exchange of ratifications of this treaty; and those who shall remain in the said territories after the expiration of that year, without having declared their intention to retain the character of Mexicans, shall be considered to have elected to become citizens of the United States.

In the said territories, *property of every kind, now established there, shall be inviolably respected.* [Italics mine. A.R.] The present owners, the heirs of these, and all Mexicans who may hereafter acquire said property by contract, shall enjoy with respect to it guarantees equally ample as if the same belonged to citizens of the United States.

ARTICLE IX. The Mexicans who, in the territories aforesaid, shall not preserve the character of citizens of the Mexican Republic, conformably with what is stipulated in the preceding article, shall be incorporated into the Union of the United States, and be admitted at the proper time (to be judged of by the Congress of the United States) to the enjoyment of *all the rights of citizens of the United States*, according to the principles of the Constitution; and in the meantime, *shall be maintained and protected in the free enjoyment of their liberty and property, and secured in the free exercise of their religion without restriction.* [Italics mine. A.R.]

ARTICLE X. [Stricken from the treaty.]

Article IX was amended by the United States Congress, condensing a much longer set of conditions into one paragraph. Originally, it had been stipulated that Mexicans "be admitted as quickly as possible," "lo mas pronto posible," not as in the amended version, "at the proper time"; the rights and property of the Catholic Church were fully spelled out in two succeeding paragraphs. What was contained, then, in the only article of the original document that was totally deleted, Article X?

In the volume *Algunos Documentos sobre el Tratado de Guadalupe y la Situación de Mexico Durante la Invasión Americana,* No. 31 of the Archivo Historico Diplomatico Mexicano, there is the following (translated from the Spanish):

ARTICLE X. All the land grants made by the Mexican government or by the competent authorities which pertained to Mexico in the past and which will remain in the future within the boundaries of the United States, *will be respected as valid,* [italics mine. A.R.] with the same force as if those territories still remained within the limits of Mexico. But the grantees of lands in Texas who had taken possession of them and who because of the conditions in the state since discord began between the Mexican Government and Texas, may have been impeded from complying with all the conditions of the grants, have the obligation of fulfilling the same conditions under the stated terms of the respective grants, but now counted from the date of the exchange of ratifications of this Treaty; for failing to do this the same grants are not obligatory upon the State of Texas, in virtue of stipulations contained in this article.

The aforesaid stipulation in respect to the grantees of lands in those territories noted outside of Texas which might have taken possession of the said grants; for failing to fulfill the conditions of some of these grants, within the new terms which begin with the day of the exchange of ratifications of the present Treaty, according to the above stipulation, the same grants shall be null and void.

The Anglo Congress' tampering with the treaty did not end with these amendments. On May 26 of the same year, in Querétaro, Mexico, where Maximilian was to be executed nineteen years later, a protocol was signed by Mexican and U.S. representatives explaining the changes insisted upon by the United States. These most interesting elaborations follow:

1st. The American Government by suppressing the IXth article of the treaty of Guadalupe Hidalgo and substituting the IIId article of the treaty of Louisiana, did not intend to diminish in any way what was agreed upon by the aforesaid article IXth in favor of the inhabitants of the territories ceded by Mexico. Its understanding is that all of the agreement is contained in the 3d article of the treaty of Louisiana. In consequence all the privileges and guarantees, civil, political, and religious, which would have been possessed by the inhabitants of the ceded territories, if the IXth article of the treaty had been retained, will be enjoyed by them, without any difference, under the article which has been substituted.

2nd. The American Government by suppressing the Xth article of the treaty of Guadalupe Hidalgo did not in any way intend to annul the grants of lands made by Mexico in the ceded territories. These grants, notwithstanding the suppression of the article of the treaty, preserve the legal value which they may possess, and the grantees may cause their legitimate (titles) to be acknowledged before the American tribunals. (Titles: those which were legitimate titles up to the 13th of May, 1846, and in Texas up to the 2nd March, 1836.)

In this case, it was not Nicholas P. Trist but A. H. Sevier and Nathan Clifford who signed for the United States, both official representatives of the Anglo-American government.

Subsequent to these maneuvers, the United States Government, primarily through President Polk and the Department of State, began to diminish very effectively the substance of the treaty and generally to nullify the value of the treaty, and it did not rescind its claims on the land and property which it had taken by force. Specifically, the authority of the first Anglo-American representative, Nicholas P. Trist, was declared invalid, because Trist's credentials had been revoked by President Polk in October 1847, four months before the signing of the treaty. Not having had the official authority to sign the treaty, Trist's signature was meaningless and therefore the treaty itself was invalid.

However, in Volume 5 of *Treaties and Other International Acts of the United States,* edited by Hunter Miller, Document 129 quotes Polk's diary, revealing that the President considered the treaty valid in spite of Trist's lack of authority to carry on negotiations: "Mr. Trist has acted very badly but . . . if on further examination the Treaty is one that can be accepted, it should not be rejected on account of his bad conduct." The editorial comment is added, that ". . . there can be no doubt that the President had the power to adopt and confirm the unauthorized acts and signature of Trist . . . *the treaty was at the very least, a proposal* from the Mexican Government." [Italics mine. A.R.] Polk's message to the Senate on February 23 set aside, one would think, any controversy over the validity of Trist's negotiation of the treaty. It was his "duty," Polk stated, "to submit it [the treaty] to the Senate, with a view to its ratification." The President's only statement regarding the Trist issue cited Article X; it was his opposition apparently that led to its deletion: "To the 10th Article of the Treaty there are serious objections, and no instruction given to Mr. Trist contemplated or authorized its insertion. The public lands within the limits of Texas belong to that State, and this Government has no power to dispose of them, or to change the conditions of grants already made."

In pointing out that Trist had no instructions to negotiate any such terms as appeared in Article X, Polk admitted that the United States had no intention of confirming the land grants or property of the Mexican people captured by his army. By his interpretation, Texas, which had been extended to the Rio Grande, including all the land grants therein by a violent act of the federal government, was invested with all authority in the disposition of lands. Yet by conservative estimates, the federal government took over without remuneration in New Mexico alone 2 million acres of privately owned land, 1.7 million acres of communal land, and 1.8 million acres of other land between 1854 and 1930. In spite of Polk's cynical assertion of "state's rights," the federal government ignored all principles of justice and its guarantees of land rights in the Treaty of Guadalupe Hidalgo.

As to the protocol, Miller reports that "it was said that the protocol would have had no binding effect," since the protocol was "not regarded as part of the treaty . . . in any legal sense . . . or obligatory as an international act; on this point the two governments were in accord." The second explanatory note in the protocol, according to Miller, was meant only to "record the opinion of the two American lawyers," for there was no Article X to interpret or to construe as adhering to treaty text, "for none existed." In other words, the protocol was valid if the treaty was valid, but since Article

X had been deleted, then item 2 in the protocol was meaningless—the entire protocol was virtually worthless.

The blow most devastating to the cause of justice of all the points in Document 129 is Miller's note, that the treaty was "at the very least a proposal" of the Mexican Government. Given the circumstances of political maneuvering, Miller's almost offhand critique is extremely crucial, more so than may appear on the first reading. The protocol was the only document related to the treaty which was signed at the point of negotiations by authorized representatives of the United States Government. But the protocol is valid only if the treaty is valid; and if the treaty is valid, then it matters not a bit that authorized signatures were ever affixed to treaty documents. We know that the treaty was ratified by the United States Congress on March 16, 1848, and by Mexico on May 30, so that on the face of the ratifications, the Treaty of Guadalupe Hidalgo is valid. If it is valid, then the United States Government should have adhered to the terms of the agreement, but it has not. If the treaty can still be questioned, that is, considered or even proved invalid on the basis of the Trist issue, then Miller may be entirely correct, the United States Congress may have agreed only to accept a proposal—and no treaty actually exists!

If the treaty and protocol are actually invalid, then, technically, the United States and Mexico are still at war; the United States' possession of seven states in the Southwest grossly violates international law and the civil and human rights of native inhabitants of this region. The United States Government is trespassing on Chicano land. It follows that every other treaty or international agreement with Mexico is invalid as well. The final irony is that the United States proclaimed the treaty on July 4, 1848.

Setting aside this overriding problem for the moment, the treaty can be viewed from another perspec-

tive. Guadalupe Hidalgo differs from treaties between
the United States and tribal nations in that it does not
confirm the Mexican American in his land. In fact, the
protocol called into question every land grant when the
governmental language expressed doubt in the words,
"the legal value which they *may* possess," and then suggested that grantees "may" legitimize their titles in
Anglo courts. The final reference to American tribunals
was a subtle touch of tongue in cheek for, as later events
were to show, Mexicans could expect no justice in the
Anglo courts. At any rate, in no sense were areas of land
or reservations set aside for possession and use of the
Mexican American. Treaties with American Indian
tribes have invariably established reservations meant to
belong fully to the Indians and to fulfill whatever purpose they saw fit. These reservations have been perpetuated to a greater or lesser extent according to individual tribes. The native tribesmen usually had a hand
in drawing up or at least personally signing these treaties, although often some Indian might have been
coaxed into signing a treaty, even though he had no
right to do so.

The Chicano, however, had no voice in how lands,
rights, and responsibilities were to be controlled. On
paper, he was permitted to retain his holdings, but this
was a meaningless stipulation, it turned out, to the
Anglo. Mexicans supposedly could exercise an option to
leave for Mexico or remain; this was more of an invitation to leave than the proffering of a real choice. The
few thousand who repatriated to Mexico during the one
year's time allotted for mexicanos to decide left many
years of sacrifice behind, and very likely were forced to
dispose of their land and property at the lowest prices.
Of course, many mexicanos had only lived here a short
time and were glad to return to Mexico under the provisions of the treaty. Estimates indicate there were some
seventy-five thousand Spanish-speaking people in the
Southwest in 1848, sixty thousand of them in New Mex-

ico, and approximately one hundred and eighty thousand Indian tribesmen as well.

The hostility of certain Indian tribes and of the environment itself isolated New Mexico and most of Arizona from Anglo-American incursions for some time, solidifying the Spanish character of the region and subverting for a while the Anglo settlers that did appear, but delaying statehood (promised vaguely in the treaty) until the turn of the century. By contrast, Texas, a republic since 1836, was admitted to the Union in 1845; California, in 1850. Although they escaped for a while the hostility which Anglo-Americans visited on Chicanos in Texas and California, New Mexican and Arizonan mexicanos were subject to the connivances of lawyers, courts, and landowners who worked hand in hand to bend the laws to their benefit. Dr. Clark S. Knowlton, Chairman of the Department of Sociology at the University of Texas at El Paso, has fully documented the extent of Anglo greed and deceit in a number of his writings. Rampant lawlessness was the order of the era in Texas and California, with beatings, murders, and lynchings occurring on both sides but most widespread on the part of the Anglo-Americans. This aspect of Anglo belligerence and the Chicano side of the conflict are recorded by Carey McWilliams in his work, *North from Mexico*. The story of the Mexicans who revolted is a fascinating one, including Joaquín Murieta and Tiburcio Vasquez in California; Governor José Martínez and Elfego Baca in New Mexico; and John Nepomuceno Cortina of Brownsville, Texas, who terrorized and literally controlled the United States-Mexico border along 150 miles for about fifteen years. Their exploits are further evidence of the Chicano's rejection of gringo intimidation and atrocities committed to frighten the Mexican American people from their homes.

Besides the American Indian, who operates under a certain framework of treaties, the Chicano is the only

group in the United States which has a compact with
the United States Government by which certain rights
are guaranteed. Thus, besides the guarantees of the
Constitution and the Bill of Rights, Mexican Americans
should be accorded certain rights—an extra measure of
protection—just as the American Indian tribes are confirmed by treaties and other national statutes in their
specific Indian prerogatives. Of course, before an American Indian tribesman has a chance to say it, let me add
that having a treaty with the United States Government
does not immediately signify that the end of the rain-
bow is in sight, that the terms of the treaty will be
complied with, and that all will be right with the world.
The very opposite is true. Since it began making treaties with other nations, the United States has often
welched on its promises.

Article III of the Pickering Treaty of 1794 between
the United States and the Seneca Iroquois, as quoted by
Vine Deloria, Jr., in his book *Custer Died for Your Sins*
(1969), has a familiar ring:

Now the United States acknowledge all the land within the
aforementioned boundaries, to be the property of the Seneka
[sic] nation; and the United States will never claim the same,
nor disturb the Seneka nation, nor any of the Six Nations, or
of their Indian friends residing thereon and united with them,
in the free use and enjoyment thereof, but it shall remain
theirs, until they choose to sell the same to the people of the
United States, who have the right to purchase.

Deloria makes the pungent observation that "Rather
than having a choice as to whether or not to sell to the
United States, the Senecas were simply forced to sell. It
was a buyer's market."

Not only, then, do the brown men and the red men
have common bonds to the land and in blood from ages
past, we have the common experience of the white
man's deception and brutality whenever land, money,
and cultural supremacy are at stake. Note should be
made here about the duplicity toward Indians of the

United States Government, which cropped up even in a document dealing with their blood brothers, the Mexicans. In denouncing the United States for divesting Chicanos of their land and their heritage, we should also be aware that the Anglo could say of the Southwest's Indian peoples, in Article XI: "Considering that a great part of the territories, which by the present treaty are to be comprehended for the future within the limits of the United States, is now occupied by *savage tribes* . . ." the United States Government agreed to police the new border and restrain or capture and punish belligerent tribesmen. Further, adding a tinge of hypocrisy to the whole matter, the Article concludes:

. . . the sacredness of this obligation shall never be lost sight of by the said (U.S.) government, when providing for the *removal* of the Indians from any portion of the said territories, or for its being settled by citizens of the United States, but on the contrary, *special care* shall be taken not to place its Indian occupants under the necessity of seeking new homes by committing those invasions which the United States solemnly obliged themselves to restrain. [Italics mine. A.R.]

The Treaty of Guadalupe Hidalgo is the most important document concerning Mexican Americans that exists. From it stem specific guarantees affecting our civil rights, language, culture, and religion. A treaty is a formal and binding contract, ordinarily, between two countries by which specific provisions govern a number of points relating to boundaries, payment of damages, collaboration on projects of common benefit and interest, or co-operative defense. The United States Government is party to dozens of treaties of major significance in the world and, as a member of the United Nations, is subject to fulfill many provisions under the United Nations charter. Astonishingly, a promise made by a President nearly fifteen years ago and never formally ratified or codified into treaty form has enmeshed the United States in a five-year struggle in Vietnam to fulfill obligations that never stipulated involvement in a major war. Yet treaties dating back more than a hundred years, and especially one in particular of an international nature, are sloughed off and ignored by America.

Every guarantee or measure of special regard for the unique values and circumstances of our culture has been gradually and effectively eroded and sometimes, as in the hundreds of lynchings that were committed as late as 1922, viciously severed. Yet we Chicanos know next to nothing about the exact processes by which the Treaty of Guadalupe Hidalgo was made meaningless over the past century and a half. The Mexican American was involved in the treaty as a sort of silent third party—guaranteed everything but given no voice in the deliberations. Supposedly the Mexican Government spoke for him and secured certain rights and assurances of his safety with the United States Government, but the Mexican officials were negotiating from weakness; they could do no more than the United States allowed —"It was a buyer's market." It is clear, moreover, that at least one provision dealing with land grants proved too constricting on Congress, and that was quickly deleted a month after the initial treaty was signed; Mexico could only acquiesce.

Examining minutely what happened in the decades after 1848, reconstructing precisely the means by which Chicanos were destroyed, physically, economically, and psychologically, would be essential in establishing the case that Chicanos have against the federal government and against Anglo-America. We must next ascertain in what form retribution can be made for violations of Articles VII and IX of the Treaty of Guadalupe Hidalgo and how recompense can be insured for rights and benefits denied by the unilateral deletion of Article X from the February 2 document.

The objective is to discover how Chicanos can redeem the quality of life that full compliance with the provisions of the Treaty of Guadalupe Hidalgo would have created for the Mexicans trapped behind the enemy lines. The value of the civil, cultural, and religious rights specified or implied in the treaty is unquestionable and should lend impetus to a thorough investigation and, eventually, to litigation, perhaps by one of the new advocate groups of Chicanos in the Southwest. The United States Government entered into an agreement with Mexico and, under the provisions of the treaty, with the Mexicans who were destined to become the first Mexican Americans. The United States should be required under law to make restitution for the damages and losses the Chicano people suffered as a result of treaty violations.

But naïveté would be the kindest charge made of such an assertion if I did not add that the possibility of developing a case or cases in which Chicanos seek recompense for past Anglo atrocities and discrimination is exceedingly slim. And yet the history of the American Indian tribes is highlighted as much by legal battles nowadays as it was by battles at Wounded Knee and Little Big Horn in the past. These court decisions have concluded in multimillion-dollar settlements in behalf of these other native Americans. Why not for the Chicano? Chicanos simply have not discussed seriously enough or assessed fully the potential of such a venture. The publicity alone would be worthwhile, but, of course, publicity is only a secondary objective. Would such a case be worth fighting for—possibly for many years? Would enough Chicanos be willing to support it? Can realistic objectives be set in seeking retribution? What chances would there be of success? Where would one start? What issue should be the first to be broached? Or should we seek a lump sum and simply ask that we be allowed, as Indian tribes are, to allocate and spend our funds as we see fit within the required guidelines of law? Who would receive retribution: a certain age group such as elementary-age children; or the elderly; or a whole community according to need; or individuals if they had just claims, perhaps an old, yellowed grant deed?

One thing is absolutely sure: we have every right to make demands, and as a people we can never demand too much. We Chicanos have not begun to insist on what our people deserve from the federal and state governments, from local civil authorities, and from the corporations and the members of their boards who became rich on the muscle and sweat of Chicanos mixed into the cement and steel of their empires. Recompense for the gringo's treachery and exploitation must be made to the Chicano. Our people must demand of the Anglo society full repayment through its government, its churches, and its foundations and charitable groups for opportunities lost, for labor wasted and exploited, for talents suppressed, for intellects squandered, for lives aborted by disease and harsh living conditions, and for the losses incurred when cultural and linguistic assets have gone unused.

The bill that Chicanos have to collect from America is a big one. But of course no one can fix a value on the Chicanos who were murdered by the hundreds in the century following 1848, nor would the Chicano accept any kind or amount of remittance for those lives. Who would dare to tally up the bill for the lives of Chicano servicemen lost in the Anglo's wars? There is no possible way to evaluate the damage to our self-respect and our Chicanismo, which the Anglo would have us lose entirely so that we could then be acceptable by Anglo standards. And what of that special asset, the Chicano family life, which the Anglo has sought to destroy through his distorted sense of parenthood and privacy; through welfare programs that break up husband and wife; through his obsession for material goods; and through social aberrations such as teen-age economics, dependency on deodorants, automobiles, desexualizing colognes, castrating clothes, and low-brow media and advertisements.

It is really difficult to foresee at this point what would occur if the Chicano could force the United

States Government to comply with the provisions of the Treaty of Guadalupe Hidalgo. One extreme would be for us to demand the return of about seven states in the Southwest, for a start. But a great deal would depend on whether we could support with fundamental data the harm and losses that have been incurred; that is why a study of how Chicanos were exploited and subjugated would be of the essence. Beyond the incalculable areas of lives, human dignity, and family life that have been destroyed, there are many other more concrete issues: employment, education, political representation, land rights, housing, and health. A new relationship should develop between the Mexican American people and the federal government, one in which the Chicano would be given the status not only of an American citizen but of an American citizen with special rights of language, culture, and responsibility. Chicanos should develop a new bond among themselves and a new status with their government and with the rest of American society. Then we could more readily embrace Chicanismo and absorb or reject whatever aspects of Anglo society we wished. We would strive for broader control over the institutions and programs designed for us and for greater self-determination toward the future. In fact, we might even redeem some of those Chicanos who had given up la raza as a lost cause. We would be in a unique position, but with much stronger potential to contribute something to this country, where there's still so much redeeming to be done.

7

WHO IS THE ENEMY?

A GROUP of Chicanos once met to discuss the question, "Who Is the Enemy?" at a conference sponsored by the Center for the Study of Democratic Institutions. At the round table sat some of the veteran articulators of Chicano thought, including Dr. Ernesto Galarza, Bert Corona, Dionicio Morales, Grace Olivarez, Armando Rodriguez, Arturo Cabrera, and Bert Acosta, all residing and working in California at the time, 1967, except for Mrs. Olivarez, of Arizona.

Their colloquy developed with this sequence of ideas: Mrs. Olivarez said that we face a nebulous enemy, that we don't know who to identify as the enemy. Morales warned against the Tio Tomases, the Uncle Toms, who tell the Anglo one thing and the Mexican American another to maintain their security with both groups. Corona spoke of the Establishment, the center of real power and decision-making, which has excluded the Chicano from the rights and benefits of society but ably exploited us at the same time. Rodriguez condemned our educational system, and Cabrera rapped barrio communities, which have not achieved political control of their schools. Galarza warned that he had found from experience that pinpointing the enemy held certain dangers, and Acosta seconded his remarks but insisted that such risks must be taken.

Their conversations remained rather vague and general, yet bared the fact that Chicanos have many enemies, that no one single barrier or problem stands in our way, and that there are many complicated and frustrating hurdles to surmount. Very often, as one of the group indicated, the Chicano has been his own worst enemy. Any of us can recount a number of incidents when internecine warfare scuttled a beneficial project or aborted a movement to unify factions within a community. The Chicano is no less resentful of someone threatening his territory and no less fearful of losing authority or power which he has laboriously amassed over the years than any person of another ethnic or racial group. We, too, become institutions unto ourselves and often forget the needs and desires of the whole pueblo in our own scrambling to maintain position and status.

But my purpose is not to recount tales that we ourselves know all too well. What I would rather do, and what Chicanos must also do, is make a conscious assessment of the enemy who very often has used our internal problems to his benefit, as well as devising his own methods to hinder our development as individuals and as a group. I speak of the Anglo, of his institutions, of his manipulation of the media and of minds. Granted, the Anglo may often act from ignorance or possibly ill-founded good will, but as the black and red men can attest, gringo pseudoliberals and guilt-ridden do-gooders have betrayed us and taken advantage of us time and again. We have heard enough stories of the helpful, sincere Anglo who comes into a barrio to lend a helping hand, then turns around to write a book or thesis on his "observations," as if he had just spent a few days at the microscope; or the consultants who have recently found Mexican Americans a negotiable item in proposal writing and suck every dollar they can from the federal agencies to conduct studies; or, until recently, the conferences to which Chicanos were invited—to have our

brains picked—and which then resulted in programs
and papers outlining what Anglos were going to do to
solve our problems. An illustrative story concerns two
consultants, an Anglo and a Negro, sent by their firm to
evaluate an antipoverty program in a Texas town. After
two weeks they finished their report. A meeting was
called one evening of the townspeople, and a great
number turned out. The consultants held forth, explaining their charts and graphs at length, telling the people
what was wrong with their program. Then the local
chairman of the council stood and told the consultants
he was going to explain their talk to the people. In
Spanish—for only a handful of the audience had understood the gringos—the leader excoriated the consultants
and reviled them for being so presumptive as to belittle
their program but not even being able to do so in their
language. The audience smiled, laughed, and cheered
quite often, and the consultants were finally thanked for
their efforts and left, pleased at the showing they had
made. They were dismayed, however, when news
reached them a few days later that an official complaint
had been filed with the Office of Economic Opportunity
against the consultant firm, and that, unofficially, if they
ever showed their faces again they would be kicked out
of town.

Hopefully, Chicanos will no longer permit their barrios to be used as laboratories, at least not by Anglo
científicos, nor allow their brains to be picked by oppor-
tunist, Anglo social scientists, at least not for free.
Hopefully, we will demand that our terms be met if
evaluations are to be made—that our own people do the
evaluating, that our own consultants be hired, and that
programs and position papers be drawn up by our own
writers. Too many reputations and too much money
have been made by Anglo and black científicos and
writers on our account while we Chicanos have benefited nothing or, worse, have suffered great harm.

Aside from the current brand of exploiters who

thrive on poverty programs and ethnic sociology, a few other of my favorite illustrations of Anglo prejudice and connivance provide a panorama of the variety and subtlety of who the enemy is.

A San Diego newspaper reported in July 1969 that the Chancellor of the University of California at San Diego had warned that minority persons who fail as college students are the makings of campus militants bent on destroying the system. Having failed, the minority person may transfer blame for his failure to the institution. The UCSD official apologist went on to propose "experimental" schools for minorities with "intellectual requirements much below those to which *we have dedicated our lives*." [Italics mine. A.R.]

Recent studies have shown that of the less than two percent Spanish-surname persons in college, only about one-half of one percent eventually graduate. I would say that by having dedicated their lives to certain "intellectual requirements," not intellectual growth but admission standards, the chancellor and his accomplices have effectively short-changed the intellectual development of thousands of Mexican Americans. A Chicano who is aware from personal experience or investigation of the educational racism and incompetence that we as a group have been subjected to will reject vehemently the chancellor's effort to place the blame for campus revolts on Chicanos who are militant because they have failed in the classroom. It is my personal experience that Chicano college students who lead campus protests have been among the brightest of our youths. If they have failed any college course it has been Whitewash 101, which is offered at any Anglo college or university.

A language professor at Long Beach State College, Dr. Manuel H. Guerra, has commented on the proposed experimental college:

This experimental college, like the experiments in the South with black children, reveals to us the nefarious conflicts of the Anglo-Saxon conscience which is deeply committed to a point of view that does not respect American racial and ethnic differences. Not only does this frame of mind adhere to a point of racism of superior and inferior Aristotelian classes, but it endeavors to conceal and disguise its inhumanity to man in the respectability of self-righteous rhetoric, bureaucratic and authoritarian pronouncements, and the anonymous and depersonalized findings of respectable academic committees. If this is what the Chicano militant is tired of, if this is what he seeks to change, if this is what he considers *his adversary* . . . American education in general will owe a debt of gratitude to these young Americans and scholars who bring new focus and enthusiasm where there is myopia and bankruptcy.

Along these same lines, a letter to the editor appeared in the *Los Angeles Times* shortly after Chicano student walkouts had taken place in East Los Angeles in March 1968. The writer charged that new schools and more teachers would not solve the crisis but that the real fault lay in what he called "the poverty student syndrome: a complete lack, on the part of the student and parent alike, of how to pay attention in class, how to study, how to take tests, how to treat teachers, or how to organize or evaluate their own or their children's progress." Problems of the poverty-area schools will go away, said the writer, an Anglo teacher in East Los Angeles, when the syndrome "is recognized, researched, and dealt with." Once again we see the Anglo mentality projecting any cause for failure of the school system onto the student and his parents, not on the school system itself.

The legalized fiction of a border between the United States and Mexico is being utilized by American firms and farms to increase profits at the expense of U.S. citizens, especially Mexican Americans who live near the border. Capitalizing on the lower wages in Mexico (between 30 and 40 cents an hour), U.S. entrepreneurs have fashioned a new trade route over the border by which firms here manufacture parts and ship them to Mexico, where they are assembled and then returned for final inspecting, packaging, and distributing. U.S. tariff regulations provide that when finished products leave Mexico, the duty imposed equals only the value added by assembly in Mexico. AFL-CIO union officials have estimated that about 25,000 U.S. jobs have been lost and that another 275,000 may be forfeited through this trade loophole.

Both Mexican workers, who are not paid any more for working on American goods than Mexican wage laws permit, and Mexican Americans, who comprise the largest manpower source for skilled and semiskilled labor in the border region, suffer all the consequences of unemployment or underemployment. Who are the enemies here? They are operations like the Development Authority for Tucson's Expansion, which promotes the "twin plant" program between Tucson and Nogales, just across the border; the State Department itself, which condones and collaborates with American firms while American workers go begging for work; and, certainly, the Department of Labor, which has done nothing to correct the situation through mediation or stronger regulations such as requiring that before companies do migrate, they give some assurance that American workers will not lose their jobs or be denied work, a rule similar to the "adverse effect" concept enacted toward the latter years of the bracero program.

The 200th-anniversary celebration of San Diego in 1969 cost the city approximately $800,000. A room tax was instituted to help repay the city's general fund, which was touched in August for another $300,000 to revive the teetering finances of the "Fiesta 200" program.

The promotional campaign behind Fiesta 200 had touted San Diego's Spanish history and roots, crediting the Franciscan padres and the adelantados (advancers) for their pioneer expeditions and settlement of the city. But somewhere along the planning ways, as has been the case in most of these fiesta-day rituals, the contributions and living presence of Mexican and Indian peoples were forgotten or ignored. When a massive tourist scheme is at stake, money flows briskly, but money becomes scarce when schoolbooks that relate the true history of the Mexican American are needed, or when teachers who are bilingual and bicultural are necessary, or when schools which are up-to-date and well administered by a bicultural staff are demanded by the people of the barrio.

Chicanos know of the county officials in Texas who belittled the *Hunger U.S.A.* report published by the Citizens' Board of Inquiry into Hunger and Malnutrition in the United States.

In one news report, officials from three counties, Dimmit, La Salle, and Zavala, where more than half the population is Mexican American, expressed surprise. A Zavala County judge said, "We are interested in helping anyone needing it. I do not know of anyone suffering from hunger." Another official from Dimmit said, "I have read and re-read the news and am still mystified by the report. We have many poor people but I just do not believe we have any great amount of hunger. . . . We are in the heart of the Garden District and vegetables abound here. Lots of vegetables that are not of the right grade for shipping are thrown away or are given away."

Yet the *Hunger U.S.A.* study, published by the Citizens' Board of Inquiry into Hunger and Malnutrition in the United States (1968), showed that in Texas in 1968, nearly 250 million dollars in farm subsidies were distributed to .02 percent of the state's population, while the 29 percent of the state's people who are poor received only 7.5 million dollars in food assistance. In the three counties cited, which are 50 percent or more Mexican American, more than 60 percent of the families are poor, and the rate of infant (postneonatal) deaths ranged from 25 to 34 per 1,000 (four to six times the national rate for white infants). Generally, only about a tenth of the poverty families participated in a welfare or food assistance program. It is such public ignorance and callousness that starves and kills our children.

A Baptist minister, being interviewed by a Los Angeles newspaperman in April 1968, claimed that the Protestant clergy had more interest in assuring social justice than in gathering souls as they marched at the "forefront" of the fight led by East Los Angeles Chicanos to improve Los Angeles public schools. He sensed that the Catholic Church generally opposed Mexican Americans asserting themselves. His stake in the controversy and that of other ministers of the group he represented was based on the betterment of the whole community. Further bolstering their image, another minister colleague was quoted as saying that "being Roman Catholic is more of a tradition than a vital reality" for Mexican people in the United States. Another minister stated that while he and his colleagues were not seeking a privileged Protestant position among Mexican Americans, he had noted that Catholic priests in East Los Angeles had shown indifference toward the goals for change among Chicanos.

Such self-righteousness as the ministers displayed is totally unfounded; they could only succeed in driving a wedge between themselves and Catholic priests who are involved, or who might otherwise involve themselves, with Chicano aspirations. Such a wedge might even affect relations between Protestant and Catholic Mexican Americans. Their evaluation of church involvement in the Chicano revolt reflects the attitude of "we're right in the middle of the action and look at those other guys who've always thought the Mexicans were in their vestment pockets." Besides, few if any priests or ministers have long remained within ecclesiastical approbation in their missionary work among Chicanos, blacks, or Indians if they had only social justice at heart. After all, conversions is the name of the game.

In a related situation, Roman Catholic and Protestant clergy who had been involved in aiding farm workers through providing religious services, clothes, and food had the backing of church authorities before 1965. But when Chicanos began unionizing in the same fields, priests and ministers suddenly found themselves transferred, silenced, or simply left no alternative but to leave the religious ministry, although they continued to serve the spirit of the people. Of the many clergymen who have undergone official censorship or criticism for farm labor activities, the most notable I have known personally were the Rev. Ed Krueger in South Texas; the Rev. Eugene Boutilier in Washington, D.C.; Father Keith Kenny in Sacramento, California; Father Victor Salandini in Delano; and the Rev. James Drake, also in Delano. To their credit, these churchmen would be among the first to admit that they have not yet done enough nor have their churches sacrificed enough for the farm worker. The truth of the matter is that no church has fulfilled its mission to the Chicano people, the black man, or the red man, and they definitely have failed with the white man. No churchman therefore should speak or act as if he's doing the Chicano a favor by being at the "forefront" of our cause. I would rather they took a back seat instead of always trying to take the driver's seat.

In an interview in the *Los Angeles Times*, shortly after the school walkouts in spring 1969, a Catholic monsignor was quoted as saying that bilingual education really wasn't necessary as a student demand. "The real language of the majority is English. This is evident by the way they handle the English idiom while speaking before the television cameras." The problem was in getting the students to co-operate with teachers, he said. "You can't get an education marching around the building."

While the Protestant ministers were rather self-serving, the monsignor typified the Catholic Church's gross

ignorance of the Mexican Americans' struggle for independence. The conservative, patronizing attitude of
Roman Catholic officialdom abhors any threat to its
hold over the people it is supposed to serve. The monsignor exposed the Catholic Church's insensitivity to
the fact that Chicanos are not automatically Catholic
and that they may wish to exercise self-will and seek to
determine their lives apart from the padre's guidance. A
caveat to all churchmen is Dr. Jorge Lara-Braud's estimate that Spanish-speaking people in the United States
are about 5 percent Protestant, 15 percent Roman
Catholic, and the rest unaffiliated with any church.
Lara-Braud is a Mexican-born Protestant minister and
director of the Hispanic-American Institute in Austin,
Texas.

The federal establishment can usually be counted
upon to do its part to aid and abet in the destruction of
the Mexican American. Chicanos simply cannot trust
the administrative or program arms of any federal unit,
no matter how idealistic, fundamental, or beneficial its
aims and its people may claim to be. The very best
bureaucrats seem to have an uncanny knack for making
brown look like white.

In December 1968, for example, when the U.S.
Commission on Civil Rights convened a hearing de-
voted to Mexican American issues in San Antonio,
Texas, Dennis Siedman, the Employment Opportunity
Deputy Chief of Staff Personnel for the Air Force in
Washington, D.C., held this dialogue with a commis-
sion official:

Q: Our State Advisory Committee report shows that in 1966
Mexican Americans held 11.6 of the GS-11 grades (at
Kelly Air Force Base). In 1967 that figure was 12.3. And
your report I believe shows that in 1968 it was 13.7. Now
the Mexican Americans represent about 30 percent of the
GS employees, and about 44 or 45 percent of the total
work force. Would you consider that a broad and glaring
inequity?

Siedman: I think we have considered that in the report to be an imbalance in the number of people in each of these grades as related to their proportion in the population.

Q: Mr. Siedman, there is one overriding impression that I receive by reading your report, and I wonder if you would care to comment on it. It seems as though the word, discrimination, or the word, inequity, is just a dirty word that will not be used. Is there any reason why that is so?

Siedman: We put no value either positive or negative on these words. We have no evidence to indicate that there is discrimination. We have no empirical evidence to indicate that there has been discrimination and therefore the word, discrimination, does not appear. . . . I believe that we feel the lack of credibility is for the most part in the community, rather than in our employees.

Q: I am puzzled. Your report says: "The combined Air Force-Civil Service Commission survey has revealed that the community and large segments of the minority work force do not perceive the Kelly Air Force Base EEO program as a positive and viable source for improving minority employment conditions." Now you seem to be contradicting that statement.

Siedman: No, I don't think that I am. In terms of credibility, in terms of communication, and I think you made reference to that line on page 3, we are referring to the community. In terms of the EEO program as being a source of great, positive action we were not able to find that either in the community or in the work force.

After listening to someone like Siedman explain away the obvious in a cool, unruffled manner, the awesome treachery we Chicanos face from the government begins to emerge, although as yet we see only nose tips of bureaucrats protruding out of the Dantesque pools of excrement to be found within certain circles of our infernal government.

We Chicanos have our share of malinches, which is what we call traitors to la raza who are of la raza, after the example of an Aztec woman of that name who became Cortez' concubine under the name of Doña Marina, and served him also as an interpreter and informer against her own people. The malinches are worse characters and more dangerous than the Tío Tacos, the Chicanismo euphemism for an Uncle Tom. The Tio Taco may stand in the way of progress only out of fear or misplaced self-importance. In the service of the gringo, malinches attack their own brothers, betray our dignity and manhood, cause jealousies and misunderstandings among us, and actually seek to retard the advance of the Chicanos, if it benefits themselves—while the gringo watches.

Mexican Americans have organized counter groups of farm workers (with the financial backing of grower associations) against the Delano grape pickers' union; one man in particular toured the country addressing farmers' meetings and John Birch Society groups and publicly slurred the name of Cesar Chavez and the cause of the campesinos. A Mexican American legislator not long ago denounced the Mexican American Youth Organizations and its leadership by name before the House of Representatives, where none of the youths who were condemned by him for "reverse racism," were present to defend themselves. Another Mexican American, serving as a top aide in a federal agency, has been convicted and sentenced to prison for using the authority of his office to secure approval of a program's funding from which he himself would profit. Once a Mexican American begins to speak the Anglo line, or show concern first for the Anglo and perhaps as an afterthought for the Chicano, or seek personal gain at the expense of la raza, then that individual has made a travesty of our people and played into the gringo's hands.

We cannot as an aspiring Chicano nation ignore the internal problems that exist within the community. We have malinches in our midst. Some have exposed themselves by their own actions; among true Chicanos, they are well known, and their names need not be mentioned here. It is enough to describe by example how malinches harm our raza. Among ourselves, we can discuss internal issues and how to deal with them. If we thrash out a particular case with non-Chicanos present, it merely feeds the gringo's ego and may strengthen his hand later on. While los desgraciados do exist, the Chicano people's internal resources will eventually resolve such problems and dissolve barriers standing between us, wherever they may be. More and more, the Chicano understands that basically he has two enemies, one within himself and the other outside. Ideally he will conquer both enemies, but he can never progress toward mastering the outside forces unless he strengthens and broadens the concepts of raza, of Chicanismo, of Aztlán among his own.

Finding out who the enemy is takes the Chicano onto rather precipitous levels of speculation concerning the issue of racism, particularly when Chicanos are accused of being racist because they talk about la raza and Chicano, los gringos and gabachos. We are accused of racism in reverse, but the first question that comes to mind is, Who is being racist *in forward*? What Chicanos say and believe about Anglo-America is a reflection of the racist norm within American society. We assert that the Anglo is racist. Perhaps the term which would help us comprehend Anglo attitudes is that of cultural supremacist. While not excluding racial or color bias, the term suggests that even in cases where race or complexion are not obvious factors underlying the discrimination, differences in culture, ethnicity, or national origin may be the motivating factors for discrimination by the Anglo. Because we have experienced the gringo's discrimination and suppression due to our color, language, and customs, we have every reason, and in some cases more reasons than the black man, to call the gringo a racist. Something is radically wrong with the Anglo; we've observed this since he came into the Southwest, gun in one hand, Bible in the other. A Mexican Indian, when the first Anglo-Saxon appeared, remarked, "Ya chingaron el pueblo!" (There goes the neighborhood!)

The examples sketched here demonstrate the subtle methods of discriminating against the Chicano. They are provided so that the ordinary observer, and some Chicanos as well, can begin to realize what is going on and be attuned to the effects of such incidents and statements on minds which will accept whatever so-and-so says or anything that appears in such-and-such a newspaper. A slight distinction may be made between the Anglo and the gringo. Not all Anglos are gringos, and some Anglos may even be black or brown, but these can never be true gringos. The gringo may be an individual or a whole group of Anglos within a certain institution whose impact as a whole is gringoist. At the highest national level, the federal government and the sixty or seventy corporations which control the U.S. economy are gringo, yet individual agencies, department heads, staff persons, firms, executives, or workers may only be Anglos. At times it appears that a particular agency or company is purposely setting up obstacles in our path or just creating nuisances. When a White House-sponsored conference on volunteer service was held in Washington, D.C., in 1969, participants were invited from all over the country. The most astonishing fact of the whole conference to the Chicanos who attended was that they represented the largest non-Anglo group there. The gringo organizers of the conference were asking Chicanos to volunteer their services to private and public programs, but we've been volunteering or have been drafted for decades and are just now trying to get reimbursed for all that free or underpaid labor. Sometimes two or more agencies collaborate in raping the Chicano. For a while in 1968, the United Farm Workers were really pressuring the Department of Labor and the Immigration and Naturalization Service (which is part of the Department of Justice) to resolve the issue of the use of Mexican nationals as strikebreakers through lax labor and immigration regulations. True to form, each agency accused the other of wrong, and each ordered independent investigations which arrived at contrary conclusions on the basis of different findings—but the real issue was never resolved.

Seldom is an institution or its staff so constituted that everything and everyone must be changed to eliminate the sources of oppression or discrimination. Quite often, institutional policies and regulations can be at fault—entrance requirements or job tests, for example. Presumably, persons who staff the agencies have not participated in establishing the laws or policies that are, in effect, discriminatory procedures and would not oppose change, particularly change that would still fulfill the intent of the agency. In such cases, the enemy is the law or the policy which was established in the past and which can now be overturned through a specific strategy. Causing an individual to resign or be fired may eliminate the problem for a time, but Chicanos must sometimes dig much deeper than the person involved for the real source of trouble. Revolutionary change may be effected through such an approach, although this may be the most tedious and least dramatic method.

The primary example in the United States of an institution that needs to be examined from top to bottom, of necessity because there are problems at every level, is the United States Congress. No other institution in the United States has greater power to err than our Congress. Since its founding, it has exercised this awesome power a number of times. Granting it the benefit of the doubt, it may at times have used this authority unwittingly, having fallen into the clutches of a wily chief executive or a treacherous fellow senator or congressman. In the field of foreign affairs, the Gulf of Tonkin Resolution comes to mind immediately, as does a similar but much earlier incident when the United States declared war on Mexico because Mexico was defending its territory against the Yankee. In the cause of civil rights, the 1968 Civil Rights Act's section on riot control is the only section being fervently enforced; and in regard to the Chicano, laws for bilingual education fail to eliminate statutes prohibiting such schooling in certain states, and bills for a special raza agency manage only to arouse expectations which never materialize.

Congressmen are accustomed to paying lip service to minority groups and passing ineffective laws because it creates a good image, but they never create really effective programs because they do not fear the Chicano, the Indian, or the Oriental. Of all the huge institutions in the United States, Congress may truly require a complete overhaul if it is to reflect better the whole American society. A number of aged men control key committees because of the seniority system. They come from safe districts which guarantee them re-election term after term. By "safe" is meant that the district has remained virtually unchanged and untouched by what has been happening in the rest of the United States for at least a quarter of a century. Certain committee chairmen can decide the fate of a bill by simply delaying its discussion or by squelching it even after deliberations have begun. Amendment of the National Labor Relations Act to include farm workers by deleting the explicit phrase that now precludes them has been bottled up at various times—in the Senate Subcommittee on Migratory Labor, until recently with the aid of Senator Murphy of California, a newcomer in the Senate, but an old-timer in the tactical delay; in the Senate Committee on Labor and Public Welfare, of which Lister Hill of Alabama is chairman; in the House Committee on Education and Labor, and in the House Rules Committee, chaired by William Colmer of Mississippi.

"Who Is the Enemy?" is an exercise I've undertaken to make a couple of basic points. Chicanos often indulge themselves in such a game but usually with no other purpose than self-indulgence. The exercise is good therapy, for we rid ourselves of pent-up hostility and frustration and finish up with a sense of relief that we have thrashed out our problem and berated the gringo wrongdoers, even though the situation has not changed or improved. Sometimes seeking out the enemy through bull sessions results in uncovering a basic issue, and sometimes action is taken that succeeds in bringing about a change for the better. The fundamental principle involved here is the necessity for Chicanos to delve deeply into the sources of current problems. Who the enemy is may not be as important as knowing why he is an enemy. Why do Anglos—the Air Force official, the Catholic priest, or the college administrator—place the blame on us for our failure to attain Anglo standards of conduct and success? Why do they insinuate that there is something innately wrong with us that causes our problems? Does some conspiracy exist against the Chicano, or is prejudice and discrimination such an inherent and vital thread in the fabric of Anglo society that no one person or institution is at fault, but the whole structure? How, then, do you root out a cancer that has invaded the whole body?

As with many diseases, there is the danger of becoming infected. The Chicano, in trying to cope with the enemy, may become as diseased as he. But it is an endemic side effect of this enemy's pathology that to fight him means to assume some of his worst traits. We Chicanos realize that we face a "nebulous" enemy. The gringo assumes many forms and many styles and for that reason is an insidious, vicious, and vindictive force against those who attempt to be different from him and oppose his will. This realization and the revulsion against the strangling effects of Anglo society have become incarnated on many fronts throughout the United States and explain in part the causes of the Chicano uprising.

8

REVOLUTION IN THE MAKING

PREAMBLE

NOT too many summers ago, a conspiracy to inflame a revolution in the Southwest was discovered by Texas law officials, who immediately brought in the FBI. A document called the "MACHO Manifesto" had been discovered, containing violent threats against the Anglo society. Soon federal and state law-enforcement agents were scouring the Southwest searching for the MACHO leaders. In little barrio cantinas and on street corners they would ask, "Are you a MACHO?"

"Yes! Of course," came back the reply time and again. It soon became apparent to the lawmen that there were thousands of MACHOs, and that the revolutionary movement itself was vast and brazen.

Finally, a Mexican American vendido in one of the police agencies heard of the widespread investigation and alarm. He carefully explained to his colleagues that macho means manly in Spanish and that the manifesto was little more than a tongue-in-cheek declaration of independence. Of course, every mexicano they questioned responded that he was macho.

Some people say that this story is apocryphal, merely the imagination of some bato loco, a wild barrio

103

kid. I doubt that you will ever find a lawman who will admit that it actually happened. True or not, the "MACHO Manifesto" story contains certain seeds of truth vital to the understanding of the Chicano and his relationship to the rest of American society.

The society that dominates life in the United States is far removed from that of the Chicano and the Mexican American life style. The essence of machismo, of being macho, is as much a symbolic principle of the Chicano revolt as it is a guideline for the conduct of family life, male-female relationships, and personal self-esteem. To be macho, in fact, is an underlying drive of the gathering identification of Mexican Americans which goes beyond a recognition of common troubles. The Chicano revolt is a manifestation of Mexican Americans exerting their manhood and womanhood against the Anglo society. Macho, in other words, can no longer relate merely to manhood but must relate to nationhood as well.

To miss this point in the story, as the lawmen did, is to misunderstand a major thrust of what is happening in the Mexican American community. There is a hard, acerbic humor in the tale of the manifesto, a story that is mostly allegorical, insinuating a rather serious probability, yet hiding it in tones of sarcasm.

The revolt that is now fermenting among Chicanos exists on many levels. There are little, internal battles going on within individuals whose economic, educational, and social status may vary in the extremes in relation to other Chicanos. There are the undecided, the ones who question within themselves whether they will break some of the old cultural patterns and throw in their lot with the new wave of Mexican Americans, the Chicanos. There are the aggressive, militant Chicanos who have come to a deeper and more intense understanding of themselves. They have won a personal victory in themselves and broken with an old world. One by one they are finally experiencing the kind of revolts that shook off Old World control of the Americas in the last half of the eighteenth century.

Had the manifesto conspiracy been true, the law investigators would have done better to have asked, "Are you a Chicano?" in order to ascertain the depth and breadth of the conspiracy against the Anglo, for the word Chicano in many ways embodies the revolt itself. The word is little understood or recognized in certain regions; in others it is rejected as demeaning. Many see little significance in the word beyond its being a contraction of mexicano. Essentially, however, where Chicano is accepted and used as a term of personal identity and relationship to other Chicanos, there is the making of a revolution. In claiming Chicano for his own, the Mexican American has gone beyond mere nationalistic reminiscence of Mexico or red-white-and-blue patriotism—he has created for himself a new identity, a new person, a new soul, a new way of being.

PROLOGUE

The power and motivation of the Chicano revolt generate essentially from the Mexican American people. No one person can claim that his philosophy, technique, or charisma has been the cause of the ferment of revolution within the Mexican American community in the sixties. There are too many varied aspects of the cultural and economic upheaval that is now occurring in Chicano barrios and in Chicano minds to pinpoint any one cause or any one person as the root. New leaders have arisen because the people have sought to express their needs and so have selected certain men and women to lead them. It is still within the power of the people to reverse the process and unmake leaders.

The Chicano community is not a psychological or ideological monolith, in which everyone thinks exactly the same thoughts, aspires to the same goals or ideals,

and seeks objectives by the same means. Logically, a
variety of leaders and tactics have evolved in the past
decade. It is well for the majority society and for Mexican Americans themselves to realize this truth, for its
opposite has become a widely held belief that functions
much like a stereotype against the Chicano. In past
decades certain individuals have usurped authority and
responsibility from Mexican Americans; usually these
individuals have been churchmen or politicians—the
distinction has not always been easy to make. Often,
leaders have been chosen for us from among certain
pliable personalities by the dominant Anglo. Consequently, for decades millions of Chicanos have been
misrepresented in local and national affairs; our deprivation and suffering have been belittled and our character distorted by the shuffling, giggling Panchos.

The Chicano, to state the obvious, is in essence himself and no other. He is not a Negro and cannot be like a
Negro. He is not an Indian in the way that native tribesmen are in the United States. He is not an Anglo even
when he resembles the Anglo in coloring and speech.
Thus he should not and cannot act like the black, the
red, or the white man, nor does he view his condition in
life in the same way that they do. This is not to say that
the Chicano cannot adapt ideas and methods of the
black man or the Indian to his own repertoire of thought
and action, just as he can utilize certain Anglo notions
and tactics for his own benefit, but if he does borrow from
these others, he will adapt the idea or action into a
uniquely Chicano frame of reference, and it will come
out his own. But the true Chicano does not want to be a
black man, a red man, or a white man, and he rejects
the opportunity, if it can be called that, of becoming
like the rest.

This resolve is clearly explainable in the context of
the awesome phenomenon of the minority peoples revolt within the United States. Our rebellion should have
shattered forever the Anglo mythology of the melting

pot. The United States has been anything but a melting pot, because the gringo has purposely segregated, separated, and relegated the non-Anglo to an inferior and degraded status. Melting pot has meant surrender of one's past and culture to something euphemistically called American society or culture. The melting pot worked only for immigrants with a white skin who came to America. Regardless of nationality, these were willing to sacrifice a discrete identity in order to succeed and enter the polluted mainstream of American "can-doism"—can cheat, can swindle, can steal, can discriminate, can invade, can kill.

The Chicano and the two other large minorities in America were exploited or annihilated for their labor and their land and only by sheer dint of internal resources managed to survive the Anglo American's manifest destiny to destroy everything non-Anglo. That the Chicano and others did survive is indicative of the Anglo's overall ineptness and inability to fulfill his own set goals and of the Chicano's and other people's interior strengths and defenses. Suppressed by force and decimated by indifference, the Chicano now finds himself being subjected to such euphemisms as "the forgotten American," "a silent people," and "the sleeping giant." The Chicano pueblo has been anything but silent or sleeping; rather, it has been forced to bide its time, to submit to injustices where no recourse seemed available, at least within the Anglo's accepted system of law and order. While we Chicanos owe a great debt to the black people of America for striking out into untested ground, the Chicano can boast of his own personal history of rebellion and rejection of oppression. He has now reached the breakthrough point of personal liberation through a revolt of his own making.

It is true that the black revolution has guaranteed that the minority peoples of the United States get a certain amount of attention from the dominant society, whether it is pro or con. The actions of the minority groups of the nation are now front-page news, whereas only a generation ago there were rarely any activities reported. However, the current frustration and distrust within the black community concerning the progress that has been made, ostensibly by the old leadership and through the old channels, illustrate to the Chicano that he cannot now simply copy the black movement; he has to surpass the effort by the blacks if he is to endure as a Chicano and somehow contribute to the rehabilitation of the whole country.

We must have leadership of diverse background, methods, motivation, and style to achieve this goal. We do have a variety of revolucionarios, some of them in gray flannel suits and others in serape vests. They play different roles in the revolt; they have been shaped by much the same kind of life, either rural or urban in nature, but related intimately by the essential character of Chicanismo. As a people unified by certain principles and values, as well as by language and history, we cannot limit ourselves, as Anglos would have us do, to searching for one heroic leader.

Chicanos do hunger for heroic figures that are somehow themselves, but more than themselves. The cult of Emiliano Zapata is most clearly an example of this desire. Until recently, Chicanos adulated Zapata from afar, but a comprehensive work, *Zapata and the Mexican Revolution* (1969), written by John Womack, has clarified many facets of the legendary Mexican rebel leader. The account illuminates many of the events of the 1910 revolution and serves as a basis for understanding some of Mexico's current circumstances. But Chicanos should read the book for its recapturing on paper of Zapata—the epitome of the Mexican revolucionario—as a historical person and the country Mexico as a mother of men. Because so many Chicanos manifest rapport with the Zapata legend, comment on this phenomenon is relevant to understanding certain aspects of Chicanismo. Zapata is relevant not merely (as the Mexican writer Carlos Fuentes said) because all poor and oppressed peoples, including those of America, espouse Zapatismo, but because Chicanos maintain close blood and emotional bonds to the agrarian reformer. To the Mexican American, Zapata is significant more for what he represents than for what he did. Few Mexican Americans have ever read a full account of Zapata's exploits. Their knowledge of him is usually by word of mouth, and impressionistic Hollywood versions certainly leave much to be desired. Zapata, nevertheless, has enjoyed a prominent position in the Chicano mind for several years. Homes and offices of Mexican American individuals and organizations frequently display at least one popular poster, printed in red and black and inscribed, Viva Zapata or Viva la revolución! Even Anglo liberals recognize the Chicano's feelings, as the presence of the same poster on Anglo office walls indicates. Perhaps Zapata has more than a Chicano following in the United States. Womack's history should be read by Chicanos if only to acquaint themselves with the details of his background. But heroes are not made by facts.

Zapata did, and still does, draw the admiration of the people of Mexico, especially the militant Mexican students. But why should he be so idolized by Chicanos? It would seem that the Mexican American's historical context and North American experience are quite different from that of Mexico. Actually, the current Zapata cult, particularly among militant Chicanos, suggests a number of facts about us and about our growing aggressiveness. The most obvious conclusion to make is that Chicanos are seeking some kind of contemporary figure (who may be yet to come but has at least not yet been accepted by the masses from among the current leadership) who would embody the heroic proportions of a Zapata, that is, a man of the people and of the land.

The revival of Zapata as a relevant heroic person for

Chicanos is a sign that one or more similar leaders are being sought; Zapata is in a sense a model. Realistically, the Zapata cult is analogous to American Negroes reverting to the hero worship of a Nat Turner or a Crispus Attucks, men with specific status in Negro history but not the relevance of a Malcolm X, a Martin Luther King, or of others to whom black people can cry their Vivas. From the Chicano standpoint, the hero is history; Zapata the legend is more real than the present Chicano leaders. But this is still a superficial evaluation of the interest in Zapata.

A deeper insight is afforded by examining the parallel between the struggle Zapata endured and the effort now beginning among Mexican Americans. It is quite logical that the Viva Zapata element—along with traces of Ché Guevara—is present most vehemently among Chicano youth; every demonstration, school walkout, or rally is sure to include one or more signs bearing the Zapata legend. (The Ché look, often in evidence and growing strongly in the Brown Beret youth groups, reflects a searching, emotional attachment to the Cuban revolutionary but rather unclear ideological ties.) Young Mexican Americans turn to Zapata in the conceptual sense because they are definitely looking for a way out of a predicament that their elders have not been able to resolve through traditional party or socioeconomic efforts. They do not yet see a Zapata in their midst, but they sense an empathy with the cause of a man fifty years dead. They see Zapata as a man who comprehended clearly the basic needs of his people because he was of his people, and who resolved to fulfill their cause through the only means left to him and his fellow men—armed rebellion. Zapata sought a return to what Octavio Paz calls the "indigenous past," to those most permanent and stabilizing elements of the past. In so doing, Chicano youth perceive, Zapata also unburdened Mexico of its history and thus brought it, bloody and raging, from the eighteenth into the twentieth century.

The Mexican American also desires to revive and ⁂
absorb into himself the best of the past in order to confront the future with an equilibrium of purpose and
motivation. The Chicano understands that he has been
denied his past, his language, and his culture by the
Anglo-American system of education, the end product
of which is mediocrity, with the Anglo as the lowest
common denominator. He knows that his land has been
stolen and his rights and rightful opportunities withheld
by the Anglo system of laws and courts, which foster
prejudice and discrimination above justice and compas-
sion. Now he seeks to retrieve those basic values of his
past. Zapata, the rebel, is a symbol of that desire. Although not yet fully realized, but here and there promised in some men, that desire may soon be embodied in
a Chicano Zapata. Perhaps there will be a Zapata in the
South and a Villa in the North as well. At any rate,
Chicano historians of the next decade will have to
gather the bits and pieces of history which are fragmented today in order to portray the new revolutionary
hero or heroes. For the time being, the only true hero of
the Chicano revolt that is just beginning is the Chicano
people.

If gigantic heroes are to emerge, the Chicano people
will create them and establish their names, just as in the
past decade the people have begun to test and shape
leaders according to their need. In the coming and
going of leaders and spokesmen from Mexican American barrios, some have truly represented the people and
their aspirations, others have sought only to serve their
egos and to gain personal benefit. We are aware that
some "leaders" have been Anglo pawns used to oppress
and placate the Chicano masses. In recent years the
process has become more sophisticated, including certain federal appointments and the placement of a few
window-dressing Mexican Americans in private firms
and in the government, on local and even national legislative levels. There is no need to name them specifically,
for not only do they know who they are, but, more im-

portantly, Chicanos are at last finding them out for what they are; their deeds, their misdeeds, and their nondeeds have exposed them. They cry foul when anyone but themselves attempts to direct the people; they use affluence and influence as a political wedge for appointments and personal prestige; they sometimes sell themselves as leaders, but they have no following, nor do they have the true interests of the people at heart.

The Mexican American people need leaders who have advanced beyond their own shortcomings, even beyond their own ambitions, and have become, in fact, greater than themselves—have taken on the significance and proportions of their people. They reflect what some refer to as charisma, which is not what they themselves possess but what the people bestow upon them. Chicano leaders can be no more and no less than the people, but that is a great deal, for something very great has been begun by the Chicano people. The Chicano revolt is here to stay. It seems to have come about overnight, but it has been fomenting for generations.

To many Anglo-Americans, no revolution is yet in evidence from the Southwest, and, as far as they are concerned, Mexican American is a term describing a dirty little war that the United States fought with Mexico over some land. A few Mexican Americans still don't know who they are or what their fellow Mexican Americans are shouting about. But now that Chicanos have made Basta Ya! a war cry and Viva La Raza! a rallying call, much of that indifference and ignorance will change. After decades of intimidation that have forced many Mexican Americans to forsake their background, many agringados are returning to the Chicano fold. They realize the hypocrisy of their Anglo role-playing and the self-denigration it has involved, and now seek to reunite themselves with the raza they once denied. They have a long path to retrace.

Those who could not assimilate and thought themselves trapped in the barrio find that they were enslaved

by the gringo's sense of values and his obscene motiva-
tions and that they had sought liberation as Anglos
rather than as Chicanos. Chicanos are coming to understand that the barrio chante, the suburban rambler
home, the union hall, the corporation board rooms, and
the government offices can all be one as long as the
single most important principle of conduct is adhered
to—that the Chicano people and their way of life and
their dreams must be redeemed and that only Chicanos
will accomplish that redemption.

The Chicano revolt is primarily an internal conver- ↙
sion. Its depth and strength expand as individual reas-
sessments of one's personality, background, and future
increasingly reach the unanimous conclusion that all
Chicanos have traveled the same rough paths, experiencing much the same indignities and injustices simply
because we are Chicanos, and that therefore our destiny
lies in enduring as Chicanos. Some of us have adjusted
and survived better than others by learning the white
man's ways, but all of us are bound together by a commonality of language, practiced or not; a common
birthplace; a common history, learned from books or by
word of mouth; and a common culture much deeper
than the shallow Anglo reservoir of lost or suppressed
heritages.

A conversion has taken place and spreads daily
among the Chicano people. We will no longer be ignored or given second rating behind the white, the
Negro, or the Indian as a people and as a force to be
reckoned with in this country. We assert that we have
not been silent but rather that the gringo has refused to
listen, and now he must pay the price of his indifference. We proclaim that we are not a conquered people
but that the gringo has treated us as if we were subject
to him and denied us opportunities that he has lavished
on his own. This must stop. We know that unless the
need to do otherwise arises, the Anglo will choose to put

us out of his mind but that now he cannot afford to forget us.

The Chicano revolt will become more physical, more activist, and more direct than school walkouts, product boycotts, marches, and rallies. We will do violence to the established institutions and the patterns of thought and conduct of Anglo America. We Chicanos have a dual heritage of rebellion to draw upon for inspiration; we know armed revolution full well, but our sense of revolt is not destructive of one's home nor is it aimed at personal aggrandizement, that is, the amassing of wealth or power. The Chicano revolt ideally will connote a total attack on the oppressor's system of oppression; strict adherence to principle; and unrelenting will to attain land, justice, and dignity. If the Chicano resorts to physical force, as Tijerina only hinted at in Tierra Amarilla, it will be to take over the institutions of tyranny and to convert them to the proper service of the people. Will we resort to armed insurrection? Or, more to the point, will we be left no other recourse to attain our rights and our dignity?

The Chicano has found a unique identity for himself, one he will not surrender. He desires a place in the world equal to any other man's. To achieve this, he knows he must accomplish a revolution. La raza has not come to this point easily, nor have we fully arrived.

BEGINNINGS

Toward the end of 1965, the suppressed anger, resentment, and frustration of the Chicano broke out in the first radical thrusts of our movement toward liberation. That pivotal period saw the inception of at least three major fronts in the current Chicano revolt. When these events occurred, their importance was sensed by only a few Mexican Americans, mainly those directly involved. Soon, however, they would achieve national significance, bringing the Chicano people's oppression and their rebellion against their plight into public prominence. Moreover, these particular incidents, which set off certain currents of action and thought, occurred at the same time that other aspects of Chicanismo were developing. Thus, what we saw happen in 1965–66 did not occur spontaneously—the causes for reaction against the Anglo system of exploitation and indifference had existed for generations—nor did the historic events of the time originate in a vacuum. Ya Basta! had become a national Chicano battle cry. For the Chicano, only the exact day was unsure; the Chicano insurrection was inevitable.

A few hundred grape pickers struck growers in Delano, California, in September 1965 to initiate what is now the single, most important unionizing effort among farm workers in a century. During the fall of 1965, many Mexican Americans attuned to national-level politicking began an assault on the White House for recognition of the Chicano's predicament and the redemption of promises unkept when the Chicano was not invited to the President's White House Conference on Civil Rights. The next spring (1966), in protest against the Denver, Colorado, city administration's harassment of Chicano involvement in the antipoverty program, Mexican Americans demonstrated at city hall, and a "crusade for justice" was proclaimed, giving birth to a new nationalism.

These first skirmishes in the Chicano's struggle for self-conception and self-determination were grounded in efforts of the early sixties, when Chicano sophistication about his rights and power burgeoned, and his determination to change his destiny through his own efforts, even making his own mistakes, deepened into an obsession. The Chicano revolution is not merely the product of a world-wide reassertion by poor and oppressed peoples of their dignity and rights, nor is it only an imitation of the black movement. If there had been no blacks in this country, the Chicano revolt would still have occurred, because we have been at least as oppressed and even more ignored than the blacks.

Since Padre Hidalgo raised el Grito de Dolores in 1810, the Chicano has known revolution. There were Mexican heroes in the Alamo who rebelled against the Mexican Government, and blood brothers died fighting each other that year (1836). Thousands of Mexicans were slaughtered by Anglo America in the War of 1847–48; hundreds of boy cadets of the Mexican military academy in Chapultepec died defending their country against Anglo American soldiers. In California, when the discovery of gold excited Anglo greed, countless mexicanos lost their lives and their claims, and men such as Joaquín Murieta, Tiburcio Vasquez, Juan Flores, and Francisco Garcia tried to avenge them. Following the end of the Anglo war against Mexico, men such as Elfego Baca; Governor José Martínez, of New Mexico; Juan Nepomuceno Cortina, and Jacinto Treviño, of Texas, attempted to fend off Anglo incursions. Since the first agricultural strike was called in 1883 in the Texas Panhandle by cowboys led by Juan Gomez, Mexican Americans have led or been involved in the major labor strikes and unionizing efforts that have taken place in the fields.

Mexican Americans were the heart and muscle of the unionization of mining in New Mexico. The Chicano's remarkable sense of loyalty and courage has been honorably demonstrated to the extremes of death in four wars: World Wars I and II, and the wars in Korea and Vietnam. We have earned in proportion to our population more Congressional Medals of Honor (twenty-five) than any other ethnic group. Ironically, when the first Chicano to be awarded the Medal of Honor in World War II was engaged in a battle in the Aleutians which cost him his life, it was only a week before the attacks by servicemen on Mexican American zoot suiters in Los Angeles.

Traumatic as the Second World War was for millions of people, for the Mexican American the war expanded his horizons by literally drafting him out of the barrio. G.I. benefits for continuing education, preference points for government jobs, and V.A. loans for housing improved the Chicano's capability for attaining new aspirations. Alerted to his rights and awakened to the advantages of a life he somehow felt could no longer be denied him, the Mexican American advanced beyond the social and religious groups which had been his forte in prewar years to founding action-oriented organizations concerned with social problems.

The League of United Latin American Citizens, founded in 1929 in Corpus Christi and San Antonio, Texas; the American G.I. Forum, established in 1948; and the Community Service Organization, launched in 1947, were the most activist groups of the late forties and fifties, persisting and expanding in influence to the present day. These groups attacked fundamental issues of injustice and discrimination—from school segregation cases to the celebrated Three Rivers case over a slain Chicano soldier. Felix Longoria, an infantryman killed overseas, was returned to his hometown of Three Rivers, Texas, in 1947. On instructions from city officials, the only mortician in town refused to accept the body for preparation and burial in a plot in the all-Anglo cemetery. Chicano war veterans intervened, firing up support from various organizations and individuals, including Senator Lyndon B. Johnson. Finally, when the Three Rivers city fathers remained adamant, Longoria's body was given authorized burial in Arlington National Cemetery. To this day no Chicano is buried in the Three Rivers cemetery. The conflict motivated the formation of the G.I. Forum, with Dr. Hector P. Garcia as its founder. Limited court cases were won on school inequities against the Del Rio Independent School District in 1930 and against the Bastrop Independent School District in 1947.

Over the years, these and other local and regional

groups have advocated voter education and registration, especially the Forum and CSO, while LULAC particularly pushed educational issues, and CSO, social-
assistance programs. LULAC is credited with establishing the Little School of the 400, which has since been
called a prototype of the Head Start programs initiated
under antipoverty legislation. Originated in Houston by
Felix Tijerina in the early fifties, the 400 School provided preschool, Spanish-speaking youngsters with at
least 400 basic English words as preparation for entry
into an entirely English-speaking school system. CSO
was probably the earliest promoter of social services
through community action by the people to be served.
It has also striven to increase voter registration among
Chicanos, including Mexican people who had remained
in alien status or had been citizens for thirty or forty
years and had never voted.

One of the most fascinating witnesses to Chicano
self-preservation techniques and community insulation
through embryonic organizing is the Beneficencia Society, barrio groups which sprang up, wherever Mexican
people congregated, to assist one another when sickness
or death struck. Beneficencia (or Mutualista) members
contributed a small sum each month as membership
dues; the funds collected would be used to tide over a
family hit by sickness or calamity, or to pay part or all
expenses of a funeral. Such groups still operate here and
there, and occasionally while traveling through the
Southwest, I have seen a paint-chipped storefront office
with a faded sign above the door attesting to the existence in days gone by of such a neighborhood insurance
society. The innate sense of organization and the terrible need and isolation that generated them is a story in
itself.

Postwar groups cleared away much of the debris
which had lain around for generations, predating the
activities of today's black activists; they helped expose
the deeper problems that existed. Not until the sixties,

however, did the job begin of radicalizing the Chicano community and rooting out those really massive, adamantine barriers of Anglo prejudice and indifference, as well as our own self-distrust and fear of self-assertion. The calculated revolt that we now observe is but a continuation of the struggle Chicanos have maintained through a century and a half of oppression. Certain developments in the last decade have only accelerated our cause.

Our political sensitivity was sharpened by the Viva Kennedy campaigns in the Southwest and Midwest. John F. Kennedy struck a response from the Mexican American people that no other man except his brother Robert has ever matched. It was a mutual discovery, for Kennedy needed every minority-ethnic vote and all the Catholic voters he could muster. In the Mexican American he had both factors—cultural background and religious affiliation—going for him. The Mexican American responded to the youth, the dedication, and the hope that Kennedy exuded, as well as the obvious interest he had in Mexican Americans as a people. We voted for Kennedy with an impact that was rivaled only by our vote for Johnson in 1964, a sympathy vote to a great extent, but a massive vote no less, and one that held many hopes. By 1964, the Mexican American delegation to Congress grew to four, that many times higher than it had been in 1960.

While the history of the Kennedy Administration does not indicate that Kennedy actually repaid the Mexican Americans' confidence and support of him, except for general programs and one ambassadorship to a Latin-American country, the importance of the Viva Kennedy experience is that Mexican Americans tasted political power and flexed their vote power as a widely organized group. Growing Chicano awareness of the potential of their vote was especially evidenced in Crystal City, Texas, in 1963, when Anglo control of city government was wrested away by a majority of Chicanos voting for Chicanos; many Mexican Americans still look back on that event as a singular if short-lived expression of the gathering of Chicano forces for bigger battles. While a great deal was gained from the intellectual flowering attributable to Mexican Americans serving in the Second World War and reaping some of its benefits through G.I. bills, it was this broad and successful involvement in a national campaign that aroused Chicano political aspirations and prefigured the premeditated aggressiveness of the sixties and the years to follow.

The War on Poverty launched by President Johnson in 1964 gave many Mexican Americans with the desire to work for la raza community (many of whom had already been promoting volunteer or small-scale endeavors) the opportunity to operate on a full-time basis and on long-term projects while earning a living wage at the same time. The practical effect of the antipoverty legislation was that it freed many Chicanos already involved in community rehabilitation from the daily grind of first earning a living and then trying to do something worthwhile on a part-time basis. Of course, the poverty war also attracted the opportunists who had never done anything for la raza but saw the chance to make a name and to prosper from the troubles of the Chicano pueblo. I've run into many of these self-promoters, but fortunately the true Chicanos who labored against adverse odds for their people, often at their own expense, outnumbered the foul breed.

For all its good intentions, the Economic Opportunity Act of 1964 caught the Chicano relatively unprepared in terms of the sophisticated strategy plotting, lobbying, and deceit required for the pursuit of program approval and funding. We did not have the skills and experience to put together proposals in the bureaucratic form acceptable to the Office of Economic Opportunity (OEO). We did not have the knowledge of the labyrinthine ways of Washington that the Indian tribes, the Negro organizations, and the foundations had. The Chicano had to learn gradually, and more often than not he was left holding an empty bag or at most a few crumbs. Even when Chicano groups did get desperately needed program money via sound proposals, properly written and phrased, Anglo and black forces back home were usually well enough in control of Community Action Program agencies and boards to offset the efforts of the Mexican American community to get its share of the local OEO pie.

Nevertheless, the Chicano has begun to prosper in antipoverty terms. Chicanos have led state CAP associations in various southwestern states including Colorado, New Mexico, and Texas; large city CAP associations including Los Angeles and San Antonio; and, of course, a few multimillion-dollar projects in various cities or regions. The overall effects of this national impetus toward organization and education in community action are immeasurable. Many Chicanos gained invaluable skills and knowledge which have been transferred into truly barrio-roots programs; in some places, now, nonfederally funded and controlled raza projects outmaneuver and outperform the OEO-moneyed boondoggles. Creating these self-determinant activities should have been the objective of the OEO program, but, instead, self-perpetuating agencies resulted, as much a part of the Establishment as city hall. OEO is no longer the deliverer from our ills that we thought it would be; some of its earliest promoters have seen the palm fronds of triumph turn to ashes in their hands. The War on Poverty is a fantasy now; the people of the barrios and the ghettos no longer expect any good to come from Washington, whose peddlers deal in wooden horses.

For three years prior to September 1965, a former farm worker turned organizer, Cesar Chavez, had been carrying forward the tedious and exacting task of convincing farm worker after farm worker that a union could be built in the San Joaquin Valley; that Delano,

California, could be organized. The corrido, "Viva
la Huelga en General," tells the story:

> El dia 8 de septiembre
> De los campos de Delano
> Salieron los filipinos.
>
> Y despues de dos semanas
> Para unirse a la batalla
> Salieron los mexicanos.
>
> Y juntos vamos cumpliendo
> Con la marcha de la historia
> Para liberar el pueblo.
>
> *Chorus*
> Viva la huelga en el fil!
> Viva la causa en la historia!
> La raza llena de gloria!
> La victoria va cumplir!

("Long Live the General Strike": On the 8th of Septem-
ber/From the camps of Delano/Came the Filipinos./And
then after two weeks/To unite in the battle/Out came the
Chicanos./And together we're fulfilling/The march of
history/To liberate our people./Long live the farm
strike!/Long live our historic cause!/Our people crowned
with glory!/Will achieve the victory!

Delano could have been just another abortive attempt, among hundreds, to organize farm workers, but
unlike other strikes, the Delano huelga (which climaxed on July 30, 1970, with the signing of a contract
with Giumarra, the largest holdout against the table
grape boycott) has gained extraordinary importance. In
September 1965, however, only a few Chicanos thought
it would last. In time the Chavez-led National Farm
Workers Association, predominantly Mexican American, merged with the Agricultural Workers Organizing
Committee, a primarily Filipino unit headed by Larry
Itliong. The strike resulted in about a dozen major contracts with wine-grape growers in California in the first
couple of years, but a strike and international boycott of

fresh-table-grape producers ensued. Huelga was to become a national issue and to project Chavez into national recognition as a Mexican American leader.

The source of the Chicano movement's nationalistic thought and cultural revival, the Crusade for Justice, had a tumultuous beginning in Denver, Colorado. Rodolfo "Corky" Gonzales, a former prize fighter rated among the ten best featherweights in the world in the mid-fifties, had been hired as director of the Neighborhood Youth Corps, an OEO project, in 1964. Gonzales had been the first Chicano district captain for the Democratic Council in Denver, and, in 1960, his Chicano district had polled the top percentage of Democratic votes in the city. In 1963, he organized what was to become the precursor group of the Crusade, Los Voluntarios, a Chicano political-activist unit which sought more political representation for the Mexican American community in Denver.

In early 1966, the *Rocky Mountain News,* the number two daily newspaper in Denver, published reports that Gonzales was allegedly discriminating against whites and blacks in the NYC program. When Gonzales' Voluntarios organized a picket of the offices of the *News* to protest the rumors the paper was spreading, the mayor, whom Gonzales had helped elect, asked him to resign or be fired. That April 29, Gonzales told the mayor he could have his job, and he quit. Afterward, in an address to the demonstrators, he declared that "this day a new crusade for justice is born," and the name stuck. Thus, after a period of development going back to the early sixties, the ultimate moment of truth arrived, not only for one Chicano, Corky, but for a great many who sought what he sought and who had finally decided that the Chicano's destiny was not in aping the white man but in building a new nationalism around culture and self-identity.

In another direction, Chicano patience for the fulfillment of promises and for recognition from the Kennedy and Johnson Administrations ended in mid-1965. When Chicanos heard that a White House Conference, "To Fulfill these Rights," had been scheduled for 1966 but that preplanning sessions the previous fall had excluded Mexican Americans altogether, enough Chicanos yelled "Ya basta!" ("That did it!") toward Washington to arouse some concern from conference schemers lest anything jeopardize the proceedings or blacken the administration's name. The issue dangled for months; there were promises of permitting Mexican Americans as conference observers, but not as participants. As March 1966 came around, matters had not improved; in fact, insult was mounting upon insult.

A briefing by Franklin D. Roosevelt, Jr., chairman of the Equal Employment Opportunity Commission at the time, was staged for Mexican Americans in Denver early in 1966; it was to be a preliminary discussion to a bigger EEOC conference the coming March, dealing with Mexican American employment needs. The briefing was a put-down, with Roosevelt admonishing the audience for having come up with no more than three complaints of employment discrimination involving Spanish surnames. He seemed to be saying, "You have to do better than that or we'll continue to ignore you." Most of the Chicanos at that briefing showed up at the March conference in Albuquerque, New Mexico, prepared to dish out the criticism. A consensus was reached on the eve of the conference that Chicanos would no longer be talked down to. On the following morning, the fifty Chicanos who made up the entire conference presented various charges against the EEOC and then walked out, leaving the Anglos there to hold a private conference among themselves. The Albuquerque fifty accused the EEOC officials of rigging the conference for one-way communication only, of condescending attitudes, of insulting the intelligence of the Mexican American, and of discriminating against Chicanos. The EEOC, they pointed out, had not one person of Mexican American descent among its commissioners, and very few staff members, and had clearly demonstrated that it was interested only in giving lip service to the needs of the Spanish-speaking community.

Maintaining the unity forged at Albuquerque, the fifty Chicanos pressed other demands as an ad hoc committee. They demanded inclusion in the White House conference scheduled for June; the appointment of a Mexican American to the commission; acceleration of the recruitment and hiring of Mexican Americans to federal agencies at all levels, particularly at regional and national levels where few were then employed; and finally, a White House conference for Mexican Americans only. President Johnson moved to appease the Albuquerque contingent, many of whom had been active in his behalf in 1964 and to whom he had made promises, but only after another demonstration by Arizona Chicanos at a conference in Phoenix in May resulted in a kneel-in at the Western Union office there. The weekend following the Arizona telegram-in, the President announced at a press conference, almost offhandedly, as he often did, that he was calling a private meeting with Mexican American leaders within a short time.

The President invited five men to Washington for an informal discussion of the issues and to negotiate a peace that would keep the Mexicans off his back and guarantee that the Chicano element wouldn't foul up his black-oriented meeting in June. The five who came to the White House were Bert Corona, president of the Mexican American Political Association, a California-based nonpartisan activist group; Roy Elizondo, president of the Political Association of Spanish-speaking Organizations, a primarily Texas-centered organization, also fairly nonpartisan but predominantly Democratic; Augustin Flores, a past president of the American G.I. Forum from Riverside, California; Hector P. Garcia, M.D., a Corpus Christi, Texas, general practitioner who had founded the G.I. Forum; and Judge Alfredo Hernandez, a former president of the League of United Latin American Citizens, which, like the Forum, was a group with nationwide membership.

Much was promised at the May meeting on both sides. The Mexican American leadership promised to cool the natives back home in exchange for the promise of a White House Conference on Mexican American Affairs. As usual, the natives kept their promise, but for the Anglo, a promise it remained.

So much detail about this sequence of affairs between the Chicanos and the Johnson Administration is necessary to understand the full import of the events in 1965–66 regarding a White House conference. The administration never intended to have Chicanos confer jointly with Negro leaders because that might have inspired a nationally publicized coalition and highlighted the common aspirations and problems of black and brown men. Therefore, at the most, we were given a few invitations to come look but not touch. Secondly, the make-up of the quintet who met with the President, although well representative of many Chicanos, is suspect—not the men themselves but the motives of the President in selecting those particular five men. Everything and everyone between California and Texas was ignored. Indigenous leadership and organizations from Arizona, Colorado, and New Mexico, as well as from the northern states, were disregarded. Pulling one of the oldest political ploys in the book, divide and conquer, the Anglo picked our leaders for us. This interpretation suggests an insidious plotting behind the scenes, but the evidence is there: the convening of a civil-rights conference where only Negroes had any right to participate; a private session with only a handful of men from certain parts of the Southwest of a certain political bent and frame of mind; a coalition of browns and blacks nullified; and a sense of unity kindled at Albuquerque defused in Washington. We let ourselves be sucked into the trap, and we are still trying to recoup from that error. The evidence shows that there was black support for combining minds and spirits at that White House conference, but it was not insistent, and we were not persistent.

Nevertheless, as the five Mexican American spokesmen flew back to the barrios, the bureaucratic wheels were already in motion for preparation of a White House conference under a sub-task force borrowed from several agencies and pulled together by a director on loan from the Department of Labor, David North, a mexicanophile as well. The little task force ran through its early paces so well and communicated a sense of good will to Chicanos at such an active level that the pressure built up in 1965–66 was effectively reduced. So successful were the Johnsonians in appeasing Mexican American forces that nothing was heard from the barrios until the sub-task force was raised to cabinet level on June 9, 1967, and launched anew as the Inter-Agency Committee on Mexican American Affairs.

Vicente T. Ximenes of Texas, who had been named meanwhile to the EEOC as a commission member, was also saddled with the chairmanship of the committee, which included the Secretaries of Agriculture; Labor; Health, Education, and Welfare; Housing and Urban Development; and the Director of the Office of Economic Opportunity. That September, North was formally installed as permanent executive-director of the Inter-Agency Committee. The first federal agency ever established specifically for Chicanos was to be led by an Anglo; no "qualified" Chicano could be found. It was living on borrowed staff, borrowed money, and, everyone guessed, borrowed time.

Concurrent with the formation of the Inter-Agency Committee and Ximenes' appointment as chairman, the President called for preparation of a hearing in October in El Paso. Not a White House conference, to be sure, but the propaganda immediately promoted the hearing as a more effective instrument than a conference in Washington, since Mexican Americans could speak directly to agency and cabinet members in a formal hearing. No one ever explained why the same structure couldn't have been ordered by the President in a White House setting, but as it turned out, there were other considerations.

The 1966 White House conference had caused the administration many problems, and another major debacle prior to an election year could not be permitted. It was necessary to placate the Chicano and at the same time give him nothing. The El Paso hearing fulfilled that need. Most of the old-line organizations played along with the scheme, but there were many others who rejected the administration's political cynicism and gimmickry. The front page of *La Raza,* one of the first of the Chicano press newspapers, ran a cartoon prior to the hearings illustrating what the editors called, "The newest game, El Paso . . . different from any other game in that it has no rules." *La Raza* was partly right. A new game was being played with the Chicano, only there were a great many rules; the point was that only the administration knew what they were.

Other currents were moving among Chicanos which were generally unobserved on the public level. An exception was the sudden explosion of the Spanish and Mexican Americans in northern New Mexico under the leadership of Reies Lopez Tijerina, Texas-born ex-farm worker and evangelist preacher who had moved to New Mexico in 1963 to begin the formation of the Alianza Federal de Pueblos Libres (Federal Alliance of Free City States). For the first time, Mexican American resurgence manifested violent, armed opposition to injustice. Alianzistas took over a federal campsite in October 1966 and assaulted the Tierra Amarilla courthouse in June 1967 with rifles and hand guns. A number of Alianza members, including Reies Tijerina, were arrested following each incident; court trials were to last into late 1969 when Tijerina, after winning one trial related to the Tierra Amarilla incident, was sentenced to two concurrent terms of from one to five years, and from two to ten years on charges dating back to the courthouse takeover. By the fall of 1968, the Alianza movement was changing its mode of operation to regain lands stolen or fraudulently taken from the original grantees since 1848. The Alianza movement is no surprise to those aware of the history of the people of northern New Mexico—the people who first settled the region, contending with native tribesmen hostile to their coming; who were driven off in the 1680s but returned in 1692 to recolonize and merge with the people and culture native to the land; who in the early 1840s repulsed two Texas attempts to invade the region; and who rebelled in 1847 against the civil government imposed by the United States after the military takeover of the country at the outbreak of the war against Mexico and killed the Anglo Governor. Nor can New Mexico ever be the same after Tijerina and the Alianza. In 1968, the Alianza adopted a new strategy. Taking the name of the Constitutional party, the Alianza attempted to run Tijerina for Governor. When he was made ineligible because of the federal charges pending against him, another Alianzista ran instead; he didn't win, not that first time.

For many years, Dr. Ernesto Galarza, a persistent activist in farm-labor struggles for the past three decades, had conceived of a unified Chicano community. His heart had been closest to the sufferings of the farm laborer; he has written three books on the subject, worked for the Department of Labor, and been a senior consultant on Mexican American affairs and labor relations for the Ford Foundation. Early in 1967, he intimated that negotiations were progressing with the Ford Foundation for the establishment of a region-wide organization that would conduct its own national programs and contract funds to local groups proposing local projects. The unifying thread of this effort was the cause of la raza unida.

Dissenters to the federal bureaucratic performance being staged by the Inter-Agency Committee convened prior to October 1967 to prepare a conference of dissident groups that would coincide with the El Paso hearing. Thus, two events were held in El Paso on the last weekend of October 1967, nearly at the same time and to a great extent with many of the same participants. But the style and spirit of the two were in great contrast and foretold the character of the Chicano movement to come. Only one of the events was to plumb the true meaning of the revolution that was about to lunge into its next stage.

The Inter-Agency hearing plodded along on an outwardly well-structured format, replete with opening speakers, plenary sessions, small group discussions, luncheons, banquets, and receptions (while Chicanitos a few blocks away ate their one meal of the day, tortillas and beans). The "rump" conference, as hearing officials termed it, convened at a church hall in El Segundo, probably one of the worst slums in the United States, but for that week, one of the most highly policed areas in the region—policed by garbage collectors on orders to make sure that none of the usual litter showed in the streets. "El Segundo," which seems to refer to the Second Ring in Dante's *Inferno*, "a place where light was mute . . . that abyss of screams, and moans, and lamentations," is the name for the barrio slum that lies between downtown El Paso and the bridges to Juárez, Mexico. It is infested by presidios (tenements) clutters of one-room apartments that look down into inner courtyards where refuse and human waste collect in standing pools of slimy water, while at one end open toilets reek of a heavy, lingering stench. *Presidio*, by the way, is from the Spanish word for prison, a word expressive of the bitter cynicism bred in the people by the environment in which they exist.

Into such a setting came the Chicanos who had refused to participate in the hearing and others who, although not invited, intended to dissent in some way. The barrio people and youths from the college campuses came also, rubbing shoulders and learning from each other. A few persons, such as Galarza and Maclovio Barraza (a member of the Executive Board, Southwestern Region, United Steel-Workers of America from Phoenix, Arizona), read statements at the hearing and then boycotted the rest of the sessions. Others, such as Corky Gonzales and Bert Corona, simply ignored the invitations. Reies Tijerina was apparently too controversial a person and never received an invitation. Cesar Chavez stayed away altogether, attending to strike duties in Delano but sending a telegram to the raza conference. Most of these figures and many other Chicano activists adopted the theme of la raza unida for the conference in a planning session on Saturday, October 28. Reies Tijerina was there that morning and prophetically told the group, "What we say today will be engrained in the minds of all men." True to his prophecy, the phrase, *La Raza Unida,* became a rallying call. Dozens of conferences have been held since October 1967, using that theme, but not one other hearing has been held such as the one that the Anglo government staged.

On the morning of the 28th, an interesting side light occurred which characterized the true purpose of the hearing. That Saturday coincided with the signing of the Chamizal Treaty, by which a century-old claim over a few hundred acres of dust and gravel was settled in Mexico's favor; nearly 120 years ago to the day, Mexico had ceded millions of acres of land to the same Anglo government. The Rio Grande had shifted its course over a century ago, and President Johnson was meeting with President Gustavo Díaz Ordaz for elaborate ceremonies to conclude the land transfer. The participants scrambled over each other to get out to the airport in time to see El Gran Patrón arrive for the pompous ceremonies. Sessions scheduled for that morning were simply forgotten, and the hearing terminated in a rout.

Still, la raza bared its deepest feelings at the airport. As the President introduced his wife and members of his entourage, he named Governor John Connally, of Texas. For a moment a few claps were heard but then boisterous, resounding "boos" bawled out from a large segment of the crowd. Connally and Johnson were given notice that the likes of the Governor would not be tolerated by right-thinking Chicanos. It must have been a shock to El Patrón to realize that Chicanos just might hoot him and his compatriots to his face; it was certainly the first time anything like this had ever happened.

As in all the significant events of the Chicano movement, there was ample cause for the booing inflicted on the Texas Governor. On June 4, 1966, melon-pickers, under the lead of Eugene Nelson, a United Farm Workers organizer had struck eight growers in the Rio Grande Valley. The huelga resulted in one contract, with a Mexican American grower, but little other progress was made. At the end of the summer of 1966, a farmworkers march from Rio Grande City to Austin, the state capital, was organized. Connally attempted to curtail the march by heading the marchers off on Labor Day at New Braunfels, just north of San Antonio, but he only intensified the Chicanos' resentment toward him. That disdain unleashed itself at El Paso.

To a great degree, the booing of the Texas Governor reflected the change in party alignment that has been occurring among Mexican Americans in the past decade. The revolution in politics is attributable to an expanding middle-class element that tends to adopt more conservative-party figures, as well as the frustrated rejection of the always-promising-but-never-delivering Democrats. Many Mexican Americans have either switched to the Republican party or have simply sat out elections, or have voted for the man rather than the party. Or is it purely coincidental that these same two Texans at the El Paso airport bowed out of the 1968 elections?

What I consider to be the most important outcome of this convocation is the assertion by young Chicanos of a dominant role in the revolution that is being welded, Chicano by Chicano, day by day. Sometime around 1966–67, Chicano youths became aware of each other on the campuses and in the barrios through the attraction of such spokesmen as Tijerina, Gonzales, and Chavez; they were also aware that black students and ghetto youths were "getting themselves together." In California, especially, where there were more Chicano college students than in other states, a number of organizations erupted: United Mexican American Students, Mexican American Student Association, and many other similar ones. In Texas, the Mexican American Youth Organization (MAYO) became the pre-eminent youth force. It was quite obvious to the few Chicano collegians that Chicanos had been systematically—by a system, not necessarily by individuals making choices— cut off from receiving an education beyond high school. At many California colleges, foreign students from Latin America often outnumbered Mexican American undergraduates. At the Inter-Agency hearing, the teen-age and young adult Chicanos were a silent minority within the minority. By contrast, Chicano youths, college students, dropouts, and batos (barrio toughs) were the new wave of la raza unida. Treated as an afterthought at the hearing, the Chicanitos threatened to sweep the old-timers out of the way at La Raza Unida Conference. One young Californian told me in a dry, humorless way, "The young Chicanos see this conference as the last chance older Chicanos have to come through. If nothing happens from this you'll have to step aside or we'll walk over you." A half year later, a militant, barrio youth group that wore the Brown Beret, inspired the first major blowout, a student walkout, on March 5 in East Los Angeles at five predominantly Mexican American high schools.

After El Paso, a new phase of organization and aggressiveness developed that Chicanos had not known before. From La Raza Unida Conference there developed lines of communication between student groups all over the country; an increased group awareness and sense of national purpose touched everyone who was in El Paso that weekend, and from it came the final push for the formation—with Ford Foundation money—of the Southwest Council of La Raza, the first major Mexican American corporation founded for the purpose of funding other Mexican groups as well as carrying out its own programs.

The Southwest Council came into full operation in September 1968 with Herman Gallegos as director, and offices in San Francisco, where Gallegos chose to operate, and in Phoenix, where the central offices were established. Maclovio Barraza was selected as the first chairman of the board of directors. The Council in turn funded projects in San Antonio, Los Angeles, and San Francisco-Oakland. Economic development of the barrios in the Southwest has been the Council's prime objective. Its work has been rather methodical and long term. It has tried to encourage Chicanos with similar interests and professional skills to identify as Chicanos in order to augment and strengthen the movement toward unity. Operations went smoothly until early 1969, when the Ford Foundation and most other foundations in the country came under congressional attack for financing politically oriented programs or activist groups. The Southwest Council had a political-education project of its own going but pulled in its horns under advice from the Ford Foundation; then another of its funded groups, the Mexican American Youth Organizations in Texas came under fire from Texas politicos, particularly Mexican American ones, and the

Council withdrew its funding from MAYO. Financially, it was a realistic move, but it left the youth organization penniless and forced it to abandon programs that required money to continue. MAYO went underground, and perhaps the Southwest Council might have wished it could have escaped notice at the time for sacrificing the young Chicanos for the sake of the Ford Foundation millions. But the youths, it seems, were expendable.

The Southwest Council broke ground in a big way for Chicanos in the field of self-development. It did not burst forth whole from a project-writer's pen, but rather over a couple of years underwent a gradual metamorphosis from a cocoon of an idea in the minds of a few Chicanos into a full-blown creature that could command attention and force open the foundation purse strings. The idea that Dr. Galarza and others had nurtured for years gained unanimous approval and support from the Chicanos at La Raza Unida Conference. It was obvious at the conference that while the politicos and bureaucrats held audiencias (hearings) in El Paso hotels, la raza at the church hall was discussing the gut issues: the lack of communication lines, the need for strengthening group awareness, the missing links between the people and political impact at the legislative and decision-making levels of government, and, of high priority, the necessity of clarifying objectives and establishing methods which either the whole community or segments of it could embrace.

The Southwest Council geared itself for economic development of the barrio through internal efforts, but as the experience with the Ford Foundation demonstrated, the Council and Chicanos in general still did not have the political wherewithal to weather the criticisms or to sever the dependence on the private gringo bureaucracies that the Ford Foundation and other foundations represented. Nevertheless, from the date of La Raza Unida Conference in El Paso, the Chicano revolt has picked up pace and co-ordination and numbers. The older Chicanos are still around to provide advice, but it is the youth who give it its style and urgency. For a long time, individuals and organizations within the Chicano community had been consciously striving to arouse more and more Chicanos to activist and militant participation. Many Chicanos foresaw the coming to greatness of our people, but they also encountered a great deal of blindness, apathy, and fear. Young Chicanos have known for years that they were getting the short end of the educational stick. Their parents long ago were aware of police harassment and brutality, of the economic injustice and violence that they have suffered for generations. Chicanos have cautiously kept that odd faith that tells them that the legal system, the economic ladder, and the social sphere beyond the barrio are inaccessible to them. But so many of us have been passive, fooling ourselves into trusting that matters were sure to improve someday. The church played a great role in formulating the deceit we practiced on ourselves; the schools taught it to us by rote, and the Anglo agencies of law and of welfare engrained it into our minds; we were whitewashed. I'm sure that many Chicanos actually believed that the Anglo himself would someday deliver us from our plight. But the truth is becoming clearer and clearer. The black man knows it, the red man knows it, and now we have to admit it, too. La raza can expect nothing from the Anglo—not justice, or freedom, or dignity. We must demand each thing and attain it by whatever means are necessary.

Older Chicanos had to be embarrassed when the Chicanitos, their own children, said Basta! to the Los Angeles school authorities. Why had Chicanos in East Los Angeles waited so long to tell the Anglo that he could no longer cheat the children of the adequate education which was rightfully theirs? The young people had to do it for themselves. The lesson that came out of that blowout has not been refuted; young Chicanos will lead la raza. They will make mistakes and overplay their militancy sometimes, but by and large they are going to show the older generation of Chicanos what must be done to guarantee Chicano rights and identity in the United States—nothing short of violent, social revolution.

9

BUILDERS OF A NATION—A HISTORICAL PERSPECTIVE

EMPLOYMENT was the logical issue to foment the first truly serious incidents in the Chicano revolt. The Mexican American has been generally relegated to the lowest-paying and meanest jobs in America. He has usually had to compete with the Negro even for the lowly jobs, because the Anglo has wanted it that way. Pitting the black against the brown for jobs available and showing favor to one group and not another has been an effective way to keep wages down, dissent at a minimum, the minorities in their places, and the blacks and browns too busy fighting each other to trouble the white man. During the early part of this century, Mexican Americans were recruited as strikebreakers (unknowingly to them) into the steel plants and factories of the Midwest. The importation of Mexicans for the harvest has accomplished the same thing as the recruitment of Mexican strikebreakers—ill will that lingers to this day.

For the 120 years of his own history, the Mexican American has been the last hired, the first fired. Traditionally, the Mexican American derived from an agricultural economy dependent on the earth for existence. Tierra o Muerte, the Zapatista cry for agrarian reform, was not simply revolutionary rhetoric; the mexicano literally could not survive without his land. Whether they were natives of that portion of the northwestern Mexico territory that became United States soil in 1848, or immigrants from Mexico after that date, Mexican Americans were predominantly rural- and farm-oriented; they had owned or managed farms or ranches, and with other avenues of employment closed, they naturally moved into farm work. Mexican American landowners were driven from their lands by violence and by financial breakdowns during the Depression; Mexicans who had property in Mexico lost their holdings, particularly during the revolution of 1910, and many migrated because of the unsettled political situation there. To keep alive, many resorted to the only work they knew, on farms; others moved into urban barrios, where still the only opportunity was in the most menial kinds of labor. Mexican Americans have joined in the exodus from rural areas of America to the cities. If up to 80 percent of Chicanos reside in urban centers today, it is reasonable to assume that nearly the reverse was true before the 1930s. However, the Depression years set in motion a movement to the cities which, during the past forty years, took nearly 30 million people from farms into metropolitan areas, including uncounted Chicanos.

The upward mobility for Mexican Americans, once they left the rural areas, has not been as rapid or as consistent as that of other groups. Labor statistics since the 1930 census show that although Mexican American employment in nonmanual work such as professional, managerial, sales, and clerical doubled by 1960, this meant only a 10 percent increase in the share of Mexican American employment in nonmanual jobs. In other words Mexican Americans were standing nearly stock-still while other Americans moved up.

Whereas during the Depression thirties, job opportunities plummeted, or at best remained static—and Mexican Americans were generally impeded even more in advancing in pay or in quality of job—there were rapid advances in the forties due to the manpower demands of the war effort. To some degree, industry and business could not afford to discriminate as in the past. The position of Mexican Americans in relation to Anglo workers rose appreciably in Colorado and California but remained relatively the same in Texas, where other groups had had a rapid rise in quality of jobs and in income. Similarly in New Mexico, while the relative job position of Mexican Americans was about even in relation to Anglos, by 1960 the Anglo scale of employment had risen sharply, leaving the Mexican American on relatively the same level as before, although he had made some gains.

California and Colorado offered the greatest and most rapid job improvement opportunities to Mexican Americans in the war forties. However, in the fifteen years after the war, the pace decreased as manpower needs slowed and Anglo workers moved in to fill skilled and semiskilled openings. In other words, once the brunt of the war effort had been handled, the Anglo settled back to take care of his own—and damn the Chicano. The experience of Mexican Americans with the federal government's employment policies, among the most racist in the country, can be told in the history of Kelly Air Force Base in San Antonio, Texas.

Friends and relatives of mine in San Antonio worked out at Kelly and found considerable opportunity during the war years to upgrade their skills and income at the base, which has since become one of the biggest flight-training centers in the nation. It is only now as an adult, able to grasp the significance of the events, that I learn from the same people I knew had worked at Kelly, that those were the days of separate rest rooms, separate water fountains, and of Anglo jobs and Mexican jobs. While the overt segregation has lessened, the division of jobs persists between Anglos and Chicanos.

Just as in farm work, the Mexican American was

relegated to the lowest-paying and least responsible jobs, with such subtlety and seemingly unconscious motivation that decades later, the air force base administration does not admit that any discrimination ever existed. Yet there are multitudes of Chicanos who have labored in the same General Schedule (GS) slots, or white collar, wage board, or blue collar levels for ten and fifteen years without getting an increase. Meanwhile, Anglo counterparts have gone up the ladder, and Anglos recently employed by the base have by-passed the veteran Chicano workers.

Kelly Air Force Base administrators no doubt have the same idea as the little old teacher in a California Central Valley school who had a majority of Mexican American children in her class. A visitor one day, a Mexican American, noticed that on several occasions she had asked a little Anglo boy to lead a row of Mexican American youngsters to an outdoors activity. He had asked her why, and she answered that Johnny's father was a rancher and he had to get used to giving orders to the Mexicans.

Professor Daniel Martinez reported the same kind of attitude when, during a survey in 1968 of Kelly's equal employment opportunity status, he learned from an Anglo supervisor that he had not promoted a certain Chicano worker to a crew-leader position because he did not believe that a Mexican American could lead a crew that included Anglos. The same supervisor had no qualms about promoting an Anglo of less experience to the same spot, however.

On a broader scale, employment in Texas maintains the Anglo dominance in higher paid, more responsible positions. Mexican Americans and Negroes are clustered at the lower end of the work scale. In 1960, 32 percent of Mexican American and Negro males were laborers, compared to 6 percent of Anglo males; 24 percent of Chicano males and 13 percent of nonwhite males were in professional, technical, managerial, or

skilled jobs, in contrast to 45 percent for Anglos. Again,
although Mexican American men entered professional
and technical occupations at a greatly increased rate in
the 1950s, this only brought them up to 3.1 percent
employed in that category, compared to 11.5 percent for
Anglos. At the lower end of the job scale, of the 167,000
migrant farm workers of Texas, about 95 percent are
Mexican American, and most migrate out of state; there
still exists a vast reservoir of low-paid labor which drags
down the job potential for all Chicanos.

The situation at Kelly Air Force Base reflects the
hiring and promotion picture at any given federal in-
stallation in Texas. According to the U.S. Civil Service
Commission, 18 perc⁀nt of all federal workers in 1967 in
Texas were Mexican American, which is greater than
the Chicano proportion in the population of 15 percent.
According to classification, however, Chicano numbers
fell to nearly nothing beyond the GS-11 ratings, and
only about 15 percent of those Mexican Americans in
wage board, or blue-collar positions, were making
above $8,000 annually.

While it is obvious to Chicanos that the federal government is one of the most rabid discriminators against
Mexican Americans, there exists a remarkable resistance
to alleviating the situation on the part of government
officials. Part of the reason for the federal insensitivity
to Mexican American job demands—and in fact among
most employers of Mexican Americans—is the fiction
they have come to depend on, that Chicanos will not
rebel or make demands, and that the only minority
group employers have to worry about is the Negro. To a
certain extent this is true, because too many Mexican
Americans have remained passive, and it is only recently that the word is getting out that better jobs and
better futures for our families will not come by pas-
sively waiting for them. Instead, aggressive assertion of
our rights as citizens and as workers will have to be the
new approach.

American business and industry have forced the Chicano to take the militant route simply because they have shown a sensitivity to militancy, to riots, to demands, to demonstrations, and to bad publicity. Although the Chicano is late in utilizing these tactics, there is still time to impress upon employers the necessity for them to recognize the validity of Chicano needs. Going back to Kelly Air Force Base as an example, veteran workers like Fernando Rodriguez, Armando Quintanilla, and Erasmo Andrade, after years of pressuring for nondiscriminatory promotional policies, went even further and began, through the Federation for the Advancement of Mexican Americans (FAMA), to demand extra consideration in promotions in order to bring job placement and grade levels of Mexican Americans up to par with Anglo employees. In other words, the militant Chicano employees at Kelly realized that equal hiring and promotional policies were not enough, that this would still relegate Chicanos to a disproportionate share in the jobs and grades at Kelly, so they pushed for special consideration to make up for past injustices. As one observer read the progress in promotions in the past few years, Mexican Americans might achieve a proportionate and fair share in wages and grade rank by the year 2000; that is simply too long to wait for men who have already been cheated for years.

Ironically, but expectedly, the more aggressive Chicano leaders have had little upgrading themselves, while other Chicanos, who took a back seat during the last few years, have advanced. Those few men who have fought the federal establishment relate that there have been offers in the past, but those offers were meant to buy them off at the expense of their fellow workers, and they were rejected as such. We don't need any more malinches.

Since the mid-1850s, Mexican Americans have had to suffer this offhand kind of discrimination, in which their status has been taken for granted by the Anglo boss and politician. The Mexican American for two centuries has exchanged his labor for the white man's crumbs. Anyone who thinks that the white man has profited only from the Negro's sweat and blood and from the American Indian's land and blood, doesn't know of one of the biggest land grabs in world history, of a region that now comprises about one-fifth the total area of the continental United States. American Indians and Negroes should recall that in actuality the territory claimed by Mexico was a haven for blacks and Indian tribes since slavery was outlawed in 1831. Mexican Americans have paid with their sweat and lives for the little recognition they enjoy today as citizens and as a people of the United States. For his labor alone, America owes the Chicano a heavy debt, just as it does the Negro and the American Indian. These two other minority groups have forged ahead in the retribution movement; the Chicanos have to go a long way to catch up.

The original state of the rural Chicano has altered little since a century ago when he was the peón under the gringo whip. The gringos still hold economic and political whips over us which must be wrested from their hands by the organized efforts of Chicanos in Delano, in Tierra Amarilla, and in South Texas (to mention only the most atrocious cases in the Southwest), but also in the Midwest, where the Chicano has migrated and so often has known that he must be out of town by sundown once the harvest is brought in.

The conditions of farm labor have thrust forward Cesar Chavez, head of the United Farm Workers Organizing Committee in Delano, to spearhead the farmworker's battle, not just the Chicano's, but every farmworker's. Looking back on the nearly five-year strike, it is hard to imagine that in 1965 Chavez was known only in the San Joaquin Valley, mostly by organizers, by some clergymen, a few growers, and a great many campesinos. Chavez not only has given farm workers hope, but to many others who may have written off la raza, he has fashioned a cause and provided a new perspective on the Chicano struggle for recognition and rights. Chavez, more than any other Chicano, has given breadth and depth to the aspirations of all Chicanos. But as Chavez will agree, the basic reason for his success has been the Mexican American people themselves. A leader must have people to lead. Chavez is a product of his people, embodying the most fundamental traits of the Chicano. He is patient, methodical, and quietly charismatic; he is not a bombastic speaker, but he has a way of expressing so much conviction in what he does say that the point sinks in all the more.

My recollections of Cesar Chavez include: our first meeting at a small dinner party, mainly of Chicanos, in his honor in Sacramento during the early months of the grape strike; the march from Delano to Sacramento during Lent of 1966 and the speech on the steps of the Capitol; a skirmish with "la migra" (the Border Patrol) in the Giumarra vineyards in 1968 at the beginning of the fresh table grape strike and boycott; a discussion over a root beer float in an A&W root beer stand in Delano late one night; and listening to him testify in the House and Senate in Washington, D.C., last fall at hearings on pesticide abuses. In all that time, I never detected any change in Chavez, the man.

This does not mean that Chavez did not grow mentally and spiritually during that period. The twenty-five-day fast which he imposed on himself in 1968 must have had a great spiritual effect on Chavez; it deeply affected Chicanos who briefly or symbolically joined him in his fast for nonviolence. It seemed a natural thing for Chavez to do, considering his known commitment to nonviolence and his personal integrity. His act did more than anything else to establish the nature of the farmworkers' unionizing movement. Put an end to the days of street confrontations between workers and management forces, he insists; that way is not for the farmworker. A long history of violence in previous farm labor organizing efforts in the 1910s and 1930s proved to Chavez the futility of trying to buck the growers' might. Chavez' fast disarmed the agribusiness moguls more effectively than pitched battles on the county roads around Delano.

In all his writings and speeches and in casual conversation, Chavez insists that the union is the only way for the farmworker to ever achieve social and economic security. The grower will never grant him decent wages and work conditions or permit him self-respect and self-determination; he must grab these for himself through the union. During a fall tour of Eastern cities in which boycotts were being conducted, Chavez stopped first in Washington, where he was to testify before Senate and House committees on the use and abuse of pesticides by farmers. At the Senate Subcommittee on Migratory Labor, chaired by Senator Walter Mondale, Chavez clearly reiterated his stand that the only means the farmworker had for protecting himself, either against unfair wage and job conditions or the misuse of poisons, was through collective bargaining.

While much information exists regarding the low state of Chicano employment in the United States, not much is really known or admitted about the roots of this situation, and much less is being done to attack the causes and correct the problem. It does appear that if farmworkers are to improve their lot, they will have to do it themselves. Non-farmworkers will help of course; but the brunt of the fight will have to be carried on by themselves. They know it, and they want everyone else to know it; hence the national boycott, first of grapes, then of lettuce, is as much a campaign to educate Americans about the nationwide conditions of farm work as it has been to force grape and lettuce growers to negotiate a contract with UFWOC. Basically, the Chavez-led strike has been a strike for all farm laborers, because as the United Farm Workers advance—and they have progressed further than any of the efforts attempted in the past 100 years—an increasing number of farmworker unions will spring up. Contracts will include not only guarantees of wage levels, working conditions, fringe benefits, and other items, but also stipulations about the retraining of union members to take over the machines that are sure to be used in practically every crop. Just as in other industries, management will not be allowed to handle equipment or engage in any functions of the workers; only the workers will be permitted to handle machinery—or else, huelga!

A point dear to Chavez' heart is the objective of providing the farm laborer a share in the benefits that will accrue to management with the advance of technology and science. Chavez insists that farmworkers can become skilled workers (in fact, most who are involved in the delicate processes of pruning, irrigating, and handling machines possess skills not easily come by except with years of experience) and that any loss from automation should be kept at a minimum. Well aware of the sharp plunge that manpower needs have taken in agriculture in the past half-century and of the severe displacement that has occurred in only the past decade, Chavez realizes that the future of the farmworker is with the skilled, even though many jobs in the fields will always require hand labor. A grapevine pruner works harder and longer, and must be at least as highly skilled, as the automobile assembler in Detroit (whose job I would describe as an automated ballet choreographed to avoid excess movement, overwork, and to produce a set output of autos per hour).

Why a farmworker should receive smaller wages, suffer unsafe and unhealthy work conditions, and lose out on fringe benefits enjoyed by most other labor sectors is something which only growers seem to understand. The grower argues that agriculture is entirely different from other industries in that the grower deals with perishable commodities, whereas steelmakers and auto companies produce nonperishables and can close down a factory without ruining the product. The growers should know, however, that more crops have been ruined by weather or pestilence than would be lost through a strike, which it would be to the advantage of both parties to settle quickly.

Growers warn that if farmworkers unionize, they would strike; then America's food supply would be cut down and prices would go up. The fact is that although farmworkers have been organized in but a very few areas, food prices have gone sky-high regardless. The price of food has little to do with the money being paid the people who pick it. It is the packing, the shipping, the merchandising and advertising, and the near monopoly that agribusinesses xert that determine price increases on certain items. Besides, strikes and boycotts in other industries have been viciously destructive of employers, products, and workers. No one ever really recoups the losses of a long strike; and certainly when violence has occurred, the resulting losses are irreparable. Growers accuse farmworkers of a mindless and insensitive tendency to destroy, which really doesn't make sense, since the farmworker must still depend on farm work and cannot lightly seek to destroy the land that feeds him.

Indeed, Chavez once echoed the agrarianist reformer Zapata and the land-grants reformer Tijerina, when he said, "We must turn our minds to the power of the land." If the land itself, however, cannot be owned by the people, its management and its production must at least be controlled by them. During a boycott tour of Eastern cities in the fall of 1969, Chavez asserted that because he had discovered that the goal of economic betterment for the farmworker could not depend on political action, "The boycott will do more to get political legislation than thirty years of political campaigning." Yet, even the federal government supported the growers' resistance; after the start of the fresh table grape boycott, the Defense Department purchases of fresh grapes rose 350 percent, and regulations governing the use of foreign labor (imported Mexican nationals, generally) became more favorable for California growers. In the Congress itself, a California congressman presented each of his colleagues with a box of fresh grapes, and President Nixon commented in California that he liked grapes. Efforts such as the farmworkers' union to break up the tremendous economic hold that agribusinesses have on America seem nearly impossible. For example, Senator James Eastland of Mississippi (who in 1969 received $146,000 in farm subsidies) is among those with the power to veto land reform legislation such as the proposed $55,000 ceiling on farm subsidies.

The growers' contentions boil down to the fact that they do not wish to lose control of a class of people whom they have considered subservient and docile for so many years, and whom they have depended upon to harvest their crops, that is, their incomes without paying them an honest wage for their work. The growers have become accustomed to having a peon class from which they can draw their labor force and which they can manipulate. That time is over. As Chavez once put it: "Employers will pay dearly by depending on that kind of labor [strikebreakers] and discouraging the American worker. He prevents the union from going in to help in recruiting and assuring the proper harvesting of a crop. They're a couple of centuries behind. If I were an employer I'd be signing a contract today."

Persuading growers to sign those contracts is further complicated, however, by the international dimensions of the labor issue along the United States-Mexico border. Striking grape, lettuce, or melon pickers are aware, painfully so, that their predicament places them in opposition to brother mexicanos who seek to cross the frontier in quest of the gringo dollar. The gringo, of course, created the situation; now he nurtures it and literally bleeds it for every cent of profit he can get.

El Veintiocho de abril
a las seis de la mañana
salimos en un enganche
pa'l estado de Pensilvania.

Adios, estado de Texas,
con toda tu plantación
yo me voy para Pensilvania
por no pizcar algodon.

Al llegar al steel mill worque
que vemos la locomotora
¡y salimos corriendo
ochenta millas por hora!

Ya con ésta me despido
con mi sombrero en las manos
de mis fieles compañeros
son trescientos mexicanos.

A Mexican balladeer composed this corrido in 1955. He was a migrant worker recruited from across the border for foundry work (worque) in Pennsylvania steel mills. "On April 28 at 6:00 A.M., he and his companions left the border under contract for Pennsylvania. Goodbye to Texas with all its farming," he continues, "I'm off for Pennsylvania to get away from picking cotton. Arriving at the steel mill, we saw the machinery and took off running at eighty miles per hour! With this last verse, my hat in my hands," he concludes, "I bid farewell to my loyal companions who number three hundred mexicanos."

The mexicano traveler to Pennsylvania, actually an indentured slave, of fifteen years ago, was not unlike the three mexicanos who died, in a San Antonio suburb in October 1968 suffocated in an unventilated truck, door locked from the outside, and abandoned by the driver. Serviano Cervantes, José Ochoa, and Alfredo Quintin had been cooped up in the truck van for more than half a day with forty-three other illegals—Mexicans who had waded across the Rio Grande and then had paid the driver ten or twelve dollars for transportation to Chicago, where they had been promised jobs. The three men died tragically and needlessly, but their story is linked to an even greater tragedy that affects hundreds of thousands of Mexican Americans all along the United States-Mexico border. The forty-six men, all of whom could have died in that truck, were Mexicans, here illegally, part of the uncounted tens of thousands who cross the border each year. They come for any kind of work—at lower wages and under worse conditions than other ethnic groups. And they pay the price of unmitigated misery for themselves, coupled with the disdain of fellow raza on this side of the border. Nearly two thousand miles of imaginary borderline extend from Brownsville, Texas, to Tijuana, Mexico, ample space for a clandestine border crossing. Perhaps a quarter of a million Mexicans wait at any given time for a chance to slip into the United States.

While the illegal entrant presents a major problem, the legal subterfuge of the "commuter," Mexicans with permanent immigrant visas who work in the United States but live in Mexico, presents another quandary. These commuters force domestic workers to compete in a labor market that readily accepts the lowest offer. Commuters often are used, unwittingly perhaps, as strikebreakers, as has been the experience in Starr County, Texas, in Delano, and in the Imperial Valley, California. The Senate Migratory Labor Subcommittee in its 1968 report, "The Migratory Farm Labor Problem in the United States," said of the commuter:

The Mexican aliens, as a group, are a readily available, low-wage work force which undermines the standards American workers generally enjoy throughout the rest of the country. More importantly, the normal play of free enterprise principles is subverted and prevented from operating to develop standards along the border commensurate with the American standard. So long as Mexican aliens are allowed indiscriminately to work in the American economy, and take their wages back to the low-cost Mexican economy, the growth of the American standard will continue to be stultified.

The United States Government in various ways has abetted the abuse of alien farm labor by U.S. growers. Public Law 78, the bracero program that terminated at the end of 1964, was an artificial law designed to legalize what had been going on for decades. At least the Mexican Government saw to it that P.L. 78 contained guarantees to protect its own citizens; nothing of the kind was established for U.S. citizens. Since the 1860s (as is well documented by Carey McWilliams in *Factories in the Fields*), California in particular, but other states as well, have imported foreign labor for the harvests. When the bracero program ended, growers simply turned to other legalistic ruses for the importation of alien labor, including the "green card," the immigrant visa, which has become another form of bracero law. However, while P.L. 78 contained a number of guarantees for Mexican nationals, no such protections hold for the present situation. The mexicano participates in the creation of a "jungle law" labor market; the effect on domestic workers in the fields is that much worse.

Under the Immigration and Nationality Act, the Secretary of Labor must certify that an applicant for a green card, in order to qualify for employment here, "will not adversely affect the wages and working conditions of the workers in the United States similarly employed." However, once an applicant is cleared and receives his visa, he may enter and leave the United States at will; and he may work wherever he pleases, regardless of how he may affect domestic labor conditions. And while a 1967 amendment to the act forbids a green-card holder from securing work wherever a labor dispute has been certified by the Secretary of Labor, the act does not affect commuters already working there, even those hired just before certification.

At present, there are some 650,000 to 700,000 green-card holders from Mexico in the United States. A substantial number of these visa holders are only commuters, earning money here which they spend in Mexico. A sample count on January 11, 1966, showed that of 42,641 commuters, 17,653 had agricultural jobs. Estimates of the effects of commuters on 1967 labor markets range from 5 percent in San Diego and 17 percent in El Paso, to 23 percent in Brownsville. In El Paso, unemployment in 1967 was 35 percent greater than the Texas average, yet commuter estimates were double the number of the unemployed. In fact, unemployment is generally higher along the border areas. In California's Imperial Valley, unemployment hit 10 percent, twice the state average; still, commuters comprised 85 percent of the farm work force!

No one in affluent America ever sees what these figures mean—the hovel existence that extends along the United States-Mexico border. Tourists can usually bypass the barrio slums on speedy highways; they drive quickly by El Segundo and never see the colonias. A survey released by the Department of Labor in September 1967 of major slum areas in the United States reported that employment problems—not merely unemployment, but subemployment—were most serious in San Antonio (47.4 percent) and Phoenix (third highest, 41.7 percent). Both cities are only a few miles from the border. This means that the effects of border unemployment and deprivation are being transported to the major metropolitan areas near the demarcation lines. The ripple effect extends even to the Northwest and Midwest.

Yet, the illegal entrants and the green carders are not the only factors; "white carders," who receive a three-day visitor's pass, may also abuse the privilege in order to find work, and they often remain in the United States far beyond the legal period. In 1968, twenty-five thousand white carders were deported, but that number drastically underrepresents the true number of white

carders actually employed here illegally. The section of
the Immigration and Nationality Act which prohibits
the harboring or concealing of aliens, by the way, excuses employers of white carders by stating:

. . . for the purposes of this section (274.4) employment including the usual and normal practices incident to employment shall not be deemed to constitute harboring.

The tales are many among Chicanos who know of employers and growers who were conveniently raided by
the Border Patrol seeking illegal entrants, green carders,
or white carders, just before pay day.

There are no easy solutions to the problem, which
itself is extremely complicated. Mexican Americans,
however, find themselves opposing fellow raza in a
game which up until now only the gringo grower or
businessman has been winning. The United Farm
Workers, for example, have attempted to collaborate
with the Mexican unions, supposedly very strong, to
close the border against scabs, but to little avail. The
Mexican Government will not cooperate; the exporta-
tion of Mexican labor means the importation of many
millions of gringo dollars. A number of remedies have
been suggested: a minimum wage law to cover green
carders, requiring applicants to prove residence in the
United States, and the cancellation of a green card after
a grace period during which residence must be established. In December 1967, Senator Edward Kennedy
introduced an amendment to the Immigration and Nationality Act that would require certification of each
commuter alien every six months by the Labor Department. This would assure that his working here would
not have an adverse effect on United States workers and
would not have the effect of strikebreaking. Not only do
growers oppose such a law, but retail businessmen
along the border fear the loss of millions of dollars from
commuters who do spend some of their wages this side
of the boundary.

Finally, the problem comes right back to the Chicano who lives along the border, who must accept the going low job rates, migrate each year to all parts of the nation, or simply move away to another state altogether. He is the chief victim of the unwillingness of either the United States or Mexican governments to protect the interests of their own citizens without harm to the other country's people.

However, the undisguised disregard that the United States demonstrates toward the Chicano becomes clear when the entire picture of deprivation is viewed. Not only do immigration laws favor the alien, but the vaunted free enterprise system encourages the "commuter factory." The Chicano is cheated out of even a dirty job on the United States side of the line by wage-depressing labor competition. He is denied potential employment by companies which move across the border and ship components of television sets, for example, for assembly or finishing on the other side.

Secretary of State Dean Rusk in 1961 warned that reducing the commuter movement could cause substantial harm on both sides of the border. Yet, substantial harm is being done right now to workers on this side of the border. Do they count for nothing? Commuter earnings are taken from the pockets of U.S. workers and the abuse of U.S. trade regulations by U.S. companies takes away more jobs. Why can't the United States Government through its departments of State, Labor, and Commerce protect the U.S. citizen first? Federal officials spout concern for international relations, but I submit that the real concern stems from the pressure of U.S. corporations who don't want a lucrative loophole plugged up.

The problem is international, but so far the approach is unilateral. Simply stopping the flow of several thousands of Mexican citizens across a fictional border would affect the region drastically. The only logical resolution of the exploitation of both Mexican and United States labor is a regional one, in the sense of a belt of commerce of several miles width on either side of the border within which regulations would tend to equalize prices and wages and decelerate migration across the border and beyond.

The human tragedy that pits brother against brother in a competition for even the lowest paying and least skilled jobs has to be eliminated. The final answer lies in the Chicano revolution of unionization, barrio organization, and political control. Otherwise the exploitation of our labor will never cease.

June 5, 1967. That date marks the first act of armed insurrection in the Chicano advance toward independence. Men of the Alianza Federal de Pueblos Libres—armed with shotguns, rifles, and handguns—took control of the courthouse and town of Tierra Amarilla, the small county seat of Rio Arriba county in northern New Mexico. This county, which borders on the Colorado state line, has more than 70 percent people of Spanish descent. The life is hard, dirt hard, for the majority of the people, many of whom claim descent from the first Spanish colonizers of the region—who had contended with the harshness of the winters and the terrain to establish their way of life. The Alianza was headed by Reies Tijerina, who has been the predominant voice in America seeking reclamation of lands stolen by force and guile from the original Spanish settlers and grantees. Tijerina maintains that the violations of the Treaty of Guadalupe Hidalgo are at the root of the deprivation and social disintegration of the people.

The aspirations of Tijerina surpass the small-scale objectives of most men, for he would seek to found the Free City-State of San Joaquin del Rio de Chama on the San Joaquin grant: a free, political enclave equivalent to, yet independent of, states bordering it. Tierra Amarilla might be the capital of such a sovereignty. Perhaps the Alianza and the Spanish American people could reclaim their past and assure the future if they could be masters of their land and reform their institutions according to their needs in building a new independent nation.

June 5. Twenty Alianzistas stormed into the Tierra Amarilla courthouse in search of Alfonso G. Sanchez, to make a citizen's arrest of the then district attorney of Santa Fe County. The Alianza had learned that on the night of June 2 several Alianza members had been arrested by Sanchez' men. These arrests were intended to squelch a confrontation that had been planned for June 3 in Coyote between the Alianza and the Forest Service; but this never took place. The Alianza considered Sanchez guilty of violating the civil rights of Mexican Americans; he had also been very vocal in criticizing the Alianza's professed objectives.

The year before, on October 22, Alianzistas had liberated the Echo Amphitheater campground in the Santa Fe National Forest and had arrested two Forest Service rangers for trespassing on their land. The site was strategic; it had originally been given by King Charles IV of Spain in 1806 as the San Joaquin land grant. The Alianza had proclaimed the area el Pueblo Republica de San Joaquin del Rio de Chama. Tijerina had been arrested following the campground takeover and held for forty-five days without bond. Upon release, he renewed his efforts to strengthen the Alianza and to publicize the deplorable conditions of life among the Spanish American people in Rio Arriba. Sanchez' actions on June 2 sparked the courthouse assault in which two lawmen were wounded and two other men taken as hostages, while the courthouse itself was nearly wrecked.

The Alianza leader was arrested on charges of kidnapping, false arrest, and armed assault on a jail. In one of the most shocking developments of the case a key witness to the June 5 incident, Eulogio Salazar, a fifty-four-year-old jailer, was beaten to death in January. No one has yet been charged with the murder although Reies Tijerina and twenty other Alianzistas were taken into custody on suspicion of murder; all were later released. The courthouse case did not come to trial until November 1968; during the intervening eighteen months, Tijerina had not given up his organizational efforts and had even participated in the Poor People's Campaign in the summer of 1968. Tijerina had attempted to place his name on the November 5 ballot as a gubernatorial candidate for the People's Constitutional Party, but pending litigation against him was cited as a legal barrier to his running in the race for governor. Only a year earlier, on November 11, a day short of the start of his trial on the Tierra Amarilla charges, Tijerina had been convicted by a federal jury in Las Cruces on charges related to the Santa Fe campground seizure. In the Albuquerque trial, Tijerina, speaking in his own defense, carried the case to the prosecution, asserting that violence had been precipitated by law officers when Alianza members had entered the courthouse to make a citizen's arrest of the district attorney. He pointed out that the incident at Tierra Amarilla had erupted as a result of injustices committed against Spanish Americans and frustrations built up over generations, during which their rights and their lands had been denied them. On December 13, 1968, Tijerina was acquitted of all charges.

A former evangelical preacher, born in Texas, the son of a sharecropper and migrant worker, Tijerina had devoted a major portion of his time since the acquittal to carrying his message to Chicanos at a number of conferences, often very youthful in make-up. At least he tried to, until last June 11 when his appeal bond on the first campground conviction was revoked and he was immediately jailed. He had been present at a sign-burning on the campground, for which his wife is now being tried.

His speeches had not changed in basic principles since I first heard him at La Raza Unida Conference in El Paso in 1967. Speaking extemporaneously but in eloquent Spanish, phrasing his words in the style of a

preacher, he said then that the reform of the land had
started on June 5:

As of June 5, fear is gone in New Mexico. We are free. Before
June 5, the pueblos were accustomed to terror; that is ending
now. We will have to learn from the militants (of the black
community) that the government respects nothing but power.
We are being trained through television to watch wars, violence in Vietnam. I want to say to the people of Vietnam for
the people of New Mexico that we give you a brotherly
salute, for you are fighting for your land, knowing that with
the land come other benefits. Unless we fight, and unite, we
will continue to keep getting the powdered milk of services.
What we seek is not justice in books but the justice of land.
Are we Communists? No! The justice we seek with our eyes,
our feet, our hearts is in the land. Life, language, land. Above
all things, all else goes away, but the land is always there.
That's why we took the land. A man said to two blind men,
"Here's something for you," but he gave them nothing. Soon
the two blind men were fighting for their share, which each
thought the other had. The Anglo does the same to us. We
need a spark to fire our movement. That spark is justice. We
have discovered the valor that is in the land and in justice.

In the summer of 1968, as the Poor People's Campaign began, he spoke to a group of Chicanos in an
apartment overlooking the capital city, with the Capitol, the Washington Monument, and the Jefferson Me-
morial in view. It was May 10, his first day in Washington for the campaign. He struck the same theme about
the land, the language, and justice, telling us that each
was part of the other and that he sought all as the destiny of the Mexican American. He told an anecdote
about the forging of the Liberty Bell in Philadelphia,
that it had been recast twice but each time had cracked
and on the third time had been left that way. His point
was that it was a sign of the hypocrisy of the liberty
which Anglo Americans espoused, in that that liberty
was only theirs to enjoy.

Boldly exploiting the Poor People's Campaign as a
platform for his contentions based on the Treaty of
Guadalupe Hidalgo, Tijerina defended his Alianza and

denounced the United States for violating the treaty and bringing the people of New Mexico to their present state of impoverishment and inequality under the law. He presented the following demands at the United States Department of State: that an impartial committee investigate the validity of the Treaty of Guadalupe Hidalgo; that an immediate executive order be given setting priority to the Spanish language and culture on all levels in the Southwest; that all the confiscated land grants be returned immediately; that compensation be given to the immediate needs of the victims; and that cases pending in courts directly related to the land question against individuals be withdrawn on the grounds that the treaty is a defective document. The Alianza leader spoke with the secretary of the Organization of American States (OAS), charging that because the United States had failed to take corrective measures through its courts and legislatures, the Alianza was turning to the OAS, el organismo regional, to seek justice. When Tijerina sought a meeting with Dean Rusk, the former secretary of state refused, but OAS Secretary General Galo Plaza, promised to present a document by Tijerina to the Commission on Human Rights. Galo Plaza stated: "The cause of the poor all over the world has my full sympathy; if there are no changes in the structures of government through peaceful means, they will take place through explosive means."

The agrarianist nature of the northern New Mexico struggle—a dimension still vital to many other nations, but irrelevant to the corporate-shares mentality of the Anglo American—was underscored during the campaign by Tijerina. He issued a denunciation of campaign organizers on July 11, 1968, accusing the key Negro leaders of squandering campaign funds and, more dear to his cause, of having ignored the land-reform tenets of Dr. Martin Luther King, Jr. He pointed out that Dr. King's suggestion—that portions of white-owned plantations in the South be redistributed to

Negro farm-owners through federal condemnation of the lands—had been abandoned by the new leadership of the Southern Christian Leadership Conference.

Tijerina seeks similar redistribution of New Mexico lands to the Spanish Americans of the Alianza. How extensive this reallocation would be is indicated in the suit filed in the federal court in Denver, Colorado, in December 1967 by twenty-eight descendants of Spanish Americans. The twenty-eight litigants, who were represented by Charles S. Vigil, a former U.S. attorney for Colorado, are descendants of Spanish people who held claims on land that had been ceded to the United States in 1803, 1848, and 1898. One million dollars in damages for all descendants of the grantees was sought. With descendants numbering from half a million to a million, Vigil estimated that the bill could run up to a trillion dollars. The suit refers to lands located in Colorado, New Mexico, Florida, Texas, California, Arizona, Louisiana, Georgia, North Carolina, South Carolina, and the Louisiana Purchase territory as a whole. Among the land grants cited, some involved such developments as the 260,000 acres held by the Colorado Fuel and Iron Steel Company in Colorado and New Mexico, and 400,-000 acres held by the Hughes Company in Colorado, a source of large mineral deposits.

Secluded from Anglo incursions in communal villages for most of the nineteenth century, the Spanish Americans and Mexican Americans of New Mexico, and particularly those of northern counties, were summarily choked off by the encroachment of the railroad companies in the 1870s. The land itself became prime real estate for farming and for grazing cattle and sheep. About 33 million acres in land grants dwindled within decades to less than 2 million in the hands of the original settlers and heirs to this land. In clear violation of the Treaty of Guadalupe Hidalgo, lands that had been held for generations were ordered to be registered with the Federal Land Office, with documented proof required. Many lost their lands without knowing it—until a generation later the government would dispossess a family or even whole villages of their land for conversion into federal parks or into open domain. In the 1870s, when the cattle and railroad interests needed the land, fraudulent claims could be filed that would embellish the greed of those companies with hundreds of thousands of acres for next to nothing in payment. The Spanish descendants were driven into more miserable isolation.

The actions by the federal agencies and civil courts in recent years have done little to improve the people's attitude toward officialdom. In fact, many have been forced to defend their rights through a movement like Tijerina's Alianza out of sheer frustration. The U.S. Forest Service represents an example of the conflict of cultures in New Mexico between an essentially folk, agrarian society and the legalistic, industrial nature of the Anglo American society. Tomás Atencio, of Dixon, New Mexico, formerly with the Colorado Migrant Council, has documented the circumstances of the cultural clash in New Mexico:

In 1964, I was involved in community development in El Rito. A group of unemployed men was organized and encouraged to initiate a self-help project. Among them were experienced woodsmen and some of them had previously worked with the Forest Service. They chose to form a working cooperative and to appeal to the Forest Service for a forest thinning project. They intended to utilize the thinnings for a by-product small industry. The project reached a disappointing conclusion when the Forest Service announced this group of unemployed Mexican Americans had to submit a competitive bid. The notion of having to go through bidding procedures scared the group. It disbanded abruptly, and another effort to rehabilitate human beings was stifled by a government bureau.

On the other hand, the Forest Service responds to established business and industry by curtailing the number of range and revegetation projects in favor of areas for recreation. In 1968, Colorado was allotted $2.4 million for recreation, but only $240,000 for range and revegetation; New Mexico was allocated $1.2 million for recreation, but again only about $240,000 for range and revegetation. A man in Peñasco, New Mexico, possesses a document concerning the sale of forest land to a timber company; this stipulates that the seller will maintain rights to grazing, timber, and firewood within the land, rights that were honored by the company. When the land was sold to the United States Government, the clause was omitted. The land now is virtually lost as far as those seemingly inconsequential rights are concerned, for the Forest Service is strictly enforcing the present contract. The small farmers and cattle growers believe the Forest Service is deliberately trying to exterminate them in the name of improving range management by reducing grazing allotments. In 1966 one area was reduced in its grazing allotments by 20 percent; in another, year-round permits for cattle and free permits for milk cows, bulls, and horses were abolished; and one other region has lost all free permits. Families, already reduced to subsistence farming, are encouraged to sell their cattle. No wonder, Atencio has said, that the native population of New Mexico sees "the forest ranger in his olive drab uniform as an American occupational trooper guarding the spoils of the Mexican-American War. There is an enemy in those hills. It is that forest ranger."

Generations of families who have lived from the land and find in it more than life, indeed the reason for existence, have come to this predicament: as many as a quarter of the able-bodied men are unemployed; there are not enough jobs to go around; the major business that is developing, tourism, is Anglo dominated; the average annual income in the northern counties is about $1,000; on the state level, average income reaches $2,310; Spanish American youngsters leave school early at three times the rate of Anglos; although Spanish-descent youths therefore fail Selective Service examinations, they still comprise 59 percent of New Mexicans drafted (even though the Spanish-surname community makes up only 30 percent of the state population). In Albuquerque it was found recently that only 12 of 292 II-S (student) deferments were for Spanish Americans. There are only six Spanish surnames among the 326 medical doctors in Albuquerque. Of sixty-six bank presidents in the state, one is of Spanish descent. Housing and sanitation in the Spanish villages is substandard if not primitive.

In spite of the highly publicized "violence" in which Alianzistas have been implicated, the Alianza continues to make formal requests of lawful authorities for retribution or return of the lands stolen from the descendants of the Spanish settlers. A letter dated November 28, 1969, was sent to President Nixon by Wilfredo Sedillo, Alianza vice-president. A stiff-bearded patriarchal macho of a man, Sedillo, along with Ramon Tijerina, Reies' brother, and a few others maintain the Alianza movement's new thrust toward political involvement along the lines of a third party. The letter is a magnificent expression of respectful regard for authority, but deadly somber in its allusion to the specter of violence:

In view of our understanding that the Treaty of Guadalupe Hidalgo of May 30, 1848, is just a proposal and not a valid treaty to end the Mexican-American War with the conditional surrender of Mexico that, if it were valid, would have been completely honored and thusly continued to completely protect the Indo-Hispano and Indian property rights in Spanish and Mexican land grants of the Southwest, and in view of the fact that we abhor the resuming of violence which seems inevitable without such valid treaty, we are enclosing here a copy of the map of the proposed "La Republica de Aztlán" as adopted by the seventh annual convention of the Alianza Federal de Los Pueblos Libres so as to terminate this war that seems to make Indo-Hispanos of the Southwest subjects of a foreign nation (the United States of America).

The convention directed that the map be sent to you together with the request that the independence of Aztlán be recognized, which is hereby done. The implication that Indo-Hispanos of the Southwest advocate violence of any kind toward the United States, for which many of us have fought and died in its wars, should not be inferred from this request. On the contrary, since the Treaty of Guadalupe Hidalgo appears to be invalid—to our regret—we strongly urge that our request be granted for the complete termination of this war and the potential danger to the United States of America and to the whole Western Hemisphere.

We look forward to hearing from you.

Sedillo referred to a conference held in November 1969 in Albuquerque at the Alianza headquarters. A large map had been sketched on paper and pinned to a plywood board depicting the territory known as Aztlán to the Chicano. A line extends from the present northern border of California across Nevada, Utah, and Colorado, down the eastern border of Colorado to a line cleaving Texas nearly in half, and then along the Gulf Coast including the present border line between Mexico and California, Arizona, New Mexico, and Texas.

In all the Alianza's efforts to obtain a just solution to what they consider a life-or-death issue, the White House, the State Department, and other federal agencies have turned a deaf ear. "We have been told the Treaty is just a proposal," Sedillo has written. "If this is so then Mexico and the United States are still at war— all they have to do is give us back our land." The Alianza spokesman traces his familial roots in New Mexico to 1601, three years after the first settlement at San Juan de los Caballeros in the Chama River Valley by Juan de Oñate. "We have no basis as a nation to go to the United Nations," Sedillo says, "and Mexico is a welfare nation from the United States, so she will not help. Franco has been contacted, but we have had no answer from him. So now we will embark on political action."

Tijerina finds himself at a crossroads, perhaps an impasse, today. On December 24, 1970 he was sentenced to concurrent terms of from one to five years and from two to ten years on the charge of assault with intent to kill or maim jailer Eulogio Salazar and for false imprisonment of Deputy Sheriff Pete Jaramillo during the June 5 raid at Tierra Amarilla. This vigorous orator, mellifluent in Spanish and strongly accented in English, this impassioned man in speech and in action, is languishing in a federal prison. Visitors had found him often in low spirits when he had been in New Mexico prisons, speaking of compromise with authorities or promising renewed efforts for the liberation of his people when he is released. Whatever the destiny of Reies Lopez Tijerina may be (ending in the triumphant achievement of his goals or obscurity in jail and afterward), the impoverished Chicanos of northern New Mexico have found a new path.

Signaling a fresh change of the wind in Rio Arriba, a letter arrived a few months ago in my mail from the Northern New Mexico Support Committee reporting on the existence and persistence of the Cooperativa Agricola del Pueblo de Tierra Amarilla. Twenty families pooled their land—about six hundred acres of the ancestral Tierra Amarilla land grant—and began preparation of three hundred acres for spring, with the rest given over to grazing. Reverting to the fundamental communal farming that their forefathers implanted in the region centuries ago (a system affinitive to the way of life of the Indian peoples who preceded them), the Tierra Amarilla farmers intend at first to share the food rather than to market it. Hunger and malnutrition are the primary enemies to be overcome. The Co-operative owns two tractors and has three others on loan. A youth group, the Comancheros, who affect the style of the Brown Berets and the MAYOs, also volunteer for duty in the fields along with the Co-op members. The people are seeking private financial support, dollars and cents, to re-create part of the past lest the future never come. As Tijerina put it, they have discovered "the valor that is in the land and in justice."

10

A NEW FAITH—HOPE FOR CHANGE

JUSTICE. In northern New Mexico, in the whole Southwest, justice could be based solely on land, its products, its permanence, and its beauty. And there is another justice that depends not on legalities but on what we refer to as "la raza," a cultural entity rather than a purely racial sentiment. Rodolfo "Corky" Gonzales—a short stocky Chicano who has in recent years become a poet and a playwright after years of earning his living and a reputation with his fists—began to preach a new faith to Mexican Americans in Denver, Colorado, as far back as 1963. He founded Los Voluntarios, a Chicano group which a year later effectively protested police tactics against raza. As owner of a bail-bonding business, he had financed in 1959 a barrio newspaper called *Viva*, the first of its kind in the city. The Crusade for Justice, which began in April 1966, soon published *El Gallo*, one of the first Chicano newspapers. The organization and its newspapers became a central dissemination point for raza thought and action.

It can be said, in truth, that the Crusade, and Gonzales specifically, have instilled the Chicano revolt with much of its spirit and ideology. Back in 1967, Gonzales was probably the first Chicano leader to oppose publicly the Vietnam war. His opposition is not from pacifist convictions but from the nature of the war, which is taking a fatal toll of Chicano lives in order to subdue a people as oppressed and impoverished as Chicanos themselves. The concept of Aztlán originated at the Youth Liberation Conference held March 27–31, 1969, at the Crusade headquarters with a group of Chicanos who prepared a position paper regarding the Chicano movement that was to issue from the conference. From the Crusade also, through the genius of Manuel Martinez—perhaps the best true Chicano muralist in the nation—came the mestizo head: a three-profile head depicting the Indian mother, the Spanish father, and the fusion of the two—the mestizo, el Chicano.

To Gonzales, Chicano nationalism is "the key or common denominator for mass mobilization and organization." Commitment to the concept of la raza and the Plan of Aztlán, Gonzales has said, implies a commitment to social, economic, cultural, and political independence. "Our struggle then must be the control of our barrios, campos, pueblos, lands, our economy, our culture, and our political life. El Plan de Aztlán commits all levels of Chicano society: the barrio, the campo, the ranchero, the writer, the teacher, the worker, the professional—to la causa." Nationalism is not merely an instrument of organization, Gonzales is saying, but a necessary readjustment of our own values that the Chicano must make away from Anglification, if la raza is to survive whole and sane in a fragmented and insane environment.

Very conscientiously, Gonzales and Crusade members make every effort to instill a sense of raza, of brotherhood, of Chicanismo, into the youngest and the oldest Chicano and in every way possible. At a conference, Gonzales will stress the use of the Chicano handclap rather than the more common Anglo applause; the Chicano style is simply to begin at a slow, even pace, then accelerate until there is a final burst of applause.

Usually this form of clapping conveys the audience's approval more readily than straight applause. It seems more deliberate, communal, intense, and dramatic. Crusade meetings, such as the Fishermen's meetings each Wednesday evening at the Downing Street center near downtown Denver, forego parliamentary procedure for consensus. Young or old can participate in what amounts to a family gathering—a strictly non-Anglo form of discussion.

In December 1969, during a teachers strike in the Denver City schools, the Crusade conducted a Freedom School for some 150-200 Chicanitos from all over the city. Basic curriculum subjects—math, English, and history—were provided by volunteer teachers-on-strike and Crusade members. But courses in Chicano history, in Chicano culture, and in Spanish were also taught, or rather communicated, principally by Gonzales and Crusade instructors. A similar program had been offered the past summer with great success and no dropouts! The program had a dual purpose, to continue the regular instruction of the students but also to Chicanoize them. This little poem was left on a classroom desk by Ruth Nuñez, twelve, following a lesson that ranged from basic Spanish to pachuquismo:

> "Poesía Aztlán"
> Viva la raza
> Don't let them down
> Be proud of your color
> Brown, brown, brown.

Down the halls of the Crusade building, the young students aged six to sixteen years old would come, yelling, Chicano Power! Even some of the teachers, Chicanos who had earned their certificates and had taught for years in the Denver school system, were themselves radicalized by the classes.

Those young people, and a few of the older ones

who had forgotten, expressed a hunger and a thirst for the life-giving sustenance of that which made them what they are, Chicanos: not just tacos, mariachis, and la virgen de Guadalupe, but their color, which they might be led to deny was bronze, their language, which had nearly been ripped from their tongues, certain inclinations of spirit in the family and among carnales (fellow Chicanos), and a complex psychology governing relationships within and without the family. A 1967 study by Dr. Manuel Ramirez, III, at Sacramento State College reveals some of the attitudes among Chicanos relevant to family life and community living. In comparison to Anglo views, Mexican American college students responded more positively on the following statements:

For a child the mother should be the dearest person in existence. More parents should teach their children to have unquestioning loyalty to them.

Some equality in marriage is a good thing, but by and large the husband ought to have the main say-so in family matters.

It helps a child in the long run if he is made to conform to his parents' ideas.

The word of an adult should never be questioned.

It doesn't do any good to try to change the future, because the future is in the hands of God.

The stricter the parents, the better the child.

There is hardly anything lower than a person who does not feel a great love, gratitude and respect for his parents.

Young people get rebellious ideas, but as they grow up they ought to get over them and settle down.

No weakness or difficulty can hold us back if we have enough will power.

Obedience and respect for authority are the most important virtues children should learn.

This and other studies have shown, however, that Mexican American values have been affected by Anglo, middle-class attitudes. Specifically, a decrease in the authority of the male was evident. But in regard to child-rearing, while conformity to the Chicano community's norms of conduct and submission to authority were obvious, there were also conflicting attitudes toward these latter values as a result of the mounting experience in asserting civil rights.

Dr. Ramirez' analysis suggests that internally Chicanos must adapt, not discard, many attitudes that otherwise repress activist involvement in the movement. An inordinate tendency to submit to authority, built in as a defense mechanism over the generations, I believe, makes it extremely difficult to convince Fulano de Tal that for his own good and for that of his people he must engage in resisting the Texas Rangers, the welfare department, the governor, or the president. He has been taught all his life that such activity is taboo, so that submission seems to have become a part of his nature. But he must be persuaded that it is cultural suicide to remain apathetic, that in order to preserve the values of his raza, he has the duty to change the person or the framework of authority so that he can honestly and sincerely submit to it. Thoreau said of the United States Government in 1848 when he opposed the War on Mexico, "I cannot for an instant recognize that political organization as *my* government which is the *slave's* government also," and Chicanos find themselves precisely in the role of being the Anglo American government's slave, as do other raza in the Latin American nations.

The concept of raza derives from a belief in the inherent relationship of one man to another, with each man willing to take the initiative, but at the same time insisting on an individual independence. The interdependence of men is another way to look at it, while each man must accept blame or praise for what he does. While raza look to the future, they willingly accept the present situation to a great extent as preordained, so that each individual understands a role that he is to carry out in his position. When great adversity befalls us, we may tend to accept it, wait it out, hope for the best or for another chance later on. Such a complexity of thought may establish a general attitude of wait and see, lo que Dios quiera (as God wishes). How does a revolution touch such a Chicano, move him to action?

Although less and less a factor, but still demonstrative of the Chicano mind, is the attitude toward sickness. While Chicanos will readily admit to a modern acceptance of diseases caused by a more or less obvious contact with something or someone from which disease may be contracted, it is harder to bring out their reversion to age-old views such as the presence of el mal ojo (the evil eye) or susto (fright), which can produce maladies such as sudden fevers and headaches that raza may find otherwise unexplainable. An old remedy is cotton thread tied around the right wrist and another around the left ankle; another protection is amulets worn by adults and children to ward off el mal ojo. I recall as a child my grandmother placing an egg cracked into a bowl under my bed when I was suffering from a fever, or having someone massage my forehead and temples with a fresh egg to relieve head pains. Because it resembles an eye, the egg was meant to draw out el mal ojo, whatever was causing the illness. Certain herbs or roots might be prescribed for sickness allied with a psychological trauma, although it was never called anything like that by past generations. I've drunk bitter-tasting teas as a youth which were meant to cure almost anything, and looking back they did seem to work, perhaps more so because of the threat of having to drink more of the acrid brew if one didn't recover. Of course, in regard to health problems, less attention is given nowadays to the old folk cures, although there are still curanderas, old women with a unique and mysterious aura about them, who prescribe cures for everything from a boil to impotence.

In a survey conducted a few years ago by Sister Mary Immaculate of Our Lady of the Lake College in San Antonio, Texas, the growing disparity between first- and third-generation Chicanos is quite apparent. The trend is toward increased Anglicization of mores in regard to family life, education, courtship, and marriage. Notably, there is a trend toward smaller families; greater individual functioning rather than functioning as family members; an increase in the desire for education and better work opportunities; somewhat more participation in clubs; a preference, still, for family celebrations; a devotion to la virgen de Guadalupe, but anti-pious religiosity still among the males; and a stronger role for women in schooling and work, along with a greater sharing of authority and responsibility in the family. A detailed analysis of this and other studies, such as that of Dr. Ramirez, would indicate that there is a strong tendency toward assimilating certain Anglo influences, but also retaining a number of Chicano values, a kind of ambivalence which is the other side of the coin in regard to the Chicano liberation efforts. The overall effect can be described as a trend toward middle-class orientation—adopting Anglo values in order to be more in tune with nonraza friends made at higher educational levels or on the job, thus a tendency to avoid boat rocking, to avoid asserting a style of life that one has tried to forget because one may be embarrassed in front of non-Chicano acquaintances or one's employer.

In the field of folklore, tales such as that of *La Llorona* convey a variety of sentiments and beliefs of the Chicano people. *La Llorona* is the story of human frailty and divine vengeance. In a small Mexican village long ago, a woman discovered her husband in an affair with another woman and in revenge she killed her three little children and hid their bodies. But she hid them so well and in such a jealous rage that afterward she could not find their tiny bodies. God condemned her to search for the bodies so they could have proper church burial or she would never have peace.

With that story firmly implanted in my little mind, should I be naughty as a little boy, my mother would shush me, tell me if I heard the wind in the trees or noises outside the house, it might be la llorona searching, searching, for her niñitos, and unless I behaved, la llorona would carry me away. If you listen to the wind in the trees, particularly in the Southwest, it does seem to be a woman calling out for someone, for rest, at least it does to me.

Another story, *The Little Serpent and the Girl,* imbues a creature with powers of speech and magic and a girl with great beauty and innocence. It seems that a little girl found a tiny snake and took him home, feeding and caring for him. One day, the snake, grown quite large, said to the girl, "I am too much for you to feed and care for, let me go now to the forest." Though very fond of the snake, the girl knew it would be best for him to return to his forest home. As she left him in the woods, the snake told her, "If you ever need help, just call me." As the girl grew into maidenhood, she became very beautiful. Two neighbor women grew envious and plotted to tell the king that the young maiden had said she could turn anything into gold or silver. The king had rocks piled high and brought the young woman, demanding that she make them gold. She denied that she had such a power, and insisted she was only a poor, innocent girl. The king, enraged, had her eyes taken out, left her in the forest, and gave the eyes to the two wicked neighbors. The maiden remembered what the snake had said and called to him. He came, but by this time he had grown immense, with a head here and a tail there beyond the horizon. Hearing her plight, he licked her hands. One hand would turn things to gold; the other, to silver, he told her. She heard a woodsman nearby and when she called him he took her home, but his wife refused to help her because they were so poor. The girl told the man to bring two rocks, and when he did, she changed them to gold. With the gold, she asked that he go out and buy her a pair of eyes, even a dog's or cat's—it didn't matter. This he did. In fact, the same old women sold him the girl's very own eyes, which they had kept in a little box. The woodsman brought the dried-up eyes to the girl and she asked him to take her back to the spot in the forest where she had found him. When he left, she summoned the snake again. Shown the eyes, the snake licked them and replaced them. They were even more brilliant and attractive than before! Upon returning to the woodsman's home, she heard that the king was sending his soldiers to slay a giant snake that had been devouring the forest animals. She rushed to the woods and told the snake that he must flee for his life. Right away he left, slithering through the forest. The young maiden lived in her little home in peace from then on, but often she would recall her old friend, the little snake, with sadness.

These and hundreds of other stories and fables convey part of the rich cultural background on the folk level. They suggest that the Chicano has inherited a diverse folk background, an ageless, word-of-mouth form of knowledge, a rich resource for the genius of art in Chicanos.

The function of culture in a person's life is "all-encompassing," according to Marcos de Leon, a California educator. "Culture," he has written,

comprises a group's ideas, habits, values, attitudes, institutions; it possesses physical and material aspects with sanctions in technology and economics. To give the group cohesion and direction, it provides social institutions, education, and political structures; culture sets up systems of belief, relating men to the universe. Aesthetics is very much an integral part of it . . . the graphic and plastic arts, folklore, music, drama and dance. And finally, there is language, the symbolism of abstract thought, the vehicle of knowledge, of belief, of legal systems, and of tribal institutions.

"A culture," Dr. Ernesto Galarza has similarly described, "is characterized by a) the uses it makes of its material environment; b) the accepted or tolerated relations between the individuals that compose it; c) the symbols, conventional signs, and utilities of everyday behavior; and d) the values by which the society measures itself as to moral performance." Dr. Galarza concludes that according to this pattern there is but one culture in the United States, the culture of the American people. There are no subcultures, as some observers would posit, but an "entire society that is manifestly capable of spawning slums and breeding poverty." Dr. Galarza adds that "it is not the subcultures that are in trouble. It is the culture, the American culture itself."

Dr. Galarza thereby spreads the blame around, but from my point of view, because one of the functions of culture is evaluating conduct, placing the blame for the destructive efforts directed against the Chicano's life style is certainly in order. Thus we must consider, as Dr. Galarza rightly says, the entire structure to ascertain where the roots of conflict and division lie. Examining the Anglo American "culture," or that predominance of thought and activity in the United States that passes for culture, I contend that the intimately connected prejudices against people of other colors and other cultures are at the center of Anglo genocidal tendencies. The instances of rejection of the Chicano and discrimination against him because of his different culture, that is, language, life style, and so on, are numerous and variously recounted here.

Anglo "culture" has resulted in the creation of huge industries around the goal of a kissing-sweet breath. A value system based on such goals as this is then projected through commercialization in the mass media to a degree that the male is castrated and the female desexed. One must smoke a certain kind of cigarette to be manly or use a special cologne that comes with karate lessons to be attractive. A female must wear a brassiere that crosses her heart or use a deodorant that lasts five days in order to be womanly. One can almost feel pity

for the Anglo who, in order to be part of the Pepsi
generation, must drink an uncola, use left guard, drive a
horse transformed into a car, pull on a cigarette that
filters out almost all the cancer-dealing tars, rinse his
mouth so he'll be kissed again, and slick his hair with a
cream so that she'll be glad he came back.

Let an Anglo describe his own kind. Nicholas Johnson, a member of the Federal Communications Commission, writes in his book, *How to Talk Back to Your
Television Set* (1970):

We learn that the great measure of happiness and personal
satisfaction is consumption—conspicuous when possible.
"Success" is signified by the purchase of a product—a
mouthwash or deodorant. How do you resolve conflicts? By
force and by violence. Who are television's leaders, its heroes,
its stars? They are the physically attractive, the glib, and the
wealthy, and almost no one else. What do you do when life
fails to throw roses in your hedonistic path? You get "fast,
fast, fast" relief from a pill—headache remedy, a stomach
settler, a tranquilizer, a pep pill, or "the pill." You smoke a
cigarette, have a drink, or get high on pot or more potent
drugs. You get a divorce or run away from home. And if, "by
the time you get to Phoenix" you're still troubled, you just
"chew your little troubles away."

It does appear that enough Mexican Americans have
perverted themselves to accept wholly the Anglo "culture," a poor substitute for the Chicano way of life, so
as to achieve economic and social success. It is almost
impossible to avoid all Anglo influences, nor are all
Anglo ways and advances in science, psychology, and
the arts to be rejected out of hand; but in the light of
the profile I've just sketched, the Chicano must be very
selective. Consistently, I place quotation marks around
the word culture when it is preceded by the word Anglo
because America has yet to develop a culture worth
emulating and passing on to posterity. For the Chicano
to accept the Anglo "culture" or to lose his own identity
in it would be tantamount to our glorying in the Aztecs
because they invented a ball game that almost all In-

dian tribes played in Mexico and Central America. Culture is made of more than that.

The North American culture is not worth copying: it is destructive of personal dignity; it is callous, vindictive, arrogant, militaristic, self-deceiving, and greedy; it is a gold-plated ball-point pen; it is James Eastland and Richard Nixon; it is Strom Thurmond and Lyndon Johnson; it is a Mustang and old-folks' homes; it is Medicare and OEO; it is an $80 billion defense budget and $75 a month welfare; it is a cultural cesspool and a social and spiritual vacuum for the Chicano. The victims of this culture are not merely the minority peoples but the dominant Anglo group as well; everything that passes for culture in the United States is symptomatic of a people so swept up in the profit motive and staying ahead of the Joneses that true natural and humanistic values may be destroyed without their knowing it. Nationalistically, Anglo America has come to believe that it is the supercountry, that it can do no wrong, that its might does make right. The United States suffers from a lack of perspective, a lack of humility; it is spoiled and immature without showing any signs that it is growing out of that stage.

But the Anglo problem can be seen even more clearly from the standpoint of the discrimination and injustice perpetrated upon the Chicano because of his color. For many decades, the issue of color has been suppressed by both the Chicano and the Anglo as a real substantive cause for conflict and difference. Jack D. Forbes, a California historian who claims he is descended from Powhatan (chief of the Indian tribe that first had contact with the Pilgrim Fathers), has incisively struck to the heart of this issue, pointing out that "scholars and social workers dealing with the Mexican Americans ignore their Americanoid racial characteristics and regard them as simply another European-type minority group with certain cultural and linguistic problems; in doing so, they help the Mexican Americans in *their* escape from the realities of their native American heritage." Color is as much a part of our culture as is language—this distinction is forced upon us; it is inescapable in American society. In a negative sense, the proof of this fact is that Chicanos have been discriminated against for both reasons, among others. In other words, the Anglo recognizes various components in other peoples as different from him; he assumes these qualities to be a cause for him to discriminate, that is, to give preference to those who do not have these different qualities. In so doing, the corollary follows—that to be non-Anglo is to be inferior; to speak other than English is to be inferior; to be brown or black or yellow is to be inferior. Convey the idea that all the good things of life belong to those who are not inferior in those certain ways, and, by and by, those other-than-Anglo people will make every effort to disavow their different traits. But color is extremely difficult to conceal, so all manner of subterfuges are invented—what Carey McWilliams and Jack Forbes refer to as the "White-Spanish myth." Within the Chicano community itself, the prejudice of color operates detrimentally. The lighter-complexioned will be favored over the darker-skinned children. A young girl will have made a better marriage for having married the guero instead of the Indio suitor. A light-complexioned Mexican American girl rejects offers of marriage from two Anglos for fear that "if there should be any dark children, I don't want my husband blaming me and calling them 'my children.'"

"Border City," the pseudonym for a town along the Texas-Mexico border, revealed a number of insights about the value of Mexican American culture to Ozzie G. Simmons, who conducted a study in the border locale in 1958. Simmons perceived that Anglo stereotypes of what Chicanos are tend to be reciprocated by Chicano stereotypes of the Anglo. Chicano stereotypes of the Anglo, however, "take into account the Anglo Americans' conflict as to their [Chicanos'] potential equality and present inferiority," but are much less elaborate than those of the Anglo toward him because Chicanos "feel no need of justifying the present intergroup relation . . . the very nature of their dependent position forces them to view the relation more realistically than Anglo Americans do." Chicanos, Simmons indicates, tend to fulfill the conduct expected of them by the Anglo. Anglos, in turn, expect Mexican Americans to be assimilated, but only if Mexicans become "just like Anglo Americans"; there is no middle road for the Anglo. The sociologist concludes:

If the full acceptance of Mexicans by Anglo Americans is contingent upon the disappearance of cultural differences, it will not be accorded in the foreseeable future. . . . In viewing cultural differences primarily as disabilities, we (Anglos) neglect their positive aspect. Mexican American culture represents the most constructive and effective means Mexican Americans have yet been able to develop, for coping with their changed natural and social environment. They will further exchange old ways for new only if these appear to be more meaningful and rewarding than the old, and then only if they are given full opportunity to acquire the new ways and to use them.

We come full circle to the little Chicana's poem about "Brown, brown, brown." Accept our color, the poem says, have pride in it as part of our culture along with language, history, tradition, folklore, land and blood. How well this is understood by Chicano youths is evident in the statement issued by activist youth groups at a liberation conference in Denver:

Nationalism is an awareness that we are not Caucasian, not Mexican-American or any label the system puts upon us, but that we are a people with an ancient heritage and an ancient scar on our souls. We are oppressed first because we are Chicanos, because our skin is dark. But we are exploited as workers by a system which feeds like a vulture off the work of our people only to enrich a few who own and control this entire country. We suffer a double oppression. We catch a double hell.

The essence of cultural nationalism is the full acceptance of this fact, that we are oppressed because of the
color of our skin and because of the nature of our being,
and that as a consequence, inevitably, our sole means of
preservation and equality before all men is in that color
and in that raza. Gonzales has said that anyone who
would wish to become a part of Anglo society is "sick,
because Anglo society is sick." His epic poem, "I Am
Joaquin," published in 1967, relates the internal effects
of Anglo society on Gonzales as well as the counter
influences and the realization of a new direction for the
rebirth of a new spirit:

> I——am, Joaquin.
> I am lost in a world of confusion,
> caught up in the whirl of an Anglo-Society.
> Confused, by the rules
> Scorned, by the attitudes,
> Suppressed by manipulation,
> and destroyed by modern society.
> My fathers,
>   have lost the economic battle
> and won,
>   the struggle of cultural survival
> and now!
>   I must choose . . .
>   between, the paradox of
> . . . .Victory of the spirit despite
> physical Hunger
>   Or
>   To exist in the grasp of the
> American Social neurosis, sterilization
> Of the soul and a full stomach.
> - - - - - - - - - - - - - -
> And in all the fertile farm lands
>   the barren plains
> The mountain villages, smoke
>   smeared cities
>   we start to move
> Mejicano, Español, Latin, Hispano, Chicano
>   I look the same
>   I feel the same
>   I cry and. . . .
>   Sing the same.

I am the masses
   of my people and I refuse to be
   absorbed.
I am Joaquin
The odds are great
but my spirit is strong.
                    My faith unbreakable
                    My blood is pure
                    I am an Aztec Prince
                    and Christian Christ
          I SHALL ENDURE!
          I WILL ENDURE!

When the Poor People's march advanced to Washington, D.C., Juanita Dominguez, of the Crusade, wrote new words to a corrido called "La Rielera," composed during the 1910 revolution. It is in the spirit of a new people with a new awareness of themselves. It says as much of what nationalism and what the Chicano revolt is about as anything else that can be written or said:

Chorus I:
   Yo soy Chicano, tengo color
   Americano pero con honor
   Cuando me dicen que hay revolución
   Defiendo mi raza con mucho valor.

1. Tengo todita mi gente
   Para la revolución
   Voy a luchar con los pobres
   Pa' que se acabe el bolon.   *Chorus I.*

2. Tengo mi par de caballos
   Para la revolución
   Uno se llama el canario
   El otro se llama el gorrion.   *Chorus I.*

3. Tengo mi orgullo y machismo
   Mi cultura y corazon
   Tengo mi fe y diferencias y
   Lucho con gran razon.

Chorus II:
   Tengo mi orgullo, tengo mi fe
   Soy diferente, soy color cafe
   Tengo cultura, tengo corazon
   Y no me los quita, a mi ni un cabron.

CHORUS I:
> I am Chicano, brownskinned, an American but with
> honor. When they tell me the revolution has started, I will
> defend my people with all my courage.

1. My people are all united, for the revolution. I will
   fight with the poor to end oppression.
   > *Chorus I.*

2. I have my pair of horses for the revolution, one is
   called the Canary, the other, the Sparrow.
   > *Chorus I.*

3. I have my pride and manliness, my culture and love,
   I have my faith, I'm different, and I fight with great
   reason.

CHORUS II:
> I have my pride, I have my faith, I'm different,
> my skin is brown. I have a culture, I have a heart,
> And no one can take them from me, no, not any bastard.

The fact that a young woman composed those words
illustrates an aspect of Chicano culture undergoing
radical change from the internalized force of group
assertiveness—the relationship between men and
women in the Chicano movement. I would be writing
but half a book if the Chicana were accorded no special
credit in these pages. The Chicana is half the movement. It may seem that when reference is made to Chicano activism, the emphasis is on the masculine alone.
That tendency is mainly attributable to my being
macho (male) and naturally viewing the Chicano revolt as a male-dominated phenomenon, but I must caution myself every so often, for that could not be further
from the truth. Organizations and headlines certainly
are dominated by the men, but the Chicanas, Mexican
American women, have been beside their men, sometimes even shoving them forward a little bit. What Chicano in recent years has not experienced at some conference or meeting the scathing but truthful words of a
Chicana, demanding to know why the men don't take
action on this or that issue, "or must the women lead the
way and the men hide behind our skirts."

Chicanas today are far different from their grand-
mothers and even their mothers in certain aspects as a
result of the explosion of the small universe which once
enveloped the Chicano community. The woman of the
Chicano revolt believes that Chicano liberation must
also include Chicana liberation. Thus within the overall
Chicano movement toward self-determination and creation of a new identity, a struggle is going on between
our women and our men. It is not a mortal struggle nor
a divisive one, because the women are saying that they
want to be recognized by the Chicano macho as a companion in the revolution. Young girls are relating to the
folk heroines of the Mexican Revolution—La Adelita,
subject of a revolutionary corrido, who exemplified the
soldaderas (women who accompanied the rebel armies
as camp soldiers, sometimes taking arms themselves).
They recall the name of Juana Gallo, a mexicana who
led the men of her village to avenge a federales attack
against her village, and of La Marieta, Maria del Car-
men Rubio de la Llave, a guerillera under Francisco
Villa.

Chicanas have even more recent history of their
contributions to the reassertion of Chicanismo among
our people. A weeks-long strike in the early 1950s
against a zinc mining corporation in southern New Mexico seemed on the verge of collapse. The struggling
miners, predominantly Mexican Americans, faced certain defeat when a court injunction forbade them from
picketing the entrances to the mines. Their wives and
daughters took over the picket signs and although many
were arrested, others replaced them until the company
conceded. The union men, in co-operation with their
women, secured a significant victory, but the women
also won something. As the movie depicting the strike,
Salt of the Earth, so vividly expresses, the women
gained a new respect from their husbands, fathers, and
sons. The crisis forced the women to overstep restric-
tions that had persisted in the traditional macho men-

tality of the Chicano but which had to fall in the face of pressures that threatened to engulf the entire family. These were the Adelitas of the mines.

In the Delano grape strike, women, among the most skillful workers in the vineyards, played a major role from the beginning. Dolores Huerte, a slight, slender Chicana and the mother of seven children, had been active in Community Service Organization projects in the early sixties and had aided Cesar Chavez in the formative two or three years before the huelga began in 1965. She has figured as a strong negotiator for the union in several bargaining sessions with grape-growers and had been effective as a boycott organizer and speaker, particularly before women's groups. Her petite size is disarming, for she is an uncommon Chicana, one of the most formidable personalities in the Chicano movement. She was at Robert Kennedy's side when he claimed victory in California and steps away when the fatal bullets struck him.

Five Mexican American women, members of the National Floral Workers Association, knotted themselves in a twenty-five-foot chain fastened to posts at the entrance to a flower farm they had struck eight months before for union recognition, better wages, and better working conditions. Considered agricultural workers, they were not included under National Labor Relations Act protections. It was an early morning in February 1969 near Brighton, Colorado, when they made their desperate move in violation of a court injunction which had strictly forbidden further picketing of the farm. A morning fog hung in the dawn air. A farm employee cut the chain, but the women didn't budge. Suddenly, a sheriff's deputy approached and sprayed the women with tear gas. The noxious vapors lingered in the foggy, still morning, felling the women, who were unable to move quickly enough because of the chain and the gassing which had rendered them nearly sightless. Other women rescued them by dragging them from under the cloud of gas. With no recourse to the law which had enjoined the picketing and ordered the gassing, the strikers were forced to quit.

There will be Juana Gallos before long, and it's not a question of whether the Chicanos will allow them to appear; they will appear regardless of macho sentiment. It's evident, in the presence and activism of Chicanas at conferences and in demonstrations, that they no longer want to play a passive role in the Chicano community —"to limit her world to domesticity, making frijoles, tortillas, limpiando la case, cuidando los niños," as young Elvira Saragoza has written in *Bronce*, an Oakland barrio newspaper. "She wants to expand, to have the domestic role together with the intellectual role. She wants to be able to use her *cerebro* (mind) because she knows that she too can think, and be creative. She is not an inferior, insubordinate being and she is tired of being treated as one."

Perhaps the most overwhelming reason that machos of the Chicano movement must understand what a girl like Elvira is saying comes, naturally, from a woman, Enriqueta Vasquez, a writer for *El Grito del Norte*, a Chicano newspaper published in Española, New Mexico. "The Mexican American movement is not of just adults fighting the social system, but it is a total commitment of a family unit living what it believes to be a better way of life in demanding social change for the benefit of mankind." Because the Chicano is at the center of the Chicano revolt, Enriqueta points out in *El Grito*:

. . there should not have to be a woman's liberation movement within it. . . . When the man can look upon "his" woman as human and with the love of brotherhood and equality, then and only then, can he feel the true meaning of liberation and equality himself. When we talk of equality in the Mexican American movement we better be talking about total equality beginning where it all starts, at home.

The Chicano macho has to concede that he has usually relegated la mujer to the kitchen or to having kids and has never allowed her to express herself. Perhaps it is true, as some Chicanas say, that the Chicano passes on to his woman the frustrations and mierda that befall him during the day. Being unable to fight back at the Anglo boss and to assert his manhood for fear of economic reprisal, he, as the breadwinner, the one most immediately subject to the gringo's supremacist attitude and actions which assail the Chicano mind and spirit, may lash out at the one person who is not at all to blame, or he tries to exert his machismo within the four walls of his home. And when he becomes involved with a cause that encourages, insists upon, and challenges his manhood and pride in la raza, he tends to forget that the bountiful cup of la raza is the Chicana and that the love and spirit of our people is perpetuated by her love and her spirit.

When I first picked up a tabloid newspaper called *El Rebozo*, my first reaction was that here was a waste of effort and resources which could have been put to better use as part of a total Chicano community newspaper. Two San Antonio Chicanas, Andrea Gomez and Sylvia Gonzales, were primarily responsible for its first issue and they made it clear that the newspaper was intended, along with arousing Chicanas to la causa, to make Chicanos aware of las mujeres in the movement. Even the name, *El Rebozo,* strikes a uniquely Chicana tone, as the editors explain: "The traditional garment of the Mexican woman symbolizes the three roles of the Chicana · . . 'la señorita,' feminine, yet humble . . . 'la revolucionaria,' ready to fight for la causa . . . 'la madre,' radiant with life."

What Chicanas have to answer for themselves, individually, is whether they can live more than one of these roles at a time. For many Chicanas it is apparent that the traditional role of "radiant mother" is no longer enough to fulfill her womanhood. Nor does the idea of merely being a helpmate appeal any more to some of the Chicanas who wish to be liberated from the home. What does inspire them is the challenge of working for la causa side by side with the men, of being appreciated for their ideas and their spirit, of being entrusted with important duties besides handling registrations or taking minutes. La mujer Chicana is asking that the men experience a cultural shock—the fact that Chicanas themselves will no longer be docile. Chicanas want to improve themselves, to continue their education into college, to break from the strict family bounds that have suppressed their own aspirations for generations.

I don't for a moment doubt that the Chicana is also conscious of the attrition that has occurred among Chicanos who have gone to college and met for the most part only gabachas (Anglo women), and, too often, married them. In a sense, the Chicano culture has suppressed the full development of our women. Then, because they lack the opportunity of other women who take higher education for granted, they are excluded from the best setting for catching a promising young Chicano. Miss Saragoza cries:

What does this pale creature have which attracts our machos? Do our men feel that they have mastered something? Tamed something? Or that they have mastered white racism? What is it? We don't know. We don't understand! We just say to our men, "Look at what you have, your brown women. Help them! Don't abandon them because when you do, you are throwing away a great deal of yourself!"

Such questions or accusations as these are troubling enough, for they arise out of basic psychological problems within machos who have not come to terms with themselves, or derive from circumstances such as educational barriers which are even greater for Mexican American women than they are for the men. But even more disturbing is the subordination of our women into the most menial tasks, even in the movement. We don't throw her away, but we abuse her spirit and belittle her worth.

A brilliant exposition of the Chicana's role in the movement, and perhaps of women in society generally, is from Mary Lou Espinosa of Milwaukee, Wisconsin. In "La Madre de Aztlán," a statement composed in the fall of 1969, she says:

Equality respects the function of
man as father
woman as mother
and both as an independent
human capable of change.

A Chicana woman springs out of her
Indian and Spanish cultural and
historical heritage.
From Indian comes strong mother figure
From Spanish comes dominant father figure.

True woman's liberation must happen first
in the mind of the woman. . . .

Socio-economic and political
conditions can help the process of woman's full
assertion in the movement and
in society, but the woman has first
to want to make herself free.

A woman, a mother, knows life
from within because of her function.
Our society is sadly masculine oriented;
it does not know life from within
because men alone make it.

Creative solution to social change
comes with people who have
creative life within themselves,
a free woman can creatively
contribute with radical solutions
because she knows life from within.

Well, the Mexican Revolution might never have carried forward as far as it did had it not been for the soldaderas. I've heard one story about them. At first the macho rebels would scoff at the women who wanted to accompany them, saying there was no place for them in the revolución; but many women persisted, following their men at a distance. When men returned from a battle, wounded and hungry, the tender care and nourishing food provided by the women soon won them over. Many soldaderas must have fallen victims to combat which enveloped the camps or from the hunger and deprivation which were frequent camp mates in the winters of the revolución. By the same token, it probably will avail los machos nothing to reject las mujeres who are insisting on becoming revolucionarias; they will do so in spite of opposition. I cannot speak for la Chicana nor will I presume to delineate her role in the new Chicano community; she will play the traditional roles, but there will be new ones which she will carve out for herself. But, just as in the Mexican Revolution, I suspect that the Chicano revolt, in all its phases and its efforts, will have to draw upon the indomitable energy and commitment to the Chicano family of la mujer de la raza.

11

NO FUTURE WITHOUT THE YOUNG

THE Chicano uprising would have been truncated had there not developed spontaneously in various parts of the Southwest a new, invigorating thrust among Chicano youth. Chicanos born and nurtured in the barrio, who had made their way onto college campuses, generated the most dramatic manifestations of youthful discontent. Correspondingly, education was the catalytic agent.

Chicanismo burst on the college campus only recently because of this most disturbing fact: very few Mexican American students were going on to college. The influx of Chicanos into higher education following World War II and the Korean War had dwindled. Besides, Chicanos had never attended college in numbers great enough to arouse attention or foster even a sense of camarada. The 1966–67 school term seems to have been a turning period during which Chicano college students became aware of each other and caught the fire of what was happening in Delano, Tierra Amarilla, Denver, and El Paso. Looking around them, the college-going Chicanos realized how obvious it was that they had been thinned out, systematically, if not purposely, along the educational ladder and cut down to a handful

on most campuses where Chicanos might be expected to
attend in large numbers. In most California state colleges, foreign students from Latin America often outnumbered Mexican American undergraduates. A vicious circle of Anglo creation—deficiencies caused by
cultural and language discrimination, and the withholding of opportunity on the basis of those defects—
became blatantly apparent. Chicanos banded together
under various names—United Mexican American Students, Mexican American Student Association, and
Mexican American Youth Organizations, among many
others. They caught the spirit and pace of the Black
Student Unions, the Students for a Democratic Society,
and the Third World Liberation Front. But while they
supported these other manifestations of student unrest,
they soon concluded that their cause was distinctive
and that they must fight for special consideration, special courses, and integrated curriculums that were not
all-Anglo or all-black but Chicano, too. They realized
that in many ways their situation was undoubtedly
worse than the blacks; they would have to strive that
much more to have their way as Chicanos.

Culture, history, language—the roots of the Chicano
—have been suppressed and forgotten by the Anglo society's chief instrument of character assassination, the
educational system. In rebellion against this studied
form of cultural genocide, students, not the lawmakers
or agency directors or expert educators, have forced
more and more school systems throughout the Southwest and increasingly in northern states, to respect and
relate to us our Chicano heritage.

A group of Chicano college students were discussing
with me their recent efforts to establish a Chicano studies program and arouse greater involvement of Chicanos in the United Mexican American Student organization on campus, one of the largest in the University
of California system. A professor, a Mexican American
himself, joined us. Under one arm he carried a number

of books and pamphlets. He pulled one of the booklets
out. It was a copy of the Constitution of California of
1849—in Spanish. The professor asked the young people if they had ever seen a copy like it before. None of
them had. That was 1969.

For the past one hundred and twenty years, that
Constitution had been suppressed, unknown to almost
all the Mexican American people of the state and no
doubt the country. The forty-eight members of the
Constitutional Convention in Monterey in 1849 included Spanish and Mexican delegates, including Val-
lejo, Cabrillo, Guerra, and Dominguez. The Constitution was published in both Spanish and English; in fact,
all California laws and documents were published with
bilingual texts until the Constitution of 1879 violated
the first Constitution, and in turn, the Treaty of Guadalupe Hidalgo. During the two-month deliberations, a
suggestion was made that Negroes, Indians, and their
descendants be excluded from having voting rights. The
motion failed when the Spanish-speaking delegates
acidly pointed out that if such a clause were passed,
Manuel Dominguez, one of the Convention delegates,
would be deprived of the vote. The required vote of the
people was not taken in 1879 or in 1894, when gringo
politicians made English a prerequisite for registering
to vote, thereby depriving Chicanos of the vote anyway.

For more than a century these and other hidden
facts and names should have been the proper matter for
instruction in history or social studies classes, at least
throughout the schools of the Southwest. Instead, Chicanos have been handed a steady diet of unilateral history which proclaimed only what the Anglo did and
how he discovered everything in North America. In
Texas, history books convey the idea that the existence
of Texas began in 1836 with the revolt against the Mexican Government. Yet, Juan de Oñate had passed
through what is now El Paso in 1598 on an expedition

that was to take him up to found Santa Fe, New Mexico, the first permanent settlement by non-Indians in the North American continent. And San Antonio, the site of the Alamo Mission, was settled in 1718 by the Spanish.

To compound their criminal attack upon a people's culture, gringo educators have robbed millions of Chicanos of their mother language by either outlawing Spanish altogether, often making us illiterate in both Spanish and English, or by causing Chicanos to feel shame in the use of their mother tongue. To understand the hatred and revulsion that Chicanos now feel against the Anglo schools, the Anglo need only try to imagine his reaction and resentment were someone to tell him that he could no longer speak English without shame or fear of punishment.

Since the first major walkout of Chicano students in East Los Angeles in March 1968 there have occurred dozens more: On March 20 in Denver; on April 9, 700 Chicanos left classes at Lanier High School in San Antonio; during the spring semester 1968 at college campuses all over California; in June 1968, Chicano graduates held a commencement at San Jose State College apart from the regular Anglicized ceremonies; during spring 1969, in Kingsville, Texas, 116 Chicano students were arrested in a walkout; and in fall 1969, Abilene, Texas, students struck against the schools there. On September 16, el diez y seis de septiembre, a national boycott (planned the previous March at the Denver youth conference) caused hundreds and thousands of Chicano youths to boycott schools all over the Southwest. The tactic may become a regular part of the annual school calendar for Chicano students. Of the latest insurrections, the most thorough victory was won by high school through elementary grade Chicano youths in Crystal City, Texas. Nearly all Chicano students boycotted the schools there from December 10 to

January 5, 1970; the city school board, dominated by gringos, capitulated to the students' demands.

In no instance of school walkouts or boycotts have Chicanos failed to include a demand for more relevant courses, bilingual teachers, and Chicano teachers, administrators, and counselors. In some way they have asserted their cultural aspirations, sometimes involving the serving of Mexican food such as tacos, along with hot dogs and hamburgers on lunch menus. On the high school level the demands of students at Edcouch-Elsa High School in the Rio Grande Valley provide an overall view of the kinds of needs and problems which young Chicanos have decided must be resolved and for which they are striking. The Edcouch-Elsa strike involved most of the Chicano students, who represent 90 percent of the student body. Other towns where Chicanos comprise the majority in the high schools include: McAllen and Weslaco, 70 percent; Edinburgh, 80 percent; Kingsville, 70 percent; and Crystal City, 85 percent. A typical "laundry list" of demands reads as follows:

That Chicano students be permitted to speak Spanish on school grounds without fear of punishment;

That courses in Mexican history and culture be included in the regular school curriculum;

That discrimination by teachers, administrators, and counselors be stopped;

That entering students be made aware of college preparatory classes;

That more student counselors be hired, especially of Mexican American background;

That teachers be forbidden to use profanity or abusive language in the presence of students;

That students be allowed to select their own candidates for student council offices;

That intimidation, threats, and penalties be stopped related to students participating in outside school clubs or organizations;

That excessive and unfair penalties be abolished for minor infractions (Edcouch-Elsa students listed suspensions for missing appointments with teachers or not standing at pep rallies as examples);

That no disciplinary action be taken against students or teachers in the strike;

That tardy or absent students be allowed to remain in class until excuses are verified and that pass regulations be clarified;

That cafeteria lunch prices be lowered or the quality of the food improved;

That greater attention be given to the education of migrant workers' children;

That school facilities be improved through remodeling or construction of new buildings.

While some of the demands seem trifling, they stem nevertheless from strongly felt needs of the students themselves, and some are at the heart of the Chicano students' revolt against the Anglo system of instruction.

In Crystal City, Texas, the site of what is the most thoroughly successful Chicano boycott to date, the median education level of Mexican Americans twenty-five years and older had increased by a half grade between 1950 and 1960—from 1.8 to 2.3. At that rate, Chicanos might reach an eighth grade median in another 120 years. The more immediate causes for revolt in Crystal City schools concerned the method of selecting cheerleaders and baton twirlers and the fact that candidates for homecoming queen could be selected only from daughters of alumni, a kind of "grandfather's clause" in reality, since Anglos were the only ones to graduate in Crystal City for decades. The underlying causes, of course, were discrimination and tokenism. On December 9, seventeen hundred Chicanos walked out of classes, and stayed out until the school board, whose chairman had been the industrial relations supervisor of the Del Monte packing plant (a chief employer of Mexican Americans in what is called the Winter Garden District), capitulated to the students' set of demands. Because of the strike, the Crystal City schools will move in the direction of establishing bilingual instruction and Chicano studies programs.

The success of the Crystal City confrontation had its beginning in May 1967 when José Angel Gutiérrez, whose home town is Crystal City, and four other Chicano radicals at St. Mary's College in San Antonio founded MAYO. MAYO did not begin to exert a state-wide public impact until 1968 when most of the school walkouts in Texas were either directly related to MAYO organizers or indirectly related because of the ferment for change that MAYO had initiated. In Crystal City, Gutiérrez and MAYO in general were classified as "outside agitators," despite the fact that although not all the MAYOs involved in the walkout were hometowners like Gutiérrez, most were from South Texas, which means anywhere from El Paso to San Antonio to Corpus Christi to Brownsville and the areas in-between. Through the Southwest Council of La Raza, MAYO had also tapped the Ford Foundation for $8,527, but in June 1969 Mario Compean, one of the original founders and at the time MAYO chairman, announced that MAYO could no longer accept the money because Ford Foundation officials had stipulated that MAYO eliminate any political activities. MAYO had suffered a terrific buffeting by Mexican American políticos for its "hate literature" and "reverse racist" ideology. At the same time, foundations generally were under congressional scrutiny concerning their funding of politically motivated groups or projects. Unfortunately for the Chicano, the foundations were hit by strong pressures after millions of dollars had been given to black organizations for the kind of activities that, by mid-1969, were forbidden to MAYO.

For a while, MAYO was forced to go underground,

which brought about its complete break with the traditional methods of defense and accelerated its espousal of direct, aggressive, search-and-destroy tactics. The stipulation by the Ford Foundation revealed to MAYO and many other Chicano activists that the Chicano people could no longer look to incumbent politicians for support and that the Chicano revolt had failed to recruit many Mexican Americans still subservient to the Anglo patrón.

MAYO and other organizations of its kind, particularly those of a youthful character, are criticized for being retrogressive, for endangering all the progress that has been made since the Second World War. But since World War II, what has happened in the educational advancement of the Chicano? The 1968 report of the governor's committee ranked Texas as 31st among the 50 states in median level of education and 42nd in the number of high school graduates. It is 39th in the amount of money it allocates to public schools, even though in per capita property valuation, it is 8th on the list. The percentage of Texans aged 20-49 who had dropped out of school are as follows:

Anglos	33.1 percent
Negroes	60.1 percent
Chicanos	78.9 percent

While these figures are based on 1960 census data, another figure indicates that Chicanos have a distance to progress toward achieving equity in schooling. From 1950 to 1960, Anglo median years of schooling increased from 10.3 to 10.7; Negroes, 7.6 to 8.7; but Chicanos, 4.5 to 6.2. According to these figures—compiled in a study by the U.S. Commission on Civil Rights from 1950 and 1960 census information relating to persons 14 years of age or more—if Chicanos were able to maintain this rate of increase (1.7 years), by the year 2000 about half the Chicano school population might be graduating from high school but not necessarily ad-

vancing to higher education. Negroes and Anglos meanwhile would have a more favorable position in terms of
years completed in school. Furthermore the commission
report indicated that nearly one-fourth of Mexican
Americans in Texas 25 years or older have not had even a
year of education (in itself a misnomer); and nearly 40
percent of Mexican American adults are functional il-
literates, that is, with less than a fifth-grade education.
The comparison between the 1950 and 1960 census
shows slight progress but reveals also that the conditions which prevented Chicanos from achieving a quality education for at least 25 years before World War II
are still inordinately harmful, and that so little has actually occurred that it is no wonder the youths are so
militant, so aggressive, so unlike their elders.

Crystal City Chicanos have established beyond any
doubt that only overt confrontation accomplishes anything within the Anglo system of education. Nearly two
thousand Chicano students from the first through the
twelfth grades took a holiday, until the school board
realized it could not afford to resist a movement that
virtually brought the school system to a halt and which,
in the long run, would have brought about its collapse.
The Chicano students forced the school board to negotiate a settlement of the dispute, not through deliberation among the school board members alone, but between them and the students. For the first time in the
two years since the East Los Angeles students walked
out of their classrooms, the student had a clearly defined position and voice in formulating his destiny. The
triumph illustrated on a small scale what is to come in
the Chicano student revolt. Having won this single battle in Crystal City, no one should think that Chicanos
will stop there or not advance into other areas of conflict.

Certainly, MAYO strategy foresees many more
Crystal Cities. MAYO's chief theorist and activist, Gutiérrez, displays at his age (twenty-five) the same kind

of obsession with a particular goal that Chavez, Tijerina, and Gonzales (elder statesmen of the movement
compared with the MAYOs) exhibit in regard to their
objectives. Gutiérrez, in relation to the other Chicano
revolutionaries, exemplifies the wide range of age and
strategy that characterizes the Chicano revolt. Gutiérrez could have been merely a college-educated Mexican
American and could have become a teacher (he has a
master's degree in government) or city administrator,
but he chose to throw in his lot with his people.

Anglo Texans persisted in their efforts to radicalize
and inflame Chicano anger even more in early 1968.
Governor Preston Smith permitted the ouster by Val
Verde County commissioners of a team of community
organizers, mostly Chicanos, operating in the county
under a program called Minority Mobilization Program.
MMP is a VISTA project emphasizing the involvement
of minority workers from the target region. Working
mainly in Del Rio, the MMP team included two super-
visors and eighteen organizers, all but three from Del
Rio. A protest march and arrests followed soon after the
March 14 announcement by Governor Smith's office
that the MMP would be terminated. The climax of Chicano reaction was a march and rally on March 30, Palm
Sunday, through Del Rio. In spite of a city ordinance
(enacted right after the initial protests) forbidding
demonstrations without a permit, more than two thousand Chicanos gathered in Del Rio from all over Texas
and from other sections of the Southwest.

Del Rio would have just been another march and
rally except that it brought MAYO to the forefront of
activist forces in Texas and fused many elements in the
state around the concept of la raza within a potentially
violent setting. While no violence took place (the police
were appropriately muzzled by city and state officials),
the conditions for a Chicano Selma were all there.

The beating of a Mexican American couple by an
officer of the Texas Department of Public Safety was

shunted aside by the Val Verde County court when the officer was exonerated at a hearing. MAYOs led a protest in front of the Val Verde County courthouse on February 1. VISTA workers were implicated, and on March 13 the governor requested that the then OEO director, Bertrand Harding, terminate the MMP project in the county. A funeral followed that next week in which a dead rabbit was carried through the town; the ordinance already mentioned had prompted MAYOs to stage the mock funeral, not covered by the regulation, in protest. Finally, at the Palm Sunday rally, what might have seemed generationally disparate elements of the Mexican American community came together to protest the governor's action. It was the largest demonstration of antipathy toward the Democratic administration in Texas since the 1966 elections. Notably, the only Chicano state legislators to support the Del Rio protest were Senator Joe Bernal of San Antonio and Assemblyman Lauro Cruz of Houston; among county commissioners, only Albert Peña of San Antonio. At the rally also was G.I. Forum founder, Dr. Hector P. Garcia of Corpus Christi; Father Henry Casso of San Antonio, an activist Catholic priest; and José Angel Gutiérrez, who read the "Del Rio Manifesto" at the county courthouse steps before taping the statement to its plate glass front door. Gutiérrez declaimed, reading from the manifesto:

There must be something invincible in our people that has kept alive our humanity in spite of a system bent on suppressing our difference and rewarding our conformity. It is such an experience of cultural survival that has led us to the recovery of the magnificence of la raza. . . . We cannot explain our survival and our strength apart from this heritage, a heritage inseparably linked to Spanish, the soul language of la raza. . . . We are committed to non-violence, even while living in the midst of officially tolerated violence. We are prepared, however, to be as aggressive as it may be necessary until everyone of our Mexican American brothers enjoys the liberty of shaping his own future.

The manifesto warns the Val Verde commissioners and the Texas governor that they are inviting serious social unrest by their decision; it warns Congress that the action taken against the county program imperils the concept of volunteer service; and it warns that such national complicity in the destruction of a movement for self-determination can only reveal the hypocrisy of attempts by the United States to assist underdeveloped nations.

Commissioner Peña gave the rally significance as a Chicano Selma when he told the crowd that the Chicano had come to the "bridge" in 1966 at New Braunfels during the Rio Grande Valley farmworkers march. He went on to say: "We have crossed that bridge today, and we're not looking back. We have raised the cactus curtain." The White House, however, chose to ignore the Del Rio event despite the urgings of Celso Moreno (director of Spanish-speaking affairs for the Republican National Committee at the time). President Nixon did not send a telegram supporting the Chicano protest and display of brown power. A memo circulated later to key Republicans noted that a telegram read aloud from Senator Edward Kennedy drew a lengthy ovation.

Del Rio had great psychological impact upon many South Texas Chicanos, although nationwide establishment newspapers and other media all but ignored the event. Chicanos on the West Coast heard about the rally by word of mouth usually and sometimes through the Chicano newspapers, but not until weeks afterward. In terms of the fortunes of the MMP, county commissioners' courts duplicated the action of Val Verde officials, so that a year later only three MMP projects were in operation out of a dozen original locales.

It seems now that Del Rio marked a turning point for MAYO in that along with an increase in its visibility and its membership, it marked a new sense of direction. In a widely quoted press conference Gutiérrez declared that the MAYO's enemy is the gringo who "has a certain policy or program or attitude that reflects bigotry, racism, discord, prejudice and violence." When Gutiérrez asserted that MAYO intended to eliminate this kind of gringo, he added:

You can always eliminate an individual in various ways. You can certainly kill him, but that is not our intent at this moment. You can remove the base of support that he operates from, be it economically, politically or social. That is what we intend to do.

The young MAYO spokesman concluded that if all else fails, MAYO might have to resort to killing all the gringos. The reaction to Gutiérrez' statement was immediate and ruthless. Gutiérrez had committed the cardinal sin of saying out loud what many Chicanos have been suppressing in their minds for generations. What it meant for MAYO was far from mere radical rhetoric; it was a clear statement of what MAYO intended to do in the coming months.

At a MAYO conference in Mission, Texas, in December 1969, MAYO unveiled the Winter Garden Project, a plan to redeem a ten-county area in South Texas for Chicanos. MAYO's purpose was twofold: first, to politicize as many young Chicanos as possible within a regulated format of social contact, with workshops on a variety of subjects and activities geared to impress the young people with tangible problems and objectives through symbolic means. After a Roman Catholic mass that included Chicano songs such as "Yo soy Chicano" and "De Colores"; the reading of the Gospel by a Protestant minister; and testimony from the Chicanos there, the conference youths gathered around a tall statue of Mary, the Mother of Christ, and, using spray cans, bronzed the formerly unpainted white stone. A few days later, vandals splashed white paint on the statue, but MAYOs again repainted it. A number of MAYOs served as security guards, indicating the vigilance the MAYO leaders wished to instill in the participants.

Secondly, MAYO democratized the Winter Garden

Project by involving the conference students in deliber-
ating the kinds and extent of efforts to be made this year
and establishing priorities. Gutiérrez envisions a number of projects such as Crystal City, but in the economic, political, and social arenas as well, which can
serve as models for action elsewhere in Texas or the
Southwest. Whether a strategy that is successful in
Texas, given the political and social make-up of the region, can be exported to another region is questionable;
but already through the Crystal City schools' victory
and the more recent election triumphs, MAYO has
proved that the gringo system can be beaten. Particularly where Chicanos predominate, there is no reason
for Anglos to have the balance of power and influence.
Chicanos can have their share of control, or all of it if
need be, and that would just kill the gringo.

Unknown to each other in early 1967, but assuming
the same path of militant action as an unavoidable step
for la causa, Chicano youths in East Los Angeles
formed the Brown Berets, a young people's organization
that is the barrio counterpart of MAYO and Chicano
college campus groups such as Movimiento Estudiantil
Chicano de Aztlán (MECHA). Brown Berets, or in
some areas, Black Berets (the original unit adopted the
brown color signifying la raza) are an extension in
many respects of the traditional gang structure of Chicano barrios. Gangs of the forties were styled pachuco
gangs; each had its own territory and set certain rules of
conduct within the pachuco milieu. The gangs were distrustful of anyone from outside their section of the barrio and often fought to maintain their boundaries or to
right a wrong. Until the advent of the Brown Beret and
MAYO ideology—which is in fact one way of thinking
—pachucos, or Chicano gang members, were engaged
in a self-destructive mode of life—group self-centered.
In fall 1967 one of the founders of the Berets, David
Sanchez, articulated the source of impetus for aggres-

sive action that Chicano youth would soon adopt nationwide. Sanchez, a student at East Los Angeles College at the time, condemned an education conference sponsored by the U.S. Civil Rights Commission in Washington, D.C., in mid-November 1967: "The Negro has got the nation's eye because he riots, but they ignore the Mexican Americans."

Indeed, the Civil Rights Commission considered the subject of education for Mexican Americans worth only a two-hour session late on a Friday evening. At the time, Sanchez displayed the aggressiveness that was moving himself and a few other Chicanos in East Los Angeles toward the spirit of the Brown Beret. Until late 1967, he and two other young men, Carlos Montez and Ralph Ramirez, were leaders of a group formed earlier that year, called the Young Citizens for Community Action, later changed to Young Chicanos for Community Action. Breaking with these Establishment-promoted groups, the trio formed a radically minded unit for which the Brown Beret became a badge, a symbol, and a name quickly associated with the most forceful element of the Chicano's search for liberation. Their three major objectives became: "To serve: to give vocal as well as physical support to those people and causes that help the people of the Mexican American communities. To observe: to keep a watchful eye on all federal, state, city, and private agencies that deal with the Mexican American, especially law enforcement agencies. To protect: to protect, guarantee, and secure the rights of the Mexican American *by all means* necessary. How far we must go in order to protect these rights depends upon those in power. If those Anglos in power are willing to do this in a peaceful and orderly process, then we will be only too happy to accept this way. Otherwise we will be forced to other alternatives."

The Beret credo is almost apologetic, not yet an ultimatum. It suggests a tender revolutionary spirit— unless one knows the facts of the tremendous barrier

that has been breached by the young people of East Los
Angeles. Mexican American students numbered 130,450
during the 1968–69 school year, about 20 percent of the
total enrollment of Los Angeles city schools. Among
teachers, counselors, and supervisory personnel totaling
27,000, only 2.8% were Mexican American or of Spanish
surname. In spring 1969, the Los Angeles schools
published two major studies, "Educational Achievement
and Aspirations of Mexican American Youth in a Metropolitan Context," and "Comparative Values and Achievement of Mexican American and Anglo Pupils." Not only
did Anglo educators conduct the surveys, but their findings are a neat whitewash job of those responsible for
Chicano students' achievement and aspirations. One report stated that "the proportion of Anglo pupils who
aspire to continued education is almost twice the proportion of Mexican American pupils. Of those who do
have post-high-school aspirations, Mexican Americans
tend toward trade schools and junior college, while
Anglos tend toward four-year colleges and subsequent
graduate training." One-third of Mexican American
pupils never finish high school, while in some high
schools the dropout rate of all Mexican American students is more than 50 percent. The study does not consider how elementary-school experiences may have
affected Chicano youths' aspirations, nor is there mention of the failure of teachers to provide adequate instruction for children with whom they do not wish to
communicate.

An author of both reports, Dr. Audrey J. Schwartz of
the UCLA Graduate School of Education, in response
to criticisms by Mexican American educators, was
quoted as saying that research showed that the Mexican
American student "views his fellow man with caution
and sees his future with resignation." The Anglo educator expressed the opinion that the schools "were not
deliberately" out to harm the Chicano student. And
yet, somehow, about half the Mexican American chil-

dren who entered Los Angeles High School about eight years ago will not have progressed beyond the eighth grade this year. Reports such as the Los Angeles studies would have Chicanos and the public at large believe that Mexican Americans fail in school because they just can't be like the Anglo students, who have so much more desire for education and for increased income potential.

On May 30, 1969, the Brown Berets opened a free medical clinic on East Whittier Boulevard, dedicated to the people of East Los Angeles. Sanchez, prime minister for the Berets, stated that the Berets had been formed as an emergency organization "to help solve social health problems in the community. Since there were no facilities that offer medical help at no cost, we took the initiative to fulfill the general need." The clinic has offered free medical care, psychiatric counseling, and weekly discussions on subjects ranging from child care to narcotics addiction. Doctors, nurses, psychiatrists, and counselors donate their time, while the everyday routine chores around the clinic are handled by Beret volunteers, including members of female Beret groups.

A few Chicano students, in alliance with Chicano educators and black students, are carrying forward on the university level the energy and impetus that groups such as the Berets and MAYOs exert in the barrio. More and more of the batos locos, the barrio toughs, with wits honed sharp by the need to survive against Anglo intimidation in the schools and in the streets, are enrolling in colleges as a result of community demands. They will join slightly more fortunate Chicanos who had the grades and the finances, either through their own work or their parents' sacrifice, to enter college on their own. There cannot be any distinction in the Los Angeles area, as an example of a compacted Chicano area with overwhelming educational and employment needs, between the batos of the barrio experience and the "campusinos" of the college environment. Within three and a half miles of California State College at Los Angeles, about 42,000 students of Mexican background live, yet Cal State has a Chicano enrollment of less than 5 percent and its school of education less than 1 percent. A Department of Mexican American Studies offering a Bachelor of Arts degree enhances the Cal State curriculum, as well as the curricula of several other colleges in California such as Long Beach State College and San Fernando Valley State College. Programs of this kind were achieved through Chicano student action, often in league with Black Student Unions.

In December 1968 the Black Student Union and the United Mexican American Students, since renamed MECHA, under an agreement between many college Chicano groups throughout the Southwest, made the following demands at the University of Southern California:

Admission and full tuition remission for 50 black and 50 brown qualified disadvantaged students for the spring semester of 1969;

Establishment of an ongoing program for scholarships for marginal minority students to be initiated in the fall of 1969, at which time 200 students are to be admitted;

Establishment and implementation of black and brown curricula, which have already been submitted;

The black studies course due to begin in the spring will be taught by a black man.

The latter stipulation was demanded because a Mexican American director for the Chicano studies program was already under consideration. Not untypical of California colleges, USC could account for 223 students of Spanish or Mexican American descent out of an enrollment of 19,000 students!

At California State College at Hayward in the San Francisco-Oakland Bay Area, in January 1969 Chicano students presented a more specific list of demands. Besides the matriculation of more Chicano students, the hiring of Mexican American teachers and counselors, and a brown studies program, Hayward college officials were pressed to consult with students to create an advisory council as liaison between the college and the Chicano community in Hayward; to offer facilities and co-operation with the Youth Manpower Education Program, a federally funded tutoring program to prepare and motivate students toward college; to provide office space, telephones, and a paid secretary as a step toward creating a Mexican American cultural relations center; and to recognize the Mexican American Student Confederation (MASC) as the official Chicano voice on campus.

The MASC leadership pointed out that although the Mexican American population in southern Alameda County totaled about 35 percent, only 35 of the college's 8,290 students were Mexican American; and of the previous year's 582 graduates only two were Chicanos. A similar confrontation had occurred at the University of Arizona in Tucson in December 1968 when the Mexican American Liberation Committee, which represented the 187 Chicano students on the UA campus, out of an enrollment of 23,012 students, pressed the administration with its own set of demands. And the figures roll on. At the University of California at Los Angeles in 1968 there were less than 100 Mexican American students among 26,500 students in an area that has 60 percent of California's Chicano people; University of California at Berkeley had only 77 students with Spanish surnames, most of whom were from Latin American countries, out of 26,500 students.

The issue of attrition within the first eight years of school is, without a doubt, at the heart of the problem for hundreds of thousands of Chicanos who have been deprived of a formative education and thus have been unable to compete for places in high school, let alone for seats in college. According to the Office of Education's Mexican American Education Unit, then directed by Armando Rodriguez, a Californian:

The average Mexican American child in the Southwest drops out of school by the 7th grade.

In Texas, 89 percent of Spanish surname children—Chicanos —drop out before they finish high school.

Along the Texas-Mexico border, four out of five Mexican American children are two grades behind Anglo students by the 5th grade.

In some California schools, more than 50 percent of Mexican American high school students drop out between grades 10 and 11.

Mexican Americans account for more than 40 percent of the so-called "mentally handicapped" in California.

Thus it occurs that on the seven campuses of the University of California, less than one-half of one percent of college students are Mexican American, completely out of proportion when Chicanos represent more than 14 percent of the state population.

In its report of 1968 the National Advisory Committee on Mexican American Education stated:

Money is only one problem. Perhaps an even more serious one is the problem of involuntary discrimination, that is, our insistence on fitting the Mexican American student into the monolingual, monocultural mold of the Anglo American. This discrimination, plus the grim fact that millions of Mexican Americans suffer from poverty, cultural isolation, and language rejection, has virtually destroyed them as contributing members of society.

Another problem is that we have not developed suitable instruments for accurately measuring the intelligence and learning potential of the Mexican American child. Because there is little communication between educators and these non-English-speaking youngsters, the pupils are likely to be dismissed as "mentally retarded." Common sense tells us that this is simply not so. The chasm that exists between the teacher and the student in the classroom is even wider between the school and the home, where there is virtually no communication. Such lack of understanding soon destroys any educational aspiration the pupil might have or that his parents might have for him.

The committee spoke of providing the Mexican American child with an "equal educational opportunity," but the circumstances of our children's deprivation demand more than that. The students' protests and demands clearly indicate that the young Chicanos know full well that they are already at a disadvantage when they enter high school or college, so that merely an equal chance to a college education doesn't mean an equal chance to obtain a diploma. The unequal experience he has had and which the Anglo has not had to suffer will thwart his efforts from the start. The committee describes "four imperatives": teacher preparation and bilingual ability for teachers of Mexican American students; instruction of the children in both English and Spanish in all curricula and in all grades until the student is thoroughly at home with both languages; preschool preparation of Mexican American children; and programs for adults in basic education and vocational schooling. The legislative prerogative already exists to implement such programs. The final issue is to pressure those holding federal and state purse strings to finance adequately the myriad projects that must be developed.

An overriding barrier to the provision of an adequate education for Mexican American people, one not covered by the enactment of the Bilingual Education Act in December 1967 and barely mentioned by the Mexican American Education Committee, stems from the legislative prohibition of instruction in public schools in other than the English language in Arizona, Colorado, and, until 1969, in Texas. Bilingual or bicultural instruction, therefore, is also proscribed. While all three states prohibited non-English instruction, Colorado alone has imposed the restriction on any elementary school, public or private; but both Colorado and Texas stipulated fines or administrative action as penalties for violations of the code. The Texas statute, gratuitously, allowed instruction in Spanish in grade schools of counties along the Mexico border in which a city of five thousand or more people resided as of the 1920 census. The limitation effectively eliminated dozens of towns along the border which may not have existed or were sparsely populated in 1920, as well as eliminating the majority of poor families in Chicano communities isolated from incorporated towns by a form of gerrymandering.

California maintained a restriction on the use of a language other than English in instruction until 1968 when the legislature repealed the 1879 prohibition that had originated in reaction to the influx of Chinese who, imported as railroad crews, flooded the state with new cheap manpower when most of the railroad construction ended. New Mexicans have possessed the right of a dual language system since 1848; bilingual and bicultural instruction is specifically permitted although not required in the state constitution. The guarantees—civil, political, and religious—of the Treaty of Guadalupe Hidalgo are also specified.

However, as indicated by 1969 statistics for Highlands University in Las Vegas, New Mexico, a system controlled by Anglos eventually destroys what it is supposed to preserve. Less than five percent of faculty and staff at Highlands are of Spanish descent, but the student body is about half Spanish surname. While entering freshmen include as high as 70 percent Spanish surname students, only 35 percent of the graduating classes derive from this group. Although more than half the faculty lack doctoral degrees, the university administration contends that it has not been able to find persons of Spanish surname qualified to teach at the institution. Other evidence offered in the *Revista Norteña,* a Las Vegas barrio newspaper, argued that turnover rates of from one-third to one-half indicated marked inefficiency and mismanagement of the university. As could be expected, Chicano students all over New Mexico are in revolt now also.

Colorado exemplifies the effects of the "insistence on fitting the Mexican American into the monolingual, monocultural mold of the Anglo American." In all but two counties of the state, Mexican Americans represent two to nine times their proportional representation among persons who have attained only four or less years of schooling; yet according to the count of Spanish surnames, they represent only 3.18 percent of the state's population. In the two counties, Mexican Americans amount to 48 percent and 68 percent of the residents. Of Spanish-speaking children in Colorado schools in 1968, 63.9 percent were reading below grade level compared to 27.3 percent among Anglo students; in math, 38.7 percent below grade level compared to 20.8 percent; in language, 55.5 percent compared to 30.6 percent.

The strange contrast between two Anglo educators in Texas indicates the schizophrenia that splits the gringo establishment. The Anglo educators both appeared in December 1968 before the hearing of the U.S. Commission on Civil Rights in San Antonio. Harold C. Brantley, superintendent of the United Consolidated School District, Webb County (a county forty square miles larger than Delaware), launched a bilingual education program six years ago. Supporting him were many Anglo parents at Laredo Air Force Base who appreciated bilingualism as an asset, considering their nearness to Mexico. The student population is about half Mexican American, half Anglo. Brantley derived impetus and technical knowledge for his program from the Cuban refugee schools in Miami, which were bilingually oriented. Brantley stated:

We tried to create an atmosphere in the classroom where the children from the dominant culture, speaking the dominant language, recognize that the Mexican American child has got something that they don't have, and that they ought to be interested in getting what this child can teach him. Now, can you begin to see what this does for the stature of the Mexican American child . . . when he is made to feel that he can do something that somebody else can't do, and that he has something that the Anglo child wants to learn about? Does that answer your question, what bilingual education does for the self-image of the Mexican American child?

While the Webb County superintendent expressed his insight into the value of bilingualism and the reinforcement of personality that the reassertion of one's cultural identity through language accomplishes for Chicano youth, another Texas educator reaffirms the nature of the gringo school system as a destroyer of Chicano identity. W. D. Higdon, principal of Hawthorne Junior High School in San Antonio, conversed with a commission attorney:

Q. Do you feel that there's anything in the background or characteristics of Mexican Americans which inhibits high achievement?

HIGDON: Yes, I do . . . I think that there are some facts that are not necessarily in statistical form, but to me Mexican American culture represents the merging of two cultures, the Spanish and the Indian. . . . On this side of the Rio Grande you have a merging of not two cultures, but many cultures. . . . To a Mexican or a Mexican American, they assume the position that *si dios quierre*, what God wishes. On this side to me any individual having been a product of the merging of many cultures would say *in God we trust*, not that he says that this is how it shall be and you are limited. But you have unlimited horizons.

Q. Would it be fair to say that you feel there are genetic factors involved which account for the differences in achievement?

HIGDON: I made that statement and I will stick by it. . . . I am not a historian, but looking at it from the past 2,000 years Western Europe has been a battleground, and certainly where armies trample you have genes remaining. And the very measuring stick that we are trying to use here today is fundamentally a product of Western Europe's culture transplanted in America, and that is the measuring stick that we are trying to measure the Mexican American by.

As the San Antonio educator said, he is not a historian; but then why does he attempt to rewrite history? He obscures the twenty thousand years and more of Mexican-Indian heritage which itself blended a number of philosophies and cultures into a unique civilization in the Americas. He overlooks the three thousand years of Spanish heritage extending back to the Phoenician influences (Cádiz, Spain, originally was founded by Phoenicians and called Gades, perhaps one of the oldest towns in Europe with a continuous life and name from its founding). He ignores Greek, Roman, Visigothic, and Arabian contributions. He denies the fact that the Mexican American is the confluence of these histories and that of the Anglo-European complex. For someone supposedly a professional in the art of teaching, the Anglo principal quoted here testifies not to any knowledge but rather to a prejudice against anything that does not fit into his concept of culture.

The concept of the Mexican or Mexican American as a personality subservient to the wishes of God again relies on the ploy of choosing a certain trait among a people that fits into an already biased viewpoint. The history of revolution and dissent in Mexico since 1810— including the insurrection against Spain; the revolts against the Mexican Government by Mexican rebels, Indian tribes such as the Yaqui, and Texas Mexicans in 1836; Mexico's ill-fated defense against the United States in 1847–1849; and the Chicano's own rebellion since then—assert that the Chicano is not satisfied with his lot. Many of us have swallowed the lies of the Anglo teachers, historians, and sociologists who have done everything they could to prove to the Chicano that he really has liked his predicament.

The Webb County school superintendent and the San Antonio school principal graphically contradict each other in their regard for the Chicano and his culture. I have no doubt in my mind that the Anglo in Webb County is an exception to the rule and that the gringo San Antonio educator exemplifies not merely an extreme rationale which depends on a genetic theory for justification, but the kind of thinking which is the root of the educational assault directed at the Chicano for the past 120 years.

12

THE LAW IN THE BARRIOS

CHICANO anger and resistance to injustice have been suppressed faithfully by the police, the courts, and the established authorities of the law delegated by Anglo society with counter force very often in excess of the circumstances which incited gringo reaction. Police brutality and court injustice are nothing new to the Chicano; the denial of his civil rights has traditionally been justified by law or by the semblance of law.

It was this very insensibility to the feelings and dignity of the Chicano that resulted on August 29, 1970, in the violent eruption of police rioters against the National Chicano Moratorium in East Los Angeles, causing one of the most tragic incidents we have known to occur in the Chicano community, the death of writer Ruben Salazar.

The Moratorium rally and march had been planned for months with Rosalio Muñoz, a former president of the student body of the University of California at Los Angeles who initiated the national Chicano draft-resistance movement in fall 1969, as the chairman of the organizing committee. Rosalio had been among the first Chicano youths to resist induction, along with Ernest

Vigil and Art Vasquez of Denver, and Fred Aviles of
Chicago. Chale al Draft (to hell with the draft) became
the resistance slogan, and Muñoz its most articulate
spokesman.

The Saturday of the demonstration was a typically
hazy, sunlit day in Los Angeles. Upwards of fifteen
thousand Chicanos, the largest assembly of Chicanos
yet recorded for one rally, had swelled the opening
march into an impressive blocks-long confluence of Chicanos of all ages, but mainly young ones. Most liquor
stores and other shops had been closed along the parade
route to Laguana Park in the East Los Angeles barrio
where the speeches and other events were to be held.
One liquor store remained open within sight of the
park, however. Thirsty paraders collected in and around
the store.

Exactly what happened next is unsure, but it is
known that sheriff's deputies began to disperse the
crowd. Apparently, some Chicano youths resisted or
could not comply with the orders because of the crowd.
In a matter of minutes, more sheriff's deputies converged on the store; the youths became more angered,
and the exchange of rocks, bottles, and tear gas and
billy clubs began. Other deputies surrounded the park,
and, using the incident at the store as a pretext, began
to disperse the rally crowds. Brown Berets stepped between the police authorities and the men, women, and
children in the audience. But tear gas and billy clubs
were rampant throughout the crowd. Five hours later
three Chicanos had been mortally wounded, more than
250 arrests had been made; 74 persons had been injured, including more than 25 policemen; and property
damage was estimated at nearly $1 million.

At about four o'clock, the MAYO national chairman
from Texas, Carlos Guerra, stood with other Chicanos
across the street from the Silver Dollar Cafe, several
blocks from the core scene of the violent outbreaks by
the police. He watched as a number of deputies massed

in front of the cafe. Supposedly, there had been a report
that someone in the bar had a gun. Without due warning, or so it appeared, a deputy fired a tear-gas gun four
times through a curtain which hung near the entrance.
Ruben Salazar, a former feature writer for the *Los Angeles Times,* and recently hired by KMEX-TV as news
director, through an almost incredible coincidence, was
killed when one of the ten-inch-long projectiles struck
him in the head.

Salazar was buried the following Wednesday, but
by then his death had become a national symbol among
Chicanos of police cruelty toward la raza. Demands had
been lodged by organizations and individuals throughout the nation with President Nixon and various federal
law-enforcement agencies; yet the Los Angeles County
Sheriff's Department remained the sole investigative
agency regarding Salazar's death and the rally disturb-
ances.

As recently as the fall 1968 the Sheriff's Department
employed only 106 Mexican Americans among 3,667
employees. Of those 106 employees, 81 were plain-
clothes detectives, that is, they operated under cover;
only 9 others held supervisory or command positions. As
usual, such an agency of the law, which was responsible
for the death of a Chicano, was itself in charge of inves-
tigating the case. Under such circumstances, little justice can be expected of local authorities. In fact, the two-
weeks-long inquest held in October to consider whether
Salazar's death should lead to a court indictment resulted in a decision by four of the seven panel members
that the newsman had died "at the hands of another."
Los Angeles County District Attorney Evelle Younger,
however, chose to ignore the citizens' charge and withheld further action.

The District Attorney's decision is not a new story to
the Chicano, but it will serve to exacerbate the tensions
and frustrations that convulsed the East Los Angeles
community last August.

No other group in the United States can claim as its own, two special police forces established and dedicated to suppressing it—the Border Patrol of the Immigration and Naturalization Service (Department of Justice) and the Texas Rangers. Our relationships with these and other law agencies is so familiar, in fact, that we have developed many terms of affection for law-enforcement types. For one of the most hated of lawmen, *los rinches* aptly corrupts the word Rangers.

According to Americo Paredes in *With His Pistol in His Hand*, Texas Chicanos for a long time have referred to the "rinches de la Kinena," implying their belief that the Texas Rangers were uniformed vigilantes in the pay of Richard King, of the vast King Ranch in South Texas, and of other cattle kings. Parades noted that Texas gringos maintained the following belief about the Rangers: "The Texan has no equal anywhere but within Texas itself there developed a special breed of men, the Texas Rangers, in whom the Texan's qualities reached their culmination." Two of the most obvious gringo qualities the mexicano observed prior to the beginning of the war against Mexico were the gringo's greed for land and the relentless pursuit of land and wealth at the expense of the mexicano. The Anglo learned the cattle business from the Spanish Mexican vaqueros (translated into "cowboys" by the acquisitive gringo), then turned around and stole their land and their cattle as well. But characteristically, Paredes remarked, the gringo imputed his own traits to the mexicano, labeling him a bandito, a thief, and a no-account. The Texas Ranger merely assured the rich cattle barons and politicians of Texas that the mexicano would be kept in his place, dead or alive.

Walking through the airport in Dallas is an insulting experience to a Chicano. In the center of the main lobby, there has been erected the unmistakable semblance of a Texas Ranger. On the pedestal—of course there would have to be a pedestal—is the inscription:

"One riot, one Ranger." The implication is clear. However, I'm wondering what would happen if a riot occurred in the Dallas airport. The statue, by the way, illustrates a penchant among Texas gringos to memorialize the damndest things—for example, a statue of Popeye the Sailor Man stands in Crystal City to remind one and all that it is the spinach capital of the world.

The Texas Rangers are all potential killers imposed on the Mexican American community as a deterrent to its progress or its freedom. In South Texas, during the melon pickers' strike, Rangers openly threatened farm union members and organizers with physical harm, arrested them, and manhandled men and women in the process of destroying the union.

La migra is the term conferred by Chicanos upon the Border Patrol, a racist-motivated branch of the Department of Justice that has often been considered by Chicanos as a tool of growers all along the United States-Mexico border. One of the Border Patrol's main functions is to track down illegal visitors from Mexico to the United States, catch, and return them to the other side of the border. To them, any Chicano is suspect, and, as many Mexican Americans have experienced personally or have heard from relatives and friends, he may be stopped at any time by la migra and questioned and searched.

I was in Delano in the summer of 1968, shortly after the boycott against fresh table grapes had been initiated by the United Farm Workers, when I had my first encounter with la migra along a dusty Delano road.

Cesar Chavez and one of his strike captains, Roberto Bustos, jumped into Roberto's dust-grayed blue sedan, and I scrambled into the back seat in a rush to get out to one of the grape fields which, a union observer had reported, contained scab laborers from across the border and from nearby towns such as Earlimart, Pixley, McFarland, and Wasco.

With Roberto at the wheel, we covered about five

miles in a short time, taking into account that the union
worker's car was easily recognizable to the marauding
sheriff or the highway patrol. Chavez had him patrol
along one of the Kern County roads, with Giumarra grape
fields on either side. Roberto spotted a small airplane. "La
migra," he said, and accelerated the car to try to follow
the plane's flight, which seemed to be circling a not-too-
distant field.

When we reached the area, it was obvious from the
plane's pattern that it was observing something inside
the grape field. From the road it was impossible to see
beyond the green screen of fruit-heavy vines. Cesar said
that the plane might scare out illegals working in the
vineyard and that our best chance to check them out
would be to post ourselves at a nearby intersection
where anyone's movements within a mile or two could
be observed.

Roberto parked the car just off the side of the road
near a corner of intersecting county roads. Seconds
later, a vehicle came barreling toward us, then slowed,
and again Roberto said softly, "La migra." Sure enough
a border patrol jeep pulled up and stopped in the middle of the road. One lone mexicano sat in the back in a
caged rear section of the auto. A gringo Border Patrolman and a vendido Mexican American sidekick clam-
bered out and walked up to Chavez and Bustos who
were standing in the dust at the side of the road.

"Who are you? What are you doing here? Let me
see your papers," the gringo patrolman addressed Chavez.

Cesar asked him if he was arresting him; if not, why
was he questioning him. No, he would not show the
officer any papers because he had no right to question
him unless he had a warrant. I had remained in the car
with a note pad in hand. The malinche patrolman came
around and asked through one of the open windows,
"Where are you from?" I answered, "I'm an American
citizen." He glanced around the car and pulled back his
head. Meanwhile the gringo migra officer had gotten no

place with Chavez; his compañero joined him and said, "Come on, let's go." His gringo partner walked backward away from Chavez a few steps, then ducked behind the driver's seat, of course.

Cesar called out to him, "What's your name? I have a right to know your name!"

As the jeep speeded up, spitting gravel and dust behind, the gringo yelled back, "You don't tell me your name, I won't tell you mine!"

Chicano familiarity with the police has created other terms of endearment including la chota, a pachuco expression of unknown derivation, but one I'd heard since I was a small child; los changos, literally, the apes; and los cochinos, which means pigs or filthy ones, of more recent derivation; la placa, which derives from the badge policemen wear; los jefes, taken from the Spanish for chiefs; and la jura, taken perhaps from *jurar*, to swear in, as police are sworn in for duty.

Los changos tried to open up Chicano heads when a walkout occurred at West High School in Denver, Colorado, March 21, 1969. A number of Chicanos, mostly Crusade for Justice members, including Rodolfo "Corky" Gonzales, were arrested and booked on charges ranging from disturbing the peace, carrying concealed weapons and inciting to riot, to resisting arrest, and assault. Gonzales was acquitted of all charges against him in early January 1970; others among some twenty Chicanos indicted for various reasons have also been cleared. The verdict shown by the acquittals is that what really occurred was a police riot. About the same thing happened in October 1969 when Crusade youths renamed Lincoln Park in Denver to Aztlán Park. A minor accident occurred during the festivities. A crowd gathered. One of the Brown Berets was holding back the people when a chota arrived and told him to move back; he said this was his job. When the youth didn't move back fast enough, the chota shoved and clubbed him. The Chicanos surrounded the chota, who, in a panic it seems, drew his revolver and fired a shot in the air. Everybody scattered, then when police cars arrived in force and began search-and-destroy movements through a nearby housing project, families took the youths inside and pelted los changos with anything they could lay hands on. The policía retired from the field.

It was in Denver that the long arm of the law reached my way ever so tentatively. On a visit to the rebirth place of Aztlán on November 29, 1969, with notebook and camera in hand, I sat in on the trial of Ernesto Espinoza, nineteen years old, a slight, soft-spoken young man who had been arrested on March 20 during a Chicano student blowout. Espinoza had been charged with carrying a concealed weapon, disturbing the peace, assault, and resisting arrest. It turned out that the "concealed weapon" was a mestizo head chain that had broken and that Espinoza was holding in his hand. The youth faced a jury of his "peers"—four Anglos and two blacks but no Chicanos on a panel of six, with the youngest in the late twenties.

When the judge recessed court for the day, I stepped out into the corridor ahead of most persons in the courtroom. As the public prosecutor walked out with the chota who had arrested Espinoza and was holding the doors open for jurors as they filed out, I shot two or three photographs, no flash, just available light. Nevertheless, the assistant district attorney's eyes blazed when he heard the shutter clicking. He rushed the chota through a nearby door. A group of us waited for Espinoza and his parents, accompanied by Corky Gonzales, to emerge from the judge's chambers. One of the juras came out with Espinoza's defense lawyer, an Anglo, stepping ahead of him to tell me in a low voice that I was wanted in the judge's chambers. He said something about my picture-taking, that they couldn't force me to oblige, but rather than start a stink over nothing would I just come in for a minute.

Suddenly, an instinctive action on my part to record

chotas in action had taken on a new dimension—I held my camera tight under my arm. In the judge's chambers, the prosecutor contended that my picture-taking had intimidated the jurors. My first impulse was to retort that it had been the assistant district attorney who had been intimidated. Caution, however, kept my mouth shut as the two opposing attorneys argued over the issue of a mistrial, and so on. Corky Gonzales, himself under indictment for similar charges in the March 20 incident, had bided his time as he stood behind me. He left the gringo prosecutor speechless, when he spoke up: "If you call his taking pictures intimidation, then what about your holding the doors open for the jurors; isn't that solicitation of the jurors?"

Finally, the judge ended the argument by informing the lawyers that he would decide the question of a mistrial at the next session by questioning the jurors. He told me that I was free to go. I didn't release the hold on my camera until we were out in the windy, snow-covered street. To this day, I'm certain that had a *Denver Post* photographer been there with an electronic strobelight unit flashing, he would have gone unmolested. Fortunately, the effort to harass a Chicano photographer failed.

Three major trials in Los Angeles involving several Chicanos are closely linked to each other by the abuse of the law to suppress Chicano organizational efforts. The cases involve the East Los Angeles Thirteen, the Biltmore Six, and the Catolicos por La Raza.

On May 27, 1968, law-enforcement agencies connived to bring indictments against thirteen Chicanos who had allegedly conspired to disrupt the Los Angeles public schools, charging the thirteen with fifteen separate counts of felonies punishable by up to forty-five years in prison! Oscar Zeta Acosta, defense attorney for all three groups, who unfortunately lost his bid for Los Angeles County sheriff in the June primaries, has described the "dramatic, coordinated roundup in their own homes and in their organizational offices during the last week of the [1968] primary," in the winter 1970 issue of *El Grito* magazine, published in Berkeley, California.

In the Biltmore Hotel on April 24, 1969, as Governor Ronald Reagan spoke in one of the ballrooms, incidents of arson and the cutting of electric wires were reported and later attributed to several Chicanos, but only six, all Chicano activists, suffered litigation on charges of conspiracy to commit felonies: Ernesto Cebada, Montezuma Esparza, Rene Nuñez, Carlos Montes, Ralph Ramirez, and Juan Robles.

Catolicos por La Raza chose Christmas Eve 1969 to protest against the racist, unresponsive Catholic Church system in the Los Angeles Archdiocese. CPLR supporters demonstrated in front of St. Basil's Cathedral, and, when several members sought to enter the edifice, police forced them back; there was the usual violent confrontation, and twenty persons were arrested. Ten Chicanos were eventually convicted of incitement to riot. Motion for a new trial was filed by attorney Acosta on the grounds that the jury had been tampered with. The Chicano lawyer himself was cited for contempt ten times and faced contempt proceedings as a result of the trial, which raza observers described as a replay of the Chicago Eight fiasco. Most of the litigation related to the three cases is at some stage of appeal or challenge. Meanwhile, the Chicanos involved are greatly limited in their activities and movements.

The point of law that was used discriminatively to thwart Chicano-movement activists—a total of thirty Chicanos at least—had been discussed by Yvonne Merga, who, when a third-year student at Hastings Law School, published an article in the Hastings Law Journal of February 1965 (Vol. 16, No. 3). Merga established the following legal framework that led indirectly to the arresting of so many Chicanos: "A criminal conspiracy has been defined as an agreement between two or more persons to achieve an unlawful object, or to achieve a lawful object by unlawful means. . . . Arrest or charges of criminal conspiracy would allow the enforcement agency to prevent disorder and damage to property before they occur."

Thus, under the law, the article continues: ". . . [an] overt act need not be committed by each member, and the act of one may be attributed to all the other participants. . . . If a conspiracy is charged there is no need to wait for all the participants to commit the planned acts before arrests are made." Her legal reference is to the California Penal Code § 182.

Obviously, such an interpretation of the law is highly useful to police agencies seeking to eliminate an organizational threat by any minority group, but specifically by Chicanos. California Penal Code § 182, originally directed at the individual who might hire or conspire with someone to commit a murder or robbery but who himself would not actually perform the act, has been prostituted into a handy weapon to abort Chicano activism. Without a doubt, the legal threat has affected the involvement of Chicanos in planning or preparations for almost any kind of activity. Still, events such as the Chicano Moratorium continue because they must.

Attorney Acosta, a kind of one-man ACLU, has challenged the legality of the courts to try Chicanos not only in the three specific instances but in any other cases, because the jury system in California has virtually excluded the person with a Spanish surname from service on grand and petit juries. Precedent for the East Los Angeles Thirteen challenge, ironically enough, derives from the case of *Hernandez* v. *Texas* in 1954, in which a murder conviction against Pete Hernandez was reversed on the basis of jury discrimination. Hernandez' new trial did not alter the final verdict of guilty, but his sentence was changed from death in the electric chair to life imprisonment. The higher court had ordered that the jury hearing Hernandez' case must include Chicanos. A legal form on which the framework of legal precedents was laid out and only pertinent information relative to a particular case was left blank, was prepared by another Chicano attorney, Gerald Lopez of San Antonio. The framework served as the basic groundwork for the California court challenges.

The analysis of California's jury system in twenty-two counties, conducted by the California Rural Legal Assistance, provided the substantiating information for the challenge. CRLA disclosed that in Los Angeles County, for example, during a ten-year period only four Spanish surnames appeared among the rosters of a total 210 members of the grand juries. One of the four, as it turned out, was a Negro.

In another ironic twist, the data and legal brief presented by Acosta were used by the defense lawyers of Sirhan Sirhan, the convicted assassin of Robert F. Kennedy, who was one of the few Anglos truly simpatico to the Chicano cause.

Rather expectedly, the Chicano contentions were dismissed in a November 1968 court argument related to the East Los Angeles Thirteen case by Judge Kathleen Parker, who agreed with the county counsel that the defense attorneys had failed to make a prima facie case, that is, prove a point on the basis of their arguments, even though thirty-three superior court judges had been interrogated. All the judges swore they had never deliberately excluded Mexican Americans.

Tanks, soldiers, and other weapons of war were called up on June 5, 1967, in Rio Arriba County (northern New Mexico), following the Alianza raid on the Tierra Amarilla courthouse. The overkill methods resulted in the apprehension of several families, along with single men, who were held for many hours, without charge, in a sheep pen. When a reporter asked Major General John Pershing Jolly, commander of the state National Guard, why the people were being literally penned up, he retorted: "Let's don't get involved in civil liberties. None of them has complained."

In Albuquerque, New Mexico, on March 26, 1969,

four men in a car were stopped by a Sheriff's Officer, Julian Narvaez. Pete Garcia, a former tecato (barrio for drug addict) was one of the men in the auto and was well known to Narvaez. When the chota ordered everyone out of the car, Narvaez saw Garcia, had him put his hands on top of the car, then searched him, and pistol-whipped him two or three times. Garcia turned around, the two men struggled, Narvaez, behind Garcia, fired his gun, the bullet going through Garcia's back and out his stomach. When Garcia held on, falling with Narvaez to the ground, more shots were fired, until Narvaez lay mortally wounded, and Garcia near death. Not until the trial began did the public learn that Garcia had first been shot in the back, and that in the struggle Narvaez was shot.

In January 1969 twenty Chicanos were arrested in Albuquerque on charges connected with marijuana. All had bonds set at $2,500 each. In May 1969 seven Anglos were arrested in a narcotics raid, but all were released to their lawyers, their parents, or on their own recognizance. One youth was released to his mother's arms and ordered to see the movie *To Sir, With Love*.

More than a dozen Chicano organizations were radicalized into confronting Anglo justice in Hayward in the San Francisco-Oakland Bay Area when on November 10, 1967, twenty-year-old Gilberto Garza fell under gunfire from three chotas. Las chotas had first charged that after they had run him down on the alleged charge of molesting a woman, Garza had threatened them with a gun. Instead, Garza had only a knife, but the policía reported that the oficiales had been forced to shoot. A Hayward judge declared Garza's death justifiable homicide. Out of the incident there developed a raza defense group, Latinos Unidos Para la Justicia.

One youth died when two Camp Gary Job Corpsmen were shot down by Austin, Texas, chotas. Mexican Americans turned out in force at the Austin City Coun-

cil meetings in April 1969 to protest the shootings, but
the Travis County Grand Jury had ruled already that
the policía were justified but could have used "better
judgment."

Seventeen-year-old Louis T. Pinedo was shot in the
back by changos in July 1967 in Denver. Early reports
by the policía and Denver's dailies indicated that the
youth, apprehended on suspicion of auto theft, had
been killed by a bullet in the back. The officer who
murdered the unarmed youth suffered no reprisal; it
was another case of "justifiable" killing.

In February 1968 a lead slug struck Paul Meza
Aguilera, Jr., eighteen years old, in the base of the skull
while fleeing from a Stanton, California, chota. The
reserve policeman who pulled the trigger asserted that
he had fired a warning shot after shouting to the youth
three times to stop. The Orange County Grand Jury did
nothing to bring the chota to justice.

Six Mexican Americans were arrested in an East
Moline, Iowa, tavern in December 1968 with such un-
warranted brutality—and, as had been the case for a
long while, without informing the victims of their rights
—that a number of Mexican Americans in the area near
Davenport, Iowa, organized a special group to protest
the incident and other incidents like it.

The sky over San Jose was a clear blue, assuring an
excellent background for La Fiesta de las Rosas parade
that the city fathers had scheduled for June 1, 1969. A
group of about two hundred Chicanos were aware neither of the clarity of the sky nor of the festive crowds
lining the main street. They represented some two-
dozen organizations and clubs in the San Jose area who
had come together to protest in a small way a ritual
they thought excluded them and in fact insulted them,
their families, and their history. Adalberto Jimenez,
who soon after lost his job with the city's Human Relations Commission because of his part in that day's
events, felt a sense of anxiety and a little awe, as did

most of the Chicanos there. Few of them had ever dared to express their deep feelings of resentment, of injured pride; and, of course, the motorcycle police made everyone a bit nervous.

Passing by was the float they had decided would signal their entry into the parade. The group pressed a little forward; a chota barred their way but was called away by a sergeant. Then another placa intervened, with his billy club horizontal in front of him. He sensed the pressure of the people behind the lead line, and decided then and there that he was being attacked. He pushed back, but found no give; then he began swinging. Other chotas converged on the scene. Men, women, and children, unable to move back because of the crowd, ducked, lost their balance, and fell under the clubs of the chotas. Some of the men threw themselves between the clubs and women and children who couldn't have otherwise escaped the enraged chotas. When order was restored among the chotas, six people had been beaten and required hospital treatment; seventeen were arrested. To the Chicanos in San Jose who were there, city hall and the establishment with their gestapo squads are no longer abstract or rhetorical phrases; they are as solid as the ends of the billy clubs in Chicanos' guts and cracking on their heads and shins. All they were doing was protesting an annual event which purports to glorify the Spanish heritage of California but which really ignores the contributions of the Mexicans and Indians. The event actually promotes a business angle that has proved a profitable tourist attraction.

Los changos, la chota, los cochinos have turned their overkill methods upon the Chicano. The same rationale that leads to the destruction of Black Panthers pulls the trigger and wields the club against Chicanos. Every effort to suppress the Chicano has backfired, however. Counter force has met with counter force, as Chicanos have organized to repel the peril of genocidal gringos

operating under the cover of law. Such a self-exposure
of chota criminals erupted in San Francisco last fall and
led to the coalescence of the first organization broadly
representative of many raza nationalities in the Bay
Area under the name of Los Siete de La Raza, one of
the few instances which have resulted in justice for the
accused.

San Francisco's Mission District comprises a raza
community involving people from Mexico, Central and
South America, Spain, and the Caribbean clustered into
one of the more or less level regions of the hilly city.
The section is named after Mission Dolores, founded by
Juan Bautista de Anza in 1776, and located on the
northern edge of the area. For several decades the Spanish-speaking immigrants to the city have congregated in
the Mission to find friends, relatives, and the familiar
sights, smells, and sounds of the raza ambiente they had
left behind. While Mexican Americans also live there,
the movement against police harassment and oppression
is not wholly Chicano but is grounded in the raza origins of the residents.

In most neighborhoods the sight of a group of men
moving a piece of furniture, a television set, for example, into a home arouses little if any suspicion. However, in the Mission District las chotas are accustomed
to suspect the worst; and when two plain-clothes chotas
saw a group moving a TV set from a car into the home
of Jose Ríos on May 1, 1969, they accosted the youths.
A scuffle followed with the chotas, Joseph Brodnik and
Paul McGoran. One of the policemen's guns fired and
hit Brodnik fatally; McGoran suffered a broken jaw.
Seven latinos were arrested, three of whom were not
even on the street at the time of the incident. They
included Nelson Rodriguez, Gary Lescallett, José Ríos,
Danilo Melendez, Rodolfo Martínez, José Mario Martínez, and the seventh, Gio Lopez, who remained free
"somewhere in the Third World," his latino brothers
say.

A tremendous and unprecedented movement to rally around the cause of the seven young men has developed in the Mission District. Through word of mouth, rallies, and a newspaper—*Basta Ya*—started since the incident, a coalition of various raza countrymen has been forged out of the injustice inflicted on the youths. The challenge is to persuade the people of the Mission District that they have a personal stake in the defense, for the freedom of Los Siete means the liberation of the barrio. The Los Siete de La Raza organization, the co-ordinating group for the legal defense of the seven latinos, developed a free breakfast program, recreation events, free ambulance service, draft and college counseling, and legal aid. The organization also founded and manages a restaurant, Las Sirenitas, on Valencia Street in the heart of the barrio.

On November 7, 1969, Los Siete were acquitted after eighteen months in jail. Whatever may have happened to Los Siete, the pattern of life, the level of awareness concerning the district problems among the raza, and more importantly, their new approach to resolving issues are irrevocably changed. Las chotas are responsible for the aroused militancy of the people. If the case of the seven latinos had been lost, the people would not have been crushed; they would have been even more angered. With the case won, the people have been confirmed in their avowal of aggression against the gringo system of "law and order." The San Francisco Establishment, from its would-be-governor mayor to el cochino McGoran, will know they have stirred up a nest of revolutionaries who will turn next upon the school system, the welfare system, the economic system, and the political system.

Since the May 1 death of the San Francisco chota, police attitudes toward the people of the district have not improved. *Basta Ya,* the Los Siete newspaper, detailed the Thanksgiving Day attack by chotas on the Alcaraz family who live in the outer Mission. As the family party was ending, some of the members of the family, which includes five sons and two daughters, were heading for their cars. Two of the brothers were arguing over a soccer game as they walked outside. A police car drove up; the chotas climbed out, intent on arresting the two men. One of the chotas suddenly started beating one of the men, Alfonso, about the head. Another brother, Theodore, rushed from inside the house and tried to pull his brother from the maddened cochino. In the struggle one chota was injured slightly. Theodore started to run across the street, and a chota fired at him, hitting him seven times. When the chota reached him, they picked him up and threw him against a wall. More police cars came and several chotas held the family at gunpoint. The charges included a count of assault against Mrs. Alcaraz, a widow who brought her family from Tijuana nine years ago and raised them alone, one count of assault on each of two brothers, and a charge of attempted murder on Theodore. The *Basta Ya* editors stated:

This is almost exactly the same thing that happened with Los Siete de la Raza last May 1st, (las chotas) using their guns in a situation where there was no need for the use of guns or force. In each case the police ACCUSED a person of murder or attempted murder and in each case the alleged weapon is the police officer's own gun. In each case the police tried to deal with a group of people they know nothing about, and had much contempt for—the brown people of the Mission District.

And how did the city's dailies treat the incident? *The San Francisco Examiner* ran the headline, front page:

Mob Assaults SF Policemen
Excelsior Mob Attacks 2 Cops

Thus, a chota attack against innocent people was turned into a riot instigated by the victims of chota bullets and clubs. And the slaughter goes on.

On September 1, 1969, Jesse Manuel Villa, eighteen, fell dead from four chota slugs in his body, one in the back of his head. Two San Jose policemen, Michael Zanoni and Bruce Fair, stopped Villa and three other Chicanos on suspicion of robbery while they were driving in San Jose. When they were being questioned, Villa apparently panicked and ran, but not very far.

Vincente Gutierrez died May 10, 1970, after having been picked up on a narcotics charge. The police claimed that Gutierrez, a young man living in San Francisco with his wife and baby, had died of an overdose of barbiturates (reds). Two private autopsies later disclosed that Gutierrez had suffered a terrific beating between the time he was arrested, when his wife last saw him, and the time she viewed his corpse.

The next month, two Mexican nationals, Guillermo and Beltran Sanchez, brothers, were shot to death by Los Angeles chotas when two San Leandro changos led a raid June 5 on a rooming house where a suspect in a San Leandro murder case was supposedly hiding. More than a half-dozen police stormed the building, shouting a warning as they entered. Several raza in a room panicked. One was killed inside the room; another ran and fell, injuring his leg; a third fled, but was brought down dead by chota bullets. The San Leandran whom the police had been hunting was later released for lack of evidence.

On March 3, 1971, in Milwaukee, a march spearheaded by the Latin American Union for Civil Rights (LAUCR) was broken up by billy-club-swinging police. The event culminated months of protest in behalf of Jose Puente and Ernesto Chacon who had been arrested in a similar police riot January 29, 1970, during a demonstration for winter clothing needs.

La Gente de Santa Fe have organized to combat the slaying by police bullets of Felipe Mares on May 21. Mares, twenty years old, and two other Chicanos were being held on a burglary charge in the Taos, New Mexico, jail; a deputy sheriff's gun brought Mares down during an alleged escape attempt.

Nothing has been done by civil authorities to make retribution to the families of the dead men or to bring the offending officers to justice.

In one of the most blatant examples of the attitude of the agencies of the law toward the people of the barrio, California Superior Court Judge Gerald S. Chargin, sitting in Santa Clara County Juvenile Court in September 1969, told a seventeen-year-old Chicano charged with incest:

Mexican people, after 13 years of age, it's perfectly all right to go out and act like an animal. . . . We ought to send you out of the country—send you back to Mexico. . . . You belong in prison for the rest of your life for doing things of this kind. You are lower than animals and haven't the right to live in organized society—just miserable, lousy, rotten people. . . . Maybe Hitler was right. The animals in our society probably ought to be destroyed because they have no right to live among human beings.

In exhibiting such ferocious racist hate, the judge went far beyond the social revulsion that usually arises from the crime the youth was accused of committing. The gringo administrator of justice exposed deep, personal prejudices that bring into doubt whether he was mentally composed to mete out proper justice in that case. His actions have also called into question prior trials in which Chicanos or other Spanish-speaking people appeared before him. His entire record should be examined; it would not be surprising to find that in cases involving the Mexican American, the heaviest fines and stiffest sentences possible have been levied. Judge Chargin was temporarily suspended from hearing cases following heated criticism, not only from Mexican Americans (who staged huge protest rallies in various parts of the county), but from various law organizations as well. He and others like him who characterize the Southwest court system should never have been on the bench. However, only in such overt instances as the Santa Clara County case are the prejudice and racism, which for decades have operated in the Southwest under the color of law, exposed.

A movement born out of the total Chicano revolt and in reaction against the chota system of oppression has developed among ex-convicts organizing under such names as the Mexican American Youth Organization in Los Angeles, Committee for the Rights of the Imprisoned in San Quentin Prison, and Quebrar in Albuquerque. The Chicano-centered, ex-convict groups work toward improving the conditions of penal institutions from the inside by articulating prisoner grievances, by providing guidance to prisoners, by exposing how the law has mistreated them, and by encouraging them to feel a sense of cultural pride.

Quebrar in New Mexico is mainly composed of addicts, ex-addicts, and their families. Pete Garcia, the Chicano accused of a chota's death in Albuquerque, was a Quebrar organizer. Quebrar is Spanish for to break; the organization's motto follows the theme: Nuestra cura es quebrar a la brava (Our cure is to break the habit on guts alone). To rehabilitate tecatos (barrio for an addict), Quebrar is planning to establish a Residential Treatment Center, a halfway house, a kickpad. Prevention of drug addiction among youths also involves face-to-face rap sessions.

The Committee for the Rights of the Imprisoned was founded in San Quentin in 1969. One of its founders is Eduardo "Mo" Aguirre, president of the League of United Citizens to Help Addicts (LUCHA), a statewide organization of addicts and ex-addicts. Roberto Martinez, CRI president, has pointed out one of the major reasons for the creation of CRI: Chicanos constitute the largest ethnic group in the pintas (prisons) of the California penal system. CRI is specifically concerned with prison reform but collaborates with LUCHA and MAYO in their antiaddiction programs.

A prime objective of CRI efforts is the reform of the California Rehabilitation Center in Corona. There a program has been in effect, called the resident-counselor system, what inmates call the "meat-grinder of minds." Martinez explains that one CRC resident "is pressured by the administration into documenting information (literally, informing) on another inmate for the purpose of keeping the person under surveillance in prison." Following the July 4th riots at Corona in 1969 Martinez related that about two hundred Chicanos in state prisons have been "excluded" from the rehabilitation center. Criminal cases can be given civil status, Martinez says, by committing an accused person to CRC instead of slapping him with a prison sentence if the crime was induced by narcotic addiction. However, CRC administration can exclude an inmate, that is, refuse to keep him at the institution depending on an evaluation of his progress there. A class injunction was prepared to cover 300 such exclusions that CRI considers unjustly arbitrary. CRI also seeks repeal of present narcotics laws and their replacement by humane and rehabilitative legislation, particularly in regard to the user rather than the hard-core pusher.

MAYO programs extend into educational improvement, development of cultural awareness and pride, employment assistance, and encouragement of community and political involvement. MAYO also maintains a half way house, Casa de Mayo, in East Los Angeles, where the stress is on self-help, ex-addict to ex-addict, and building community concern that the ex-addicts remain "clean."

Tecatos are known to hustle from $25 to $200 a day through stealing, conning people out of money, dealing in stolen goods, doing anything to support their habit. An ex-addict once told me that the tecato wastes a fantastic amount of energy and intelligence getting the money needed for drugs. Now it seems that a growing number of one-time tecatos and ex-convicts are finished with the old lives in which they sought to destroy themselves or others, and have turned to the service of their hermanos and their raza. All that energy and intellect will not be wasted. Primarily because of the cultural reawakening, many tecatos and convicts are being helped to revitalize themselves. The important element is that former victims, fed up with the rehabilitative or penal system that could never really work for them, have undertaken remedies that they themselves control and carry out. This is one of the most positive movements developing in the last year or two among Chicanos.

Why Chicanos represent such a high proportion of convicts in California and, it appears, in other Southwest states, usually in excess of their percentage of the population, is tied in with the miseries of a people who have often been forced into crime, who have been brutalized by los changos and then have become their victims and their wards in pintas. As now set up, prison is destructive of human values, but when it also is an extension of gringo disdain for the Chicano or the black, it becomes a monstrous, soul-devouring creation of the devil himself. The convict or ex-convict can tell this story best himself. A young Chicano who has gone the route in California from juvenile centers, to Corona, to Vacaville, to Susanville, to San Quentin has told me he would like to write a book about the Chicano de la pinta someday. It would be a fascinating story.

Reies Tijerina in an Albuquerque jail.

Six Chicanos jailed on conspiracy charges in the Biltmore Hotel incident involving the California governor.

Six raza, one more at large, in a San Francisco jail charged with killing one chota.

Pete Garcia, a former tecato, on trial for his life in another case involving a dead chota.

Twenty Chicanos convicted on various counts for activism against the Catholic Church.

To a Chicano, the only interpretation he can give to the
present conditions of these men is that they are in jail,
not for any real crime they may have committed but
because they are political prisoners, jailed because they
represented something about their people that the
gringo establishment could not understand, which it
feared, and so suppressed in the only way it knows—
imprisonment. Others, young Chicanos, who ran in fear
from a chota with a gun, were killed. La chota reigns
supreme in the barrio; he relentlessly maintains his role
of guardian of the gringo's world. He is convinced that
it is his duty to maintain law and order from the perspective of a dual system of justice—one for the Anglo;
another for the Chicano, the black man, and the Indian.
For a long time, the people of the United States have
reacted strongly, some against and others for the in-
carceration of Negro leaders or black militants; most
killings of black people have been well publicized. But
the "justifiable" homicides of young Chicanos have gone
virtually unnoticed. Why? Part of the answer must be
the disregard that the police, the press, and the Anglo
liberals have toward the Chicano; they just haven't
been impressed that young men with Spanish surnames
have had chota bullets crash into their skulls or tear
their stomachs apart.

By no means will oppression of the Chicano lessen
in the years to come. We are just beginning to confront
the armed tools of the gringo establishment. Many Chicanos, the ones in San Jose, East Moline, Austin, Chicago, Salt Lake City, Kansas City, San Francisco, Los
Angeles, Phoenix, Albuquerque, San Antonio, and all
the towns and townships in between will come to realize that the Chicano is considered subject to the Anglo
society; dissenters will be summarily punished and put
away. Los rinches, los changos, la chota, la migra, los
cochinos, have often been the best organizers of the
Chicano movement; their bestiality has opened the eyes
of many Chicanos who otherwise would not see—

because they didn't want to—the gringo chota for what he is. Bitter resentment against what Anglos call law and justice and civil rights has built up in the Chicano for generations. He now realizes that truly it is better for a man to die on his feet than to live on his knees.

13

TOWARD A THIRD POLITICS

BEAT the Anglo at his own game.

I can remember Ernesto Galarza telling this to Chicanos about six years ago at a legislative conference in Sacramento, California, sponsored by the Mexican American Political Association. What seemed like so much rhetoric coming from an old campaigner in the farm union battles of other decades is, in actuality, the very root of Chicano liberation, if it is to come. We must beat the Anglo at his own game. Until now, because it is his game, the Anglo has held all the cards, made the rules and decided how high the stakes would go. He is a rather formidable opponent for the Chicano.

Generally, the Mexican American has always had a streak of the politico in him. Misfortunes and mistreatment at the hands of political authorities, however, have often caused the Chicano to leave the politicking to those willing to sell their souls. It seemed to the Chicano that civil authorities, that is, "elected representatives," were no more possessed of a guiding spirit of soul than a stray dog sniffing at the tree trunks in the town plaza. It has been our experience for generations that the politician visited our barrios only with an election coming, and that his free tacos-and-beer fiestas were all

241

that could be expected of him in spite of his generous promises. We ate the politician's tacos and drank the beer, shook his hand, and, for a few, money in varying amounts would sometimes be left in the palm. We would smile knowingly: "Muchas gracias, licenciado, buena suerte en la campaña." And we would hate ourselves all the while we were drinking the bottle of tequila the money bought.

That more or less is the way the Chicano understood politics—at least up until the Second World War. Aspirations and a sense of power began to blossom as a result of the sudden awareness of the rights due us— rights that so many Chicanos gave their lives to assure. The creation of the American G.I. Forum in 1948, the resurgence of the LULACs after the war, the formation of CSO in 1947, the coming of MAPA in California in 1958, and, not long after, the Political Association of Spanish Speaking Organizations, illustrate the intense craving of the Chicanos for exerting a little political muscle in their own cause.

The Democratic party has traditionally been the party of the Chicano, although I have met a few long-time Republicans here and there, or at least they claimed to have belonged to the Republican party for many years. The adherence to Democratic party lines probably extends to the administration of Franklin D. Roosevelt and the fact that Democrats were in power during some of the most productive years for many Chicanos who developed an affection for Roosevelt and who certainly benefited in a limited way from the war-time expansion of employment opportunities. Deep loyalties developed among many families—loyalties that became traditional, a family heirloom, during the war years. Many thousands of Chicanos fought under a Democratic president, and those who did vote invariably cast their ballot for the incumbent chief executive. As a little boy I used to count the five gold stars that my grandmother had placed in one of the front windows.

Each World War II veteran of Chicano birth felt an allegiance to the Democrats. The allegiance was established out of wartime dependency on a president who played the role of patrón.

Historically, Texas, Arizona, California, Colorado, and New Mexico had strong inclinations in more recent decades toward Democratic party lines, particularly in the thirties and forties when, it seems, many Mexican Americans established party preference. Texas had been faithfully Democratic for generations; there, political capital was to be made as a Democrat. Moreover, Texas has been the home base for many thousands of Chicano families who have migrated out of the labor cornucopia of South Texas, spilling out to the West Coast, the North, and Northeast. A marked change in party affiliation surfaced only as recently as the mid-1960s, but not, it should be kept in mind, in significant numbers. In Texas, for example, John Tower was elected in 1966, the first Republican senator since Reconstruction days. The number of GOP congressmen at that time, three, is also serving Texas at present. Six years earlier, Richard Nixon had failed to win Texas' electoral votes by a mere forty thousand votes. At the time, 80 percent of Mexican American voters had voted for John F. Kennedy, but since then the Democratic Chicano voting base has been eroded. What many Chicanos seem to be doing is not necessarily switching party affiliation (they may remain Democratic from tradition or principle) but staying away from the polls, withholding active support, or calling to task the Democratic patrónes by voting against them. Undoubtedly, in Texas, Mexican Americans figure strongly in the 1970 and 1972 state and national campaigns, especially as a result of a growing defection among Mexican American Democrats.

It is clear that among many Chicanos the days of the patrón system are gone. Whether the patrón was Anglo or Mexican, his role as a mediator in all the problems of the Chicano and as the distributor of favors is forever over; this does not mean that the old patrónes are giving up their roles or that many Mexican Americans still do not depend on them. The men who were elected in the 1960s as protagonists for la causa cannot expect the same kind of backing they have been accustomed to from Chicanos. Witness the 1966 elections in Texas, when Tower defeated the Connally-backed Democratic candidate, Waggoner Carr, by 200,000 votes; Tower amassed 25.54 percent of the vote in eighteen predominantly Mexican American Democratic precincts of San Antonio. In the previous senatorial elections, when Congressman George Bush had run against Senator Ralph Yarborough, the Republican candidate had received only 6.54 percent of the vote in the same precincts! Waggoner's defeat, it should be pointed out, was surely related to his connection to former Governor Connally's Waterloo at New Braunfels, where Connally tried to abort the farmworkers' march in September 1966. The Democratic debacle that year in Texas also influenced President Johnson's reassessment of Chicano strength, and led to the Inter-Agency Committee and the El Paso hearing, neither of which were successful in assuaging Chicano militants.

The legislators most vulnerable to demise as patrónes because they should be most accountable to Chicanos are the five men of Mexican descent now in Congress: a senator from New Mexico; a congressman from California; a congressman from New Mexico; and two other House members from Texas. All have been elected since 1960 and thus as yet hold no powerful committee posts and, apparently, cannot present a united front in regard to certain Chicano interests. The bill granting statutory status and a new name (the Cabinet Committee on Opportunity for the Spanish Speaking) to the Inter-Agency was introduced by Senator Joseph Montoya in the Senate and by Congressman Edward Roybal of California in the House, where it passed by a vote of 315 to 81. One of the dissenters was

Congressman Henry B. Gonzalez of San Antonio. While he may have accurately assessed the bill as "a token, a false hope, and a vague promise," the difference of opinion with his other Mexican American colleagues, one would think, should have been ironed out before a vote was taken. While politics may be the art of compromise, in this case it is questionable which side was the least artful. Political ineptness and division should not be so visible, although it may exist at the highest level of legislative endeavor among Mexican Americans. As perhaps the most public of Mexican American figures, these legislators are also most subject to appraisal; from the Chicano point of view it has not been enough that they have usually followed the party line.

It was Congressman Gonzalez who berated the Mexican American Youth Organizations as "reverse racists" in a forum where the young people had no opportunity to defend themselves against their accuser—not a very democratic procedure for a person dedicated to upholding the basic principles of democracy.

And how do Mexican American legislators stand up for the contribution of the Chicano constituency at war? The best that has been said of the Chicanos being killed in Vietnam is typified by Congressman Roybal, whose Chicano electorate in the 30th Congressional District is around 10 percent of the total. In a House speech on October 8, 1969, the California congressman cited a study by Dr. Ralph Guzman, a political science professor at Merritt College, University of California at Santa Cruz, on "Mexican American Casualties in Vietnam":

Casualties among persons of Mexican American descent so far during the Vietnam War have been more than 50 percent greater than the ratio this minority group bears to our overall population. These somber statistics prove once again that the Spanish surnamed community in the United States has traditionally shouldered its share, and more, of the burden of military service in America.

Congressman Roybal reverted to the superpatriotic rhetoric about Chicanos as if we must continue to prove the loyalty and courage of the Chicano serviceman. But he said nothing about the fact that because of educational and economic deprivation, military service is the only way out of the barrio for many Chicanos. Nor did he point out that Dr. Guzman's study is the basis of a draft-resistance movement spreading among young Chicanos who consider the Vietnam War another form of gringo genocide that works two ways: against the Vietnamese and against the Chicano as well as the black.

Since New Mexico became a state in 1912, politics have incorporated the dominant racial-cultural elements—the Anglo, the Spanish American (a phrase that has enjoyed the most popularity until recently in the state), and the Indian. Almost traditionally, as if by unwritten agreement, the two senate seats have been split between an Anglo and a Spanish American. Such unspoken compromise probably dates back to 1853 when Congress, in its token way, authorized the New Mexico Assembly to hire an interpreter, a translator, and two clerks for each House—the senate and the assembly. Of the four clerks, two were to be qualified in Spanish, the other two in English. Prior to that gesture, the act governing the Territory of New Mexico had overlooked the fact that half the population was of Spanish descent. In spite of this unspoken compromise, which extends into other positions, and in spite of the presence of many Spanish-surname persons in elected or appointive positions, the most affluent and influential levels of government and private enterprise remain Anglo dominated. Chicanos and Indians remain the poorest, the least educated, the least hopeful, and minimally represented. Among many New Mexicans, certainly among Alianza members and other activist Chicanos, Senator Montoya is severely denounced as a Tio Taco. But he is not the only target of such denunciation in the state.

Of overriding importance is that these legislators by and large do not depend on Mexican American votes for their election. Congressman Roybal, as noted, has only a small Chicano constituency. A study by the Mexican American Study Project at UCLA in 1967 showed that Roybal polled 159,562 votes in the 1966 election; total Spanish-surname voter registration amounted to 17,323, a mere 11 percent of total voters registered. Assuming that all registered Spanish-surname voters cast a ballot and voted for Roybal, this still represents less than 10 percent of the electorate in favor of the Chicano legislator. While Roybal is aware of his obligations toward the Chicano community in his district, he also must represent 90 percent of the electorate, which is a mixture of other ethnic groups, conservative and liberal elements, and economically disparate neighborhoods. Ethically, he cannot turn his back on the Chicano voter, but even if Chicano voters turned their collective backs on him, it might not make a bit of difference in his election results. He would still be a winner.

A premonition of the kind of adversity developing for the California congressman, and other Mexican American legislators for that matter, is evident in what may have been a fatal political blunder. Neither Roybal nor any member of his staff formally solicited the endorsement of the Council of Mexican American Unity at the convention in February 1970. As a consequence, the convention voted down an attempt by Roybal supporters to endorse him anyway in his bid for reelection. A young law student, John Costello, reflected the convention's thinking (three Mexican American candidates were endorsed to vie against incumbent Anglo Democrats in state primary elections), saying that in eight years Roybal had been "more or less of a dormant congressman." No Chicano legislator can rest on his laurels these days. In the past he could play the patrón but be wary primarily of the Anglo politician. No more. An Editor's Note in the first edition (May 1970) of *La Raza*, an East Los Angeles magazine sums up what some raza think about Congressman Roybal: "La Raza cannot support Mr. Roybal, the Democratic incumbent and an American of Spanish surname (A.S.S.). Roybal is the classic example of a vendido político." The magazine went on to support Father Blase Bonpane, a Roman Catholic priest and university professor who entered the race for the 30th District seat. "Bonpane is more of a Chicano in spirit and heart," the magazine concluded.

When Congressman Roybal vacated his seat on the Los Angeles City Council after thirteen years to run for the U.S. House of Representatives, the blatant disenfranchisement of Chicano votes was demonstrated to him. Chicano voting strength and CSO voter registrars had given him the decisive edge in 1949 in winning one of the fifteen Los Angeles Council districts which was heavily Chicano. Almost immediately after Roybal left for Washington, the city council districts were revised. Roybal's former "safe" Chicano slot on the council, which he had been assured would remain so, was realigned out of existence. No Chicano has been represented since then, while three black councilmen were placed on the council after it was redistricted—the old divide-and-conquer trick. Roybal recalls that the Democratic party, which was then in the majority at the state capital, had also assured him that redistricting of congressional districts would offer him a sure thing in the 30th District. It did not, he reflects. In fact, he had to have a run-off with another Democrat for the new district seat. Roybal's troubles have eased somewhat. As a result of the 1970 November elections, the Democrats regained control of both state houses. In 1972, when the California Legislature redistricts to allow for new Congressional seats, they might gain a few Chicano votes, not only by assuring Roybal of his position but also by carving out one or two Chicano districts. Roybal will still be in the position of most Mexican American legislators who are most answerable to that portion of the

electorate that is ordinarily more affluent, more conservative, and predominantly Anglo. For the 1970 elections, Roybal was on safe ground, competing against the
same opponent as two years before and winning by
nearly the same two-to-one margin.

In terms of population, California Chicanos are the
least represented of all Southwest Chicano communities
at both the state and national levels. The lone Mexican
American in the 1968–70 session of the California Legislature, Alex P. Garcia of the 40th Assembly District,
was re-elected last November. The only other Chicano
to win an Assembly seat—of two Democrats running
against incumbent Republicans—was Peter Chacon in
the 79th Assembly District. Joseph Montoya had con-
tested for the 50th Assembly District, but fell far short
and lost to William Campbell. Both Chicano candidates
had run in districts of small Mexican American population. The last Mexican American legislator prior to
Garcia's win in 1968 had been erased in a heavily
Republican victory in 1966 (Philip Soto of the 50th Assembly District had lost by 200 votes). Coincidentally,
Garcia's state district represents the half of Congressman Roybal's 30th District which is most heavily Chicano. Since Mexican Americans represent more than 14
percent of the state population, Chicanos proportion-
ately should have sixteen or seventeen legislators in the
state legislature and five or six in the congressional
delegation. (By contrast, the Indiana State Assembly
boasts a Mexican American member, Joe Arredondo,
who represents Lake County, where Gary is located.
One of the handful of large U.S. cities with a Negro
mayor, Gary includes about 18,000 Mexican Americans
and 6,000 Puerto Ricans—in all less than 10 percent of
the electorate.)

While a number of cultural or historical factors may
be alluded to in explaining the underparticipation of
Chicanos in politics, the existence since 1848 of legal or
procedural barriers have been even more decisive in the

development of Chicano attitudes toward political action. Besides, there have been overt instances of voter fraud and discrimination. Only in New Mexico had English not been made a prerequisite (and therefore a barrier) to voting or registering. Yet nothing in the U.S. Constitution requires that the rights contained in the document can be fulfilled or exercised only in the English language. California violated its first constitution, the Treaty of Guadalupe Hidalgo, and the U.S. Constitution when in 1894 it deprived its Spanish-speaking citizens of equal protection of the laws by making English a requirement for registration. From 1894, Puerto Ricans were victims, along with the people of Cuba, Guam, and the Philippines, of another unjustified war against Spain. They were deprived of the right to vote in Spanish until the Supreme Court upheld the Voting Rights Act in *Katzenbach* v. *Morgan,* permitting puertorriqueños in New York to vote in Spanish (June 13, 1966).

In Texas, the poll tax operated detrimentally to citizens least able to afford or least able to derive any worth from paying for the right to vote—the preponderance of Mexican Americans. When the $1.50 poll tax was abolished by the Supreme Court in 1966, Texas imposed other impediments to registering, including that all voters reregister each year; that is, they must obtain an application, fill it out, and mail or file it with the tax assessor's office which in turn processes it and mails back a registration certificate. By a decision in the Corpus Christi District Court in February 1967, mass registrations are illegal. Only the voter himself, his parent, spouse, or child can mail or present the application to the tax assessor and only one application can be mailed at a time. Not only is the registration period very short, from October 1 to January 31, but it ends long before the May primaries and the November elections, which brings up the problem of creating interest so far in advance. Also, many Mexican Americans who take to the migrant stream miss the May primaries; thus they see no need to register. Because the Texas Chicano is included under total white voting-age population, it is difficult to assess precisely overall voting strength among the three-fifths that are registered. Negroes, on the other hand, are defined numerically, with about 400,000 registered out of some 650,000 eligible voters.

While California has not had a poll tax, its English language requirement has proved a most unfair barrier. Not until the early fifties, when the Community Services Organization funded by Saul Alinsky's Industrial Areas Foundation, instigated mass registration drives did the problem of language discrimination become relevant. Mexican Americans who spoke broken or accented English were turned away by Anglo registrars. Next, Mexican Americans were deputized as registrars, but as voter drives persisted, challenges of Mexican Americans at the polls were stepped up as well. During elections in Southern California in 1958, incidents of intimidation by Republican party workers were reported by activist Mexican American observers. Such political adversity, once again, instead of causing the Chicano to retreat, resulted in the formation of groups such as the Mexican American Political Association in 1958 and the Political Association of Spanish-Speaking Organizations in 1961, both ostensibly nonpartisan.

Chicano aggressiveness led to the California Supreme Court's decision on March 24, 1970, declaring that California citizens literate in Spanish or a language other than English may vote in state elections. The court held unanimously that the state constitution requirement that voters be literate in English violated the equal protection clause of the Fourteenth Amendment. Some 100,000 Spanish-speaking persons were affected. Two Chicanos, Jesus E. Parra and Genoveva Castro, both natives of Los Angeles, had been represented by the American Civil Liberties Union of Southern California and California Rural Legal Assistance in the case against the state.

The litigants had also sought the printing of a certain number of ballots in Spanish, but the court balked on that point, which might have led to a full bilingual electoral process. (The California statute was originally imposed in 1891 when Assemblyman A. J. Bledsoe, a member of the Committee of Fifteen, introduced the legislation restricting in the main the free access to the ballot of the Chinese. The Committee of Fifteen had been a vigilante outfit that ousted every Chinese person from Humboldt County in northern California.)

Then came the Kennedy campaign of 1959–60 when Viva Kennedy clubs sprang up all over the country wherever contingents of Mexican Americans or Spanish-speaking communities could be found. Puerto Ricans were also swept along in the tide. Among Mexican Americans the overwhelming sentiment was with the Democratic candidate. Leadership among the prominent organizations that had developed statewide followings—MAPA and CSO in California, and PASSO in Texas; or national status such as the G.I. Forum and the LULACs—fitted smoothly into the Kennedy apparatus. The Irish, Catholic, northeastern presidential contender tried for every vote, and undoubtedly the Mexican Americans turned out to vote for Kennedy as they had done for no one else. That Kennedy won and that Chicanos had made a difference were the two most important facts for those Chicanos who had registered fellow Chicanos, distributed leaflets, sold buttons, planned fiestas, and helped people reach the polls on election night. Chicano expectations soared with Kennedy's victory. They knew the political realities of patronage and favors. However, immediate results did not develop. The side effect, of course, was the election of Mexican American legislators to Congress: Gonzalez in 1961, Roybal in 1962, and Eligio de la Garza from Texas in 1964. Senator Montoya gained the Senate in 1964 replacing Fabian Chavez, a native New Mexican who abdicated the seat to run for governor against a ten-year resident of the state, David Cargo, the eventual winner.

In no instance did the Mexican American vote alone assure a Mexican American's victory. As far as constituency is concerned, the four legislators are answerable to economic and social forces controlled by the Anglo.

Not surprisingly, the basic political requirement for Mexican Americans to be elected necessitates nearly 100 percent registration, nearly perfect turnout at the polls, and, if possible, adherence to only one Mexican American candidate. Fundamental politics. Fundamental problems: Chicanos heavily populate a certain section of town, but districting, either intentional by gerrymander or coincidental, cuts up the concentration to the degree that the Chicano vote is diluted for all but ward or internal district elections; or, where Mexican Americans predominate, registration is small and difficult to increase, such as in Chicago; or a Mexican American candidate confronts another Mexican American in a primary contest that results in both being eliminated because the Chicano vote is split—and an Anglo becomes the Chicano's only choice of a candidate. A five-state review of the 1966 elections by the UCLA Mexican American Study Project bears out this general profile:

In Arizona, three liberal Democrats survived a Republican onslaught but two others were defeated for the House; Joseph Castillo, a Democrat from Pima County gained a Senate seat.

In California, 14 Mexican Americans vied for the state legislature, but mainly ran against each other, splitting the Chicano vote which eliminated them in primaries and which later resulted in a defeat in the final elections.

In Colorado, lone Mexican American legislator, State Senator Roger Sisneros, was returned for a second term. The new Hispano Party, a third party effort was incepted by Mexican Americans but carried only the home county of their gubernatorial candidate, Levi Martinez.

In New Mexico, several defeats were suffered of Spanish American candidates due to a major Republican turnout; one

Mexican American Democrat lost to a Mexican American Republican.

In Texas, Mexican Americans increased their representation in the State Legislature, retaining five incumbents but electing four more to the House and their first Senator, Joe Bernal of San Antonio to the 31-member Senate—all this in spite of a splinter group, Mexican American Democrats, and John Tower's massive win.

Arizona exemplifies the confused picture that politics presents to Chicanos. In last November's voting, Raul Castro, former ambassador to Bolivia and El Salvador, led the incumbent governor, Jack Williams, a Republican, until late precincts and absentee ballots for Maricopa County (Phoenix) came in and deprived him of what would have been a remarkable upset. While heavily Republican in state and congressional allegiance, voting GOP for governor since the mid-1950s, certain areas are widely divergent in the ballot-box results. In the 1st Congressional District comprising Maricopa County, that is, Phoenix, Republicans polled 140,000 votes in the 1964 presidential election; 102,000 in the 1966 congressional election; then up to 137,000 in 1968. Democrats amassed 113,000 votes in 1964; dropped to 49,000 votes in the off-year election; but regained their losses only up to 54,000 votes two years later. By contrast, the 3rd District went Democratic 86,000, against 60,000 Republican votes in 1964; experienced an off-year drop to 66,000, as did the Republicans to 45,000; but when 1968 came around, cast 102,000 Democratic ballots, while the opposition slipped again by 2,000 votes. In the last general elections, a Mexican American House member moved up to the Senate, but another Mexican American lost his House seat to a Negro candidate.

Mexican American voters and Indian voters could have a strong effect on some county governments. In Apache County, for example, the two groups together represent 75 percent of the electorate—if they were

fully registered. The influx of retirees from all over the
country who settle in the warm and dry Arizona climate
may be a serious factor in undercutting Chicano influence particularly in rural-suburban areas where, before,
Chicanos had been holding their own with a regular
upkeep of their population through births and immigrants. Could Arizona ever elect a Mexican American to
the United States Congress or to a high state office? The
question now seems highly speculative, especially in the
light of Raul Castro's defeat and the threat Chicanos
face from the redistricting that will probably hit by the
1972 elections.

The 1970 census population figures will result in the
realignment of congressional districts in some states.
Three southwest states, Arizona, California, and Texas,
stand to gain several House seats. The redrawing of
boundaries could directly affect Chicano votes on the
national level. In the case of Congressman Roybal, his
already meager Chicano constituency may be whittled
down even more and may even cause him serious trouble in achieving reelection. Statewide, California may
gain as many as six House seats up to a total of 44: there
are at present 23 Democrats and 15 Republicans in the
delegation. Arizona and Texas may gain one House seat
each, the former for a total of four seats where there are
now two Republicans and one Democrat, and the latter
up to 25 where only three Republican congressmen are
now members of a 24-man delegation. Expected to stay
the same are Colorado: four seats, three Democrats;
Nevada: one, a Democrat; and New Mexico and Utah:
two each, all Republicans. California and Arizona Chicanos can expect little political gain in terms of congressional input; the odds are dead set against Chicano
voting power being consolidated into new districts.
And, as the evidence shows, Chicano votes will probably be diluted on the state district level. The tragedy for
us is that Chicanos will have almost nothing to say in
the matter. National forces beyond our control will

grind us down. Population growth and shifts, our own migration, a polarization of conservative forces regardless of party label—all combine to deprive Chicanos of national and state representation. Finally, Chicanos will suffer from the loss within a given area of population, particularly in rural areas. Consequently, Chicanos will find it difficult or nearly impossible to affect political decisions in the city and in the country. The Chicano is left with only one possible role to play—the swing vote or the third party. In this regard, Chicanos can turn their limited power potential to their advantage, if they would understand it as such, by seeking to control the balance of power. In certain city districts or smaller towns, Chicanos may still wield the preponderance of power.

The taking of raw political power at the grass roots level has been an experience of somewhat ambiguous value to the Chicano. Examples of Chicano political assertion occurred in Crystal City in 1963 and in Mathis in 1965; both were takeovers of city governments in Texas. Crystal City, about 80 percent Mexican American, was shortlived as a Chicano political bastion. A result of PASSO voter stimulation, Crystal City authority was regained by Anglos in a couple of years due largely to the Chicanos' inexperience in the political process and to their failure to establish economic resources and control. The Action party instituted by Mathis' Chicanos, 70 percent of the city population, maintained its leadership into the 1968 local elections when three of the four city council seats were lost to Anglos, who had formed a counter organization, the Area Citizens. Action party spokesmen charged that the presence of sheriff's men and Texas Rangers outside the courthouse on election day had discouraged Chicano voters. During the 1965 elections, Manuel Chavez, who was elected city commissioner, reported that welfare recipients were warned about being dropped from welfare rolls if they were seen at the polls; surplus food supplies were curtailed from two to three weeks in ad-

vance of the election; cars were ticketed for minor
mechanical defects on the day of election; voting officials confused voters by asking if they had property as if
it were a prerequisite to voting; voting booths were not
provided, which forced people to vote in view of others.
Inexperience, coupled with lack of singleness of purpose, had led to fragmentation among Action party
members and the eventual downfall at the polls in
1968.

While the Crystal City and Mathis debacles were
rather thorough and have discouraged some people
from similar attempts, they have the more positive
effect of proving that organized, purposeful, and prin-
cipled Chicano political action can result in the acquisi-
tion of fundamental political authority. However, the
concomitant lesson learned was that sheer power without practical knowledge of how to manipulate it, increase it, and confirm it, is of little value. These two
experiences were preliminary attempts at the formula-
tion of a third-party tactic. The next such attempt may
be the culmination of the experiments in Chicano takeovers and may lead to a substantial political reconfigur-
ation of South Texas and, in turn, other Chicano communities.

The period 1960–68 embodied the Chicano's first
full-fledged introduction to national and state politics.
Chicano representation increased in the United States
Congress. In certain states Chicano legislators showed a
marked sophistication and expectation of permanency
in their positions, and in a couple of instances Chicanos
surprised the Anglo (and, it seems, themselves as well)
in wresting some government control from gringo
hands. That took place under Democratic party patron-
ismo. Chicanos had a hand in persuading the Texas
governor and the president to sit out the next few years.
And when Richard Nixon defeated Hubert Humphrey,
the myth of the Chicanos as one-party supporters was
discredited, if ever so slightly.

The Chicano was to learn very soon, however, that

politics under a Democrat or Republican differed not in the slightest. As a campaign consultant to Richard Nixon's California gubernatorial attempt in 1962 remarked shortly after the doleful Nixon defeat, "Neither the Democrats nor Republicans take Mexican Americans seriously." The Nixon advisor, Arthur Sutton, added that the Republican party had long ago written off the Mexican American vote as lost. "Fragmentation of the Mexican American community has allowed Democratic leaders to count on Mexican American votes without the bother of having to take their views into consideration when making party policy or when passing out patronage." Matters hadn't changed very much in 1968. Many Mexican Americans had crossed party lines to vote for Ronald Reagan for California governor, mostly in protest against Governor Edmund Brown. By early 1968, a group called California Latin American Republican Organization had been formed by leading Mexican American GOP party members whose fortunes had risen with the election of Reagan as California's governor. A Texas Mexican American, Celso Moreno, who had campaigned in years past for Democrats, had worked as a political organizer for John Tower in his Senate campaign of 1966. He became director of Spanish-speaking affairs for the Republican National Committee and spearheaded the Viva Nixon element of the GOP presidential effort in 1968. A strange thing happened on the way to the White House as far as Mexican Americans are concerned. The president's first appointment of a Mexican American to a high-level government post involved a registered Democrat, Martin G. Castillo of Los Angeles. It almost seems that the Nixon administration had chosen Castillo purposely to break up Mexican American forces in the party, for the appointment immediately ignited GOP opposition from California to Texas. Castillo had campaigned for Nixon in California, but Ray Garcia, a former field representative to the then Lieutenant Governor Robert Finch, said that Castillo had merely appeared on some panel shows with Nixon filmed in New York. A *Los Angeles Times* article on April 30, 1969, quotes Garcia: "Castillo lied to me and other Republicans to place himself in the position where he might be appointed to an important position." Castillo was formally named by the president to head the Inter-Agency and to serve as deputy director of the U.S. Commission on Civil Rights on May 27. Two days later, Commissioner Ximenes transferred the keys to the Inter-Agency to Castillo in a brief ceremony with about thirty Mexican Americans in his top-story office six floors above the Inter-Agency offices. Castillo, revealing his naïveté, admitted he was a registered Democrat but stressed that all of us there in the office were "neither Democrats nor Republicans"; rather that we were all fighting for one cause, la raza. Someone, not an employee of the Inter-Agency, expressed concern as to the job futures of the present staff. Castillo retorted that he and his nucleus of staff aides would be foolhardy to act rashly regarding dismissal of staff; and sure enough, it took about three months to clean house of most of the former personnel. Expectedly, Castillo then spent the majority of his time and energy in developing and promoting the Inter-Agency, bringing about statutory authority, and establishing an annual budget for its first year of a half-million dollars.

Other early Nixon appointments of Mexican Americans led to controversy in Texas. Albert Fuentes, Jr., of San Antonio, who was named special assistant to the Small Business Administration's new director, Hilary Sandoval, had turned to the Republican party in the early sixties and had organized the Viva Nixon promotions in 1968. In May 1969 he lost his job when he was indicted in the San Antonio Federal Court on conspiracy to defraud the federal government. Veteran Democrat Gil Pompa, also of San Antonio, had been appointed to a high-ranking post with the Community Relations Service (CRS) of the Department of Justice.

He had been involved in a complaint charging him with racial discrimination against two administrators being hired by the Edgewood School District in San Antonio. Pompa, then an Edgewood School Board member, had insisted on persons with Spanish surnames being hired to fill summer school administration positions. Pompa has since been promoted to Associate Director of CRS, the third ranking official of that agency.

That same month, Celso Moreno came under fire from prominent Republican leaders when he attended the Del Rio rally protesting the ouster of VISTA workers from Val Verde County. He was criticized for having sat on the speakers' platform, conversing with the militant Chicanos, and carrying a sign that urged: Vote Republican. Moreno has since been replaced by John Lopez of San Jose, described by a fellow Republican, a Chicano, as a John Birch member with strong anti-Democratic party prejudices. The Republican National Committee in Washington, D.C., filled its national slot of special assistant on Spanish-speaking affairs with Hugo Perez, a native of Guatemala who has lived in the United States since 1941. He was appointed to the position on January 8, 1970. Perez, by the way, believes in "dissolving the minorities into the mainstream of American life," and the learning of English as the ultimate solution to bringing about that goal.

Richard Nixon did fulfill a number of promises that he had made during the campaign, particularly in regard to placing Mexican Americans in high administrative positions, something neither Kennedy nor Johnson had ever done beyond a token one or two. A White House staff aide opening never materialized, although Republican Mexican Americans had argued for a spot there. As early as January 22, two days after Nixon was inaugurated, a Corpus Christi lawyer, Tony Bonilla, a legal counsel of LULAC, headed an eight-man panel in a Washington press conference criticizing the Nixon Administration for forgetting its promises. A White

House staff position was insisted upon and Moreno was named as a prime possibility. But it seems the White House is adamant against even having a Mexican American associated with its white portals. In July 1969 the Bureau of the Census sought me out for a special assignment that required me to photograph various Mexican American notables in Washington and throughout the country, and Mexican Americans in various walks of life in the Midwest and Southwest. Grace Olivarez of Phoenix was doing the text for a pamphlet directed to Mexican Americans. When we called the White House for permission to photograph Castillo either inside or with the White House in the background, we were told, "Absolutely not, and that's all there is to it." Our intent had been to show Castillo's relationship to the White House as a special advisor on Mexican American affairs, but instead we stirred up all the existing taboos.

Another Nixon promise come true was the appointment of Hilary Sandoval, an El Paso news distributor and Nixon supporter, to head the Small Business Administration. Sandoval, among many other Republicans, had been hopeful of a White House Conference on Mexican Americans, but, fortunately, that never materialized. The thought of another fiasco such as the 1967 El Paso affair is too much to wish on any administration, but such a recurrence should not be inflicted in particular on the Chicano. Besides, Chicanos have had their fill of government-sponsored conferences; the Johnson-promoted hearings in El Paso were a window dressing and a conscience-salving outlet for that administration, and there is no reason to believe that a White House conference under Nixon would be any different. A few months after they had been confirmed in their posts, Castillo and Enrique "Hank" Quevedo (executive director of the Cabinet Committee on Opportunity for the Spanish Speaking, who had run unsuccessfully for the California assembly in the 48th District), and other staff people became intent on convening a conference of

federal employees of Mexican American background in
the Washington, D.C., area. The plan was rather
naively instigated in the belief that a very green squad
of Inter-Agency Republicans in a still very Democratic
environment, relative to Mexican American allegiances,
could pull off such a conference, with a kind of gentle-
man's agreement that everyone would really try to help.
Scheduled for the weekend of July 26, the plans for
gathering perhaps a hundred Mexican Americans at a
site in Annapolis, Maryland, at about twenty-five dollars
a head fell through when a number of those invited
flatly refused. The ambiguity of attending as nonfederal
employees, which meant that dozens of high-priced
consultants were being hired for free, or as federal employees, which meant submitting reports or acquiring
permission to attend a meeting which had the aura of a
clandestine convocation, could not be resolved to satisfy
enough of the Mexican Americans involved. The gathering was postponed, and apparently the idea has gone
the route of a White House conference—to oblivion.

The conclusion many Chicanos have reached is that
neither party has treated the Chicano seriously or honestly in all the years we have dutifully followed the
patrón's lead. This has resulted in an insurgent element
—the third party—against old-style politics. Third parties are not new to American politics; the last presidential election demonstrated what a third party can do to
national alliances. But the concept is quite new to the
Chicano and reflects the overall revolution that is occurring within the Chicano community against gringo
ways.

The value of a third-party force from the Chicano
vantage point stems from the reality of U.S. politics and
the so-called two-party system. The two major factions
exist in essence as mutual perpetrators of a lie. That lie
is that one party upholds tenets different in some way
from the other's and that each relates to a different constituency. The parties exist to give the impression that

the needs of one or more segments of society are being
served by one party, but being deferred or ignored by
the other. Actually, the parties serve only their own
needs, which are satisfied by keeping people in a state
of suspension. The reality of political-social life in the
United States is that two major segments of society are
served for good or bad by either party at one time or
another; seldom are both served simultaneously; and
never is one served without the other suffering very real
—or at least a sense of—material and psychic deprivation. The most general description, a cliché now, is the
distinction between the haves (los que tienen) and the
have-nots (los que no tienen). To say that the difference is merely economic is simplistic and misses the
subtle nuances. The haves and their elected representatives of either party seek to retain the status quo or, if
possible, cause a retrogression of the status of the opposite segment, the have-nots. This is the usual procedure
which operates in America. It has little to do with party
affiliation; the Democrats have deceived and exploited
the Chicano people as much as the Republicans, although the Democrats have a greater debt to repay.
The Democrats have relied on the Chicano vote as a
sure thing, have divided Chicano political aspirations
when they posed a threat, and have never rewarded
adequately Chicanos' allegiance with a share of the
dividends of political success—recognition, inclusion in
decision-making, and patronage. Alliances with the two
forces known as the Democratic or Republican parties
on the level of the haves are decided on the criteria of
wealth, social standing, vested interests, and racial or
cultural supremacy; rarely are alliances made on the
basis of intellect or sensitiveness toward honesty, justice,
and equality. The third force, or the Third World, consequently, is composed of the poor, the social outcasts,
Chicanos, blacks, Indians, hippies, intellectuals, and
artists—a few exceptions notwithstanding. The two
major parties have guaranteed to each other, informally

of course, that one or the other will win an election, if
not this year, then the next. Only a semblance of change
has ever taken place. *Washington Post* columnist Nicholas Von Hoffman recently made a pungent comment
that the only thing that has changed about Richard
Nixon's promises is that they're about different things.
Otherwise, the insincerity, the dishonesty, the cynicism,
and the indifference remain the same.

The parties have assured themselves a livelihood by
limiting the choice of candidates—two. A third party,
whether it is Wallacite or Chicano (the objectives of
these two are basically similar although different in the
extreme as to motivation) runs counter to all the artificial structures and feigned ideologies the parties have
laboriously fabricated and cynically preached for decades. The defection of a Strom Thurmond, for example,
is grounded not on ideological disillusion or a conservative reawakening but on unvarnished political expedi-
ency. The truth of this from the Chicano experience is
the admission of a few Mexican Americans that they
have changed party labels because "the Republicans
were bound to get into the White House eventually."
They figured their chances were better than even to
achieve high rank—that's political realism, and I have
no quarrel with it whether a Thurmond or Fulano de
Tal is involved. The point is that Americans are deceived by party loyalties.

A writer on American politics, Walter D. Burnham,
Associate Professor of Political Science at Washington
University, asks in *Trans-Action* magazine:

Bathed in the warm glow of diffused affluence, vexed in spirit
but enriched economically by our imperial military and space
commitments, confronted by the gradually unfolding consequences of social change as vast as it is unplanned, what need
have Americans of political parties? More precisely, why do
they need parties whose structures, processes, and leadership
cadres seem to grow more remote and irrelevant to each new
crisis?

The disappearance of the parties, he warns, "as active intermediaries would only entail the unchallenged ascendancy of the already powerful, unless new structures of collective power were somehow developed to replace them." The already powerful, of course, have already come to power, and only "new structures of collective power," carefully conceived and nurtured in the proper seedbed—that is, at the local levels of political function, the cities and counties—can counter such forces, if not replace them. Historical evidence from America's political past shows that there is a tendency for "critical realignments" when parties are created or cease to exist, and a trend toward "electoral disaggregation," that is, the breakdown of party affiliation altogether. Burnham states:

American politics in its normal state is the negation of public order itself, as that term is understood in politically developed nations. We do not have government in our domestic affairs so much as "non rule." We do not have political parties as understood elsewhere in the Western world; we have anti-parties instead. Power centrifuges rather than power concentrators, they have been immensely important not as vehicles of social transformation but for its prevention through political means.

Burnham perceives that the common recurrence of third parties is evidence of the lack of political development since the Civil War. But, significantly, each rise of a strong third party has prefigured the realignment of the electorate. George Wallace's American Independent Party is an obvious current illustration, and the Raza Unida party, formed in early 1970 in Texas, forecasts the kinds of reassessment and revision of party alliances which may occur, at least in the Southwest. The Raza Unida party may signal the downfall of the Democratic (Dixiecratic) party in Texas. If 1970 didn't fragment and disperse Democratic alliances in Texas, 1972 should provide the quietus to a party which for a long time has been "remote and irrelevant" to political but nonparty developments in the state. Simply put, the people have been moving away from the parties, certainly the Democratic party, and the party leadership has just not been able to cope with or understand the movement. In fact, the appointment of Connally as Secretary of the Treasury under a Republican Administration points to the serious slippage that has already taken place.

Illustrative of the political-party lie is the existence of hundreds of "political" prisoners in the United States. These are political captives in the sense that they are victims of a process of government and opinion forming which has placed them outside the majority of citizens, government, and media. In that regard, they are non-political or nonpartisan, but according to the practices of politics, they do operate politically, that is, dealing with individuals or institutions to bring about change or no change. If all the militant Chicanos and blacks, the Indians on Alcatraz and in jails, the antiwar protesters, and the draft dodgers in Canada and elsewhere were counted, the number would reach the thousands. In suppression of Los Siete de La Raza in San Francisco, the Chicago Eight, the D.C. Nine, the New York Eight, the Biltmore Six, Reies Tijerina, Eldridge Cleaver in exile, and Huey Newton, nonpartisanship is the order of the day on Capitol Hill and across the country.

The third party is the party of the have-nots; but it also attracts the will-nots, those people who will no longer serve either party because neither party has served the people. A pertinent raza metaphor current in Chicano thought regarding third-party insurgence describes the American political system as a two-headed snake which feeds from two plates at once. The phrase, two-party system, embodies the admission that we are confronted by one system that is manipulated by two factions whose most obvious distinguishing features are the differences in the two dumb animals they have aptly adopted as symbols.

Most third-party movements, such as New Mexico's

in 1966 and Mathis' in 1965 were given short shrift in the political grinder by both major parties. A recent development in four counties of South Texas promotes the sense of cultural nationalism inspired by the concept of la raza under the name of Raza Unida party. A Texas law permits the activities of a third party at the county level as long as the party can get the notarized signatures of 3 percent of the voters in the last general election. Hidalgo County, which is more than half Mexican American, as an example, involved the solicitation of about twelve hundred persons; the others, Zavala, Dimmit, and La Salle counties, each required signatures from about eighty to one hundred people. Thus on the basis of numbers, the Raza Unida experiment seemed small scale. However, just as in the past incidents in Crystal City and Mathis, Texas, and in New Mexico where in his home county the gubernatorial aspirant could have run for any office apparently and won it hands down, on a limited scale Chicanos tend to vote heavily for their own when they have a choice. Raza Unida party leaders theorize that their movement applies pressure on both major party candidates beyond the county level to pay attention to their demands. In the past, they relate, Democrats or Republicans paid them solely for signing up Chicano people, but provided no resources for Chicanos to move up in party ranks and assert influence in party matters, including where campaign money was spent and for whom, and who the final party candidates would be.

The Raza Unida party dispenses with primaries, in which most other Texans decide their party affiliation by voting in one or the other party's primary. Instead, a Raza Unida party nominating convention was held May 2, 1970, at the time of the regular primaries in each of the four counties. Each Raza Unida county organization operates autonomously, that is, democratically. Candidates elected at these conventions run in the general election, thus saving primary campaign funds for the major competition in November. Runoffs among party candidates are also avoided. Because those signing for third party eligibility cannot vote in the primaries anyway by state law, Raza Unida organizers were careful to recruit signatures mainly from migrant workers who would ordinarily have gone al norte by primary time, but who would return by the general election.

In the four-county area, some 80,000 votes, at most, were at stake, from which Senator Ralph Yarborough had derived 14 percent of his electorate in 1964. In the spring primary, however, the U.S. Senate liberal from Texas lost by a wide margin to Lloyd Bentsen. His re-election bid fell on an off year; that is, voting tends to drop from a presidential election year. Raza Unida adherents were instructed to cross party lines; just as Republicans in the past have voted in Democratic primaries to knock off an aspiring Chicano candidate, Raza Unida voters could have voted for Yarborough. While Chicanos were given the dubious credit for the first time of having such power as to defeat a U.S. senator, Yarborough was hurt most by his detractors and enemies within the Democratic party rather than by Raza Unida partisans. Quite likely, Bentsen gained many GOP crossovers in the primaries, for the GOP senatorial candidate ran uncontested.

A strong effort to attract a large turnout of Republican voters and to win over Chicano defectors from the Democratic ranks was a promising strategy of the Republican Senate aspirant, Congressman George Bush. The pressure formerly burdening Yarborough to get out the Chicano vote to offset Republican inroads fell on Bentsen. Texas Democrats were facing the possibility, for the first time since Reconstruction, that their state might be without a Democratic senator in Washington. The Republicans, on the other hand, had fielded a formidable slate: from Paul Eggers, the gubernatorial opponent of Preston Smith, to Edward Yturri, a Corpus Christi lawyer, unopposed in the primary and vying for attorney general. Bentsen beat his Republican opponent handily nevertheless.

Raza Unida organizers had been banking on Democrats eliminating each other in primaries and then picking up the pieces to strengthen their hand. They figured that whichever way the primaries and state elections might go, there will be disaffected voters who would turn to the third party, which would present a united front with a Chicano candidate. Whereas Chicanos may be competing in primaries, even against each other, the loser and his following can be persuaded to back the Raza Unida candidate and at least reap some of the benefits of siding with a winner. In almost every county contest—county judge, county commissioners (four), county treasurer, county clerk, county attorney, and some justices of the peace who represent districts in a county—a Chicano name will show under a separate column for the Raza Unida party. The Chicano voter will not have to choose between two Anglos as usual, whether one is a Democrat or not. At present there are about seventeen Texas counties where the Chicanos constitute over half the population; each county is a prime target for a takeover through a third-party organization.

Third party advocates, such as José Angel Gutiérrez, underwent tests in municipal and school board elections in the May primaries. Gutiérrez, for example, won chairmanship of the school board in Crystal City and did not waste much time in making an impact by ordering the firing of several teachers and a school principal on complaints of racial prejudice alleged by Mexican Americans. Another of the Raza Unida victories, which also occurred in Carrizo Springs and Cotulla, was the election of a former schoolteacher, Alfredo Zamora, as mayor of Cotulla. Former President Lyndon Johnson was fond of telling Mexican American groups that he had spent some happy years teaching in the "Mexican" school in Cotulla. Zamora, coincidentally, taught at that same school. After being elected mayor, he led a Chicano protest against the city school board in early September 1970, seeking reform of the local, segregated school system. Board members responded by pairing the Mexican and Anglo schools, so that half the grades go to one school now and the other half to another, regardless of whether they live on the "right" or "wrong" side of the tracks.

Zamora, Gutiérrez, and the many others who represented the Raza Unida party (both successfully and unsuccessfully for elected office) were conspicuous by their youth and educational achievement. Zamora, for example, was the first mayor of Cotulla to have a college degree, not to mention the first to have a Chicano surname. Nominees of the Raza Unida party in Hidalgo County included Alejandro Moreno, a graduate of the University of Texas, for county judge, an administrative not a judiciary position; Homero Martinez, a Vietnam veteran attending Pan American College, for county treasurer; and Ramon Vitela, also a Vietnam returnee and Pan American college student, for county clerk. Their youth and advanced schooling were in sharp contrast to their incumbent opponents. Their very youth suggests inexperience, which requires expert advice to overcome. Chicano elected officials need to form their own organization and tap foundation resources to be able to hire consultants and staff people who can help them govern well, something which their former opponents were unable or unwilling to do.

Raza Unida party ambitions are tied in with the most militant elements of the youthful activists in the South Texas area. They have usually found, along with some of the elder Chicano statesmen including Bexar County Commissioner Albert Peña of San Antonio, and Senator Joe Bernal that state and national political figures have been unresponsive to local demands, ideas, and aspirations. The only way to assure high-level attention to grass-roots needs is to deprive the comforta-

ble políticos of the security they once had in certain
districts. Even near misses in certain elections in 1970
here only set the stage for stronger confrontations in the
next presidential election year, a year that may turn
Texas politics completely upside down—with Chicanos
pushing as hard as anyone.

Victories at the local level must first of all be confirmed by providing visible returns to the Chicano
community, and, in turn, to the whole populace, as soon
as possible. The tendency would be to wipe out all Anglo patronage that previous administrations have
handed out. This would be unwise, first because the
Raza Unida party should not itself be discriminatory; it
should distinguish between persons in office with skills
that are useful and the unskilled. Second, it would be
unwise because, according to the white man's game,
keeping a few token Anglos within the official framework could blunt later attacks and even serve to divide
the Anglos, as they have sought to divide Chicanos in
the old game they once controlled.

The potential for change in a Chicano-controlled
enclave of four South Texas counties is awesome. In
fact, the most immediate danger Raza Unida party
leaders face is the threat of overextending themselves in
their own ambitions and haste to bring about radical
change. Some of the projections cited by Raza Unida
spokesmen include: volume buying to equip coopera-
tively county and municipal offices, schools, and other
facilities and even city services; adoption of new taxing
systems that would benefit the poor but put the burden
where it can be most easily handled, on the rich farmer
or businessman; change in the conduct of the agencies
of justice, including the selection of grand juries and the
appointment of citizen police review boards. Theorists
behind the Raza Unida faction take special pains to assure that Chicano control will not mean that only Chicanos gain from political takeovers. In one sense, Chicanos should reap the initial benefits, for in any system

where discrimination of one group has been a fact of life for generations, simple equity will not guarantee Chicanos material opportunity and civil rights. Third-party Chicanos will have to attempt massive and concentrated efforts to redistribute opportunity and the resources of each community so that Chicanos will experience the tangible success of their political coming of age.

The most serious error that Raza Unida party proponents could make, I believe, is to advance into such a powerful or safe position of control that the party itself would become stultified and unresponsive to fresh ideas and younger voices. The party might think seriously of including the principle of "no reelection" for their officers and candidates, from the lowest elected or even appointive positions to the highest.

Relentlessly, the next step is to build a network of third-party organizations, developing the same kind of local-level strength throughout the numerous barrios in the nation. With a framework of pro-Chicano, nonpartisan enclaves, Chicanos could exert a true third-party force which could make or break political candidates in every southwestern state. If we cannot have the power to elect whom we wish, we may be able to keep a particular candidate from winning election; the next time candidates are chosen, the experience of the past may provide the lever to break a party central committee's hold on local politics. The time when Chicanos can wield such terrible power may be a long way off, but the coalition of the have-nots and will-nots as an inevitable force in American politics is not far off. The Liberal party in New York, which retained Mayor John Lindsay, although an unexportable New York phenomenon, indicates that the concept is replicable and desirable. The major parties can respond from the town to the state level with sound programs and well-financed opportunities for Chicano involvement, with campaign moneys and postelection patronage.

For the time being, the parties are involved only in token acquiescence to Chicano demands. I see no reason to believe that either national party will ever take the Chicano seriously until Chicanos get off the party bandwagons, establish a negotiating bloc as a third party, and, through the undisguised assertion of Chicano nationalism, engage in nonpartisan coalitions with other groups to achieve a measure of equity. Raza Unida, the concept and the party, has the potential to effect change for Chicanos because it is founded on a movement that is nationwide. The movement toward a national identity was weak and poorly articulated five years ago, but is now the motivation and rationale for Chicano uprisings all over the United States.

For the first time, a ground swell of indignation exists among Chicanos toward the "normal" processes of government, which actually are abnormalities forced upon us by the gringo. It is only natural that insurgence against the political system become a fundamental target for change in the Chicano's liberation strategy. I perceive the very defection of Mexican Americans from the Democratic party to the Republican party, not only as political realism but as a sign that Chicanos will not be politically classified as only one party by the gringo. Of itself, party realignment expresses the Chicano revolt, but the danger is that there are generally not enough who move over to the Republican party, and the few who do, are easily co-opted, bought out, sometimes with a high government post; the overall effect is to diminish Chicano cohesiveness. A few Mexican Americans become the Chicano community to the administration in power; the same thing happened during the administrations of Kennedy and Johnson. Johnson co-opted a certain California-Texas axis of powers; Nixon, a different Southern California-Texas combine. Both elaborations of the window-dressing Mexican American motif were instituted in the Inter-Agency Committee, which is now the Cabinet Committee on

Opportunity for the Spanish-Speaking, a presumptuous mouthful. As soon as the Inter-Agency passed into the Cabinet Committee, it went from an ineffective, power-less, temporary agency to an ineffective, powerless, permanent agency—for five years anyway. It assumed the same stature as the EEOC and the Commission on Civil Rights, notwithstanding the comments of former Executive Director Hank Quevedo who said, "We needed the continuity and commitment reflected in our authorizing legislation to insure that the whims of the moment do not override a systematic long-range thrust." That's political jargon which, translated, means that now it will probably take the Cabinet Committee five years to accomplish something—or nothing. As for the Democrats, I've heard that the National Democratic Committee has been looking for a full-time Chicano or-ganizer for some time, but with an $8–$12 million debt and committee chairman problems, Chicanos can expect the NDC to fumble around in its collective pocket for loose change with which to finance Chicano politicking for some time to come; we can expect even very little lip service from the Democrats.

Finally, political truth for Chicanos lies not in party affiliation but in the assumption of power as a people united under the banner of Raza Unida. Where Chi-canos hold the majority of voting power, they should control the offices and functions of power; where Chi-canos wield the balance of power as a third-party force, they should exert this authority for the good of the Chicano pueblo; where Chicanos are a minor segment of the electorate, they can still influence government through concentrated and united effort and through utilizing the assistance of stronger raza party units in the next town, the next county, or the next state.

Given the burgeoning power of the Chicano mys-tique, there is every reason to expect Chicanos to exert extraordinary leverage, even beyond our numbers, on politics at every level. And should Mexican Americans gain power in a predominantly Chicano region such as South Texas, northern New Mexico, and various parts of Arizona, Colorado, and California, the possibility of the creation of Chicano city-states becomes less of a hope and more of a crucial and real decision to be made by Chicanos in the seventies.

A great many problems are yet to be ironed out, and the bits and pieces of revolution must be set in motion. More walkouts are occurring, farm labor strikes are spreading, police belligerency is mounting, the number of political prisoners is multiplying, and new approaches to obtaining power for the Chicano people in politics and in other problem areas are developing. The assassination of John F. Kennedy dispirited many Chicanos; then the murder of his brother, Robert F. Kennedy, even as Chicanos stood at his side; and the shooting of Martin Luther King, Jr., took a heavy psychological toll among our people. The Chicano could see clearly the America he sought to challenge for equal standing and what it could do to people who sought to change the nation. With despondent eyes he looked deeply into the miasma that was his country's soul. The Chicano revolt has a long history; we have barely outlined it here. Only within the sixties has it grown in power and breadth into a major force in American society. The future direction of the Chicano people will have much to do with the future of America.

14

NEW STRATEGIES FOR THE SEVENTIES

WHEN the national magazines, newspapers, and electronic media offered their traditional end-of-the-decade reviews in January 1970, a people who had begun an awful struggle to free themselves from the gringo world and establish a unique identity in the Americas merited not one mention. The Chicano people should not permit this indifference to continue in the 1970s. The seventies should become the decade of the Chicano.

Not that the Anglo media are the bench marks of success, but they reflect the national thinking, or, rather, the lack of concern of the dominant society for the Mexican American. A Chicano once described to me a visit he paid to an Eastern newspaper editor's office: on the wall behind the news executive was a long sheet of paper with about twenty categories, beginning with inflation, Vietnam, crime, and so on, with blacks and urban decay nearly last; the Chicano had not even impressed the editor as deserving of a place on the scroll. Whenever an "interpretative" news article, that is, an article by an Anglo about Chicanos, has appeared in recent months, one or another of the various aspects of the liberation movement is given emphasis to the detri-

276

ment of the overall effort under way. Gringo books and articles about Chicanos tend to create new stereotypes as much as they seek to catch the "color" of, say, the Tijerina led, land grants movement or Chavez' unionization drive. Articles will emphasize Chavez sitting in a rocking chair (like President Kennedy's) due to ailments that developed from his long fast; or another will dwell on Tijerina's being called King Tiger, which is only very slightly derived from his name. A recent book about la raza was reviewed in the syndicated *Book World* section under the title, "I Am Not a Boy," which is the way in which the reviewer defined the word *Chicano*. And when a news article does try to tell the full story, it is squelched: for example, a story by Associated Press features writer Dave Smith, on Chicano power, was withdrawn from publication after it had been wired to subscribers for August 13, 1967, release. The followup wire from AP killing the story read: "Focus questioned. It may be reinstated in another form in the future." Smith merely considered the Chicano's deliberation of the "rewards for rioting" which Negroes had gained recently and what alternatives that left the Chicano. Could there have been some fear that the story might spread the idea among the barrios? Or was the article just too blunt about the fact that Negroes did get rewarded for the riots?

The U.S. Information Agency (USIA) quashed an article about Cesar Chavez titled, "New Voice in the Vineyard," from appearing in its August 1970 photo bulletin, sent monthly to USIA officials in 118 countries overseas. The man responsible for killing the story was R. Kenneth Towery, USIA assistant director for press and publication and a former aide to Senator John Tower of Texas, where Chavez' union organizers have been very active.

Never has the full impact or the full meaning of the Chicano movement been appreciated, but, then, Chicanos have never had the opportunity to communicate their deepest feelings and aspirations to the world. Gringo control of the media has seen to that. One artful piece in *The Washington Post* early last year dealt with the student unrest in South Texas, and was headlined, "The Chicanos Want In." The writer managed to suggest just the opposite of what most Chicanos intend. We want out:

Out of a cultural milieu which desensitizes man and woman into profit-producing machines, devoid of humanity and soul.

Out of a country which poses a military answer to every foreign issue; and despite having been born in revolution against Old World oppression, seeks to deny the same right to nations who reject Brave New World oppression.

Out of gringo patterns of injustice and prejudice which have suppressed the best talents and minds of our people and accepted only those few willing to gringoize themselves to achieve a measure of fulfillment.

Out of a system of government which is controlled by economic and social influence to reap its benefits at the expense of the poor and minority peoples.

To put this in positive terms, the Chicanos in essence desire three things:

To fulfill our peoplehood, Chicano;

To reclaim our land, Aztlán;

To secure the future for ourselves and our countrymen.

To achieve these goals Chicanos must have political, social, and economic freedom. We know that none of these basic freedoms will be achieved merely by wishing or asking for them. Therefore, Chicanos are confronted with the realities of devising new methods, perhaps techniques never tried before, of developing the resources to support those techniques, and of establishing, in some cases, new systems to supplant the worn-out and harmful gringo ones. How do we accomplish this? Outright revolution—that is, armed insurrection, appears to be only a device of the rhetoricians. Our revolt may cause violence, but we will be the chief victims of it if it occurs. The events of August 29, 1970, in East Los Angeles bear out this truth. I believe in fighting against the political structures and social practices which have suppressed us but not in a violence that endangers lives. If our revolt should lead us further toward violence, the police, the National Guard, and the armed forces are at the beck and call of the oppressive forces in the United States—that way lies the destruction of our people. The gringo reacts with excessive force against the Black Panthers, against the Young Lords, and against the Brown Berets. We must find means of revolution which accomplish the same goals that armed insurgence might.

What has been begun by Cesar Chavez, Corky Gonzales, José Angel Gutiérrez, and Reies Tijerina must be carried forward. The priority of the huelga, the spark of the Chicano revolution struck by Delano farm workers, should remain a primary goal for Chicanos to achieve. The shameful fact is that Chicanos in many cases have allowed the Anglo to pre-empt the stage in this struggle, which is so deeply rooted in our past. The success of the huelga is la raza's success; there must be a new surge of interest by all raza in changing the National Labor Relations Act and assuring other civil guarantees for farm workers and migrant laborers. In a very real sense, the predicament of the campesino underscores the predicament of all raza, for if we cannot free the Chicano of the fields, how can we free the Chicano of the barrio? They are one and the same.

The strongest current among our people is the youth — force struggling for recognition and liberation. While generational discrepancies persist among young and old Chicanos, there is a cross section of Chicanos who speak and think in similar terms about their aims and aspirations, which is quite broad as to age and economic and educational background. Nevertheless, generational breakup is one of the Anglo social norms that Chicanos have to combat vigorously. It sometimes seems, as a consequence of some Chicanos gaining middle-class status, that there is a greater commonality of thought between the very old and the very young; the middle aged are still too tied up with making it as Anglos, with being agringados or blanqueados. But these, too, can be made to come around to their senses. Si no, que se chingan.

The Chicano community is undergoing one of the most rapid changes of any people of the Americas. We can point to many causes—racial and cultural prejudice, labor exploitation, educational deprivation, and political disenfranchisement—to explain, up to a point, why Chicanos have taken so long to pull themselves together and to assert that identity and unity of purpose which would clearly manifest our peoplehood. In many ways, we have inner strengths to accomplish communion among ourselves; but we have been distrustful, unfaithful, and weak among ourselves as well. That negative aspect of our experience in Anglo America, which has taught us many of its worst traits, must now become a lesson of the past. Chicanos have to look to their own resources to accelerate the change we will effect in the seventies. If the resources do not lie in the community, we must learn how to bring them in from outside the barrio.

The upward and increasingly sophisticated evolution of Chicanismo can be even more rapid and contributive to sanity in the United States than the black movement. Chicanos can approach the crisis of races that torments America as the single group in the nation which represents, with our brother raza, broad racial and cultural integration. Chicanos must explore the multicultural and multiracial wellsprings of la raza Chicana. We must study it, write about it, speak out to the nation. We are a modern people. While the nonraza nations are dying or dead as cultural entities, the mestizo people, la raza, are but a few hundred years old. "We are a big baby," Reies Tijerina has put it in referring to the mestizos, who number some 200 to 250 million people in the Western Hemisphere today. By the year 2000, we will be twice as many as the Anglo American.

We must explore and exploit the heritage of the Spaniards, a thousands-of-years-old history and culture, with ties going back to the Phoenicians, the Greeks, the Romans, and the Arabs. We must give honor to the Spanish father, as Wilfredo Sedillo insists, and I with him. We have hardly begun to investigate the fathomless inheritance that is ours from our Indian forebears, the Nahúas, the Toltecs, the Aztecs, and the North American Indians. José Angel Gutiérrez once spoke of the Indian heritage as "our better half," that is, our Indian mother. We are the offspring, the mestizo, who finds himself in an alien culture, but who is finding himself able to adapt to both culture sources and become the modern Chicano.

Because we are interiorly integrated, the integration syndrome of black-white America has no relevance to the Chicano. For example, we do not believe that our Chicanitos must attend classes with Negroes and Anglos in order to attain an adequate education. If there must be integration, we say, let it be in terms of cash, curriculum, and control. Let the Chicano enjoy a just share of funds so that his barrio schools can hire the most qualified teachers, purchase the best equipment, and give young people the finest education possible. Integrate the history books, the literature books, the languages spoken in the classroom, so that the Chicano can identify himself there and feel pride in his being Chicano. The Anglo must let go of the total control he has maintained over the educational system, the curriculum, the hiring and firing, the discipline, and the decision-making so that Chicanos will have a say in the schooling of their children. Of course, the Anglo or black will not bow to this prescription for change. Chicano communities will have to force this change, this brand of integration. Because of the Anglo society's resistance, Chicano takeover of educational systems, not everywhere, but in many places in the Southwest and Midwest, may be that much more complete when they occur. Chicanos in Houston conducted a weeklong boycott in September, with three to four thousand raza children kept out of school by their parents. The protest of the Chicano Community won a reversal of an HEW integration order which put Chicanos and blacks together, while Anglo schools remained segregated.

In the educational context, an exemplary effort is being made in Mercedes, Texas, to build a Chicano university from the ground up. (An Indian-Chicano institution is also developing in Davis, California, near Sacramento, under the name, Deganawidda-Quetzalcoatl University.) Jacinto Treviño College, named after a Chicano whose reputation for killing los rinches cobardes (cowardly Rangers) is celebrated in corridos (Chicano songs), began classes in the fall of 1970.

Founded as an extension of Antioch College of Yellow Springs, Ohio, and financed by foundation and government moneys, Treviño College is in the first phase of certifying fifteen masters degree candidates, who will in turn become the undergraduate school faculty. The director is Dr. Leonard Mestas, a Coloradoan who completed his doctoral studies in education at the University of Colorado.

There are also twenty-two G.E.D. students ranging in age from eighteen to forty-five years old who will themselves form the core of the first year undergraduate student body. According to Narciso Aleman, a MAYO founder, now the college's administrator and a masters candidate himself, Treviño anticipates collaborating with Crystal City schools in bridging the whole community's educational needs.

Eventual site of the college is an abandoned Oblate Fathers monastery in Mission, a few miles from McAllen, where MAYO held a crucial organizational conference in December 1969. A dispute among the Oblate Fathers has withheld final liberation of the "mission" for Chicano use. Located on a slight elevation above the Rio Grande Valley floor, the mission could be no better situated for it overlooks both the United States and Mexico across the Rio Grande. In fact, the site reflects the history of the colegio's namesake, Jacinto Treviño. Treviño was born in the United States. In 1910, one part of his family was living in Mexico and the other part on this side of the border. A gringo beat up his brother. Jacinto heard that his brother had been killed by this certain gringo, the son of a rich Texan. In his grief and anger, Jacinto killed the young gringo de veras. Jacinto escaped across the border, but later was induced to return by a cousin named Pablo. Rangers ambushed him. As he and another brother Joaquin fought their way out, they shot Pablo and one of the Rangers. The story has since been perpetuated in El Corrido de Jacinto Treviño.

The 24-year-old Aleman clarifies the deeper reasons for choosing Treviño's name: "The Treviño family signifies what has happened because of an artificial boundary. Jacinto himself was not a violent man but he defended his family and himself. And the local populace identified with him." Aleman stresses the point.

"We wish to dedicate Treviño College to this spirit to this history," Aleman says. "We would like to believe that the colegio will dedicate itself through its students and faculty to los de abajo, to the poor."

With time and good fortune, for the Chicanos who created Treviño College certainly have the will, a truly Chicano institution could develop. In a sense, Chicanos have been hampered by not having had their own segregated colleges; blacks at least have had some fifty schools they could attend for a degree. We Chicanos were fooled into believing that we were white, Caucasian and thus integrated into the United States melting pot, while all the time we were actually being segregated and set apart in "Mexican" schools. But the privilege of education was withheld beyond the elementary grades. It was useful to maintain us at a certain level of ignorance so that we could not operate or compete on a level with the Anglo, thus forcing us into a worker class and a soldier class. Those are categories we still suffer for the sake of "integration," gringo style.

The Chicano brand of integration can be carried into every area of life: in economics, whether related to the workingman or the businessman; in civil rights related to voting, housing, the institutions of justice; and in politics. Events of the past five years demonstrate that the greater the resistance Chicanos meet in achieving an equitable role or a share in jobs, housing, education, and politics, the more complete and total their eventual assumption of these powers will be. This is the pattern that will manifest itself more and more in the seventies. There are regions or cities in the Southwest, and even in the Midwest and Northeast, where Mexican Americans or raza can take over the functions and power of government, where school systems can be controlled by the barrios, and where the economic life of the barrios or pueblos can be placed in the hands of the Chicanos who live there.

Coalition is one of the first avenues of action for Chicanos. The brief experience in the Poor People's Campaign demonstrated that on certain issues based on common needs, there can be coalition. In 1968 Reies Tijerina convened with black activists in California and pledged with them a black and brown coalition. Chicanos have many things in common with the black people of the United States. We can do much together and still maintain our own identity. In fact, there may be greater sense of community among the two groups than we have yet seen, simply because not enough Chicanos and blacks have taken the time to correspond and plan together. We have been pitted against each other for 120 years by the white man. It is time that we turn the tables.

But because of our Indian inheritance, Chicanos should begin to communicate with the Indian brother. Our historians and scholars should research the intermingled roots of our history and culture. The Yaqui Indians, for example, have maintained certain modes of life that are distinct from the mestizo culture, but they still are a relevant link with the Chicano past. They have endured the pressures from Mexican and Anglo governments, and have revolted against the Mexican Government several times as late as the 1920s, with some tribesmen escaping across the Sonora-United States border and settling in communities near Tucson and Phoenix. These people have an embattled history which is characterized by a fierce rejection of the white man. Still, along with their tribal customs they have retained many Spanish influences in a kind of synthesis of both the Indian and Spanish heritage. One such settlement represents about a third of the population in Guadalupe, a small unincorporated community just on the edge of Phoenix. Descendants of the Sonoran tribesmen, they are Mexican Americans in terms of identification, but they represent one extreme of the spectrum of the Mexican American people. At the opposite extreme of the spectrum are those who emphasize their Spanish origins. The Yaquis have their own customs, quite separate from their Mexican American neighbors. They retain the customary el capitan, a ceremonial leader who presides at annual celebrations, as well as other customs and dances. The Yaqui has somehow withstood many generations of the Anglo presence to preserve his tribal ways. They have even set limits on the extent of Spanish-Mexican influence. How have they done this? Is there something in their personality and way of life that Chicanos can adapt as we struggle to cope with the pressures of a dominant society which we cannot reject entirely but from which we must learn to extract its best features? Can we learn from the Yaqui experience how the fusion of Spanish-Mexican culture has occurred?

North American Indian tribes have suffered a kind of cultural shock from their discovery, an unplanned one, in March 1966, of the presence of the Tigua Indian tribe of Isleta, Texas. Vine Deloria, Jr., describes the event in his book, *Custer Died for Your Sins*. "The modern era of Indian emergence had begun," he writes, when representatives of the tribe appeared before the National Congress of American Indians' executive committee meeting in El Paso. The Tiguas had been forced to transport the goods of the Spaniards (who had been driven out of New Mexico in 1688) back to El Paso. Assigned a piece of land at what is now Isleta, down south about ten miles from present-day El Paso, the little tribe was virtually forgotten for centuries. After their appearance before the NCAI, they obtained formal recognition as an Indian tribe in early 1968 from the United States Government. "Discovery of the Tiguas rocked Indian people in several respects," Deloria relates. "Indians had been brainwashed into accepting the demise of their tribe as God's natural plan for Indians. Yet the Tiguas plainly demonstrated that Indian tribal society had the strength and internal unity to maintain itself indefinitely within an alien culture."

Haven't we Chicanos also a discovery to make, perhaps a mutual discovery, among our Yaqui brothers? Are there not other tribesmen in the Southwest with whom we have cultural and psychological bonds that could result in a mutual effort to reclaim a way of life that the gringo has nearly destroyed? One person who has expressed his affinity is Mad Bear Anderson, one of the Indian leaders in the repossession of Alcatraz Island in San Francisco Bay. At the December (1969) Moratorium Day in San Francisco, Anderson declared, "The only people who have a right to live on Alcatraz are the Indians and the Chicanos."

The realities of black urban strength will necessitate political coalitions with black organizations, but, also, Chicanos have an obligation, much like a family duty, to collaborate with Indian tribes in their struggles. The Indian mother—that side of our past that binds us to the earth, inspirits our hands and minds with the esthetic, and colors our vision with sensitivities for the humanity in man—has been neglected by many of us Chicanos. It must be one of our objectives to return to that nurturing mother in order to revitalize those values and insights which Chicanos need to achieve more profound levels of thought and motivation.

Reclamation of the barrio, from within, must be an objective of Chicanos in the seventies. For this purpose, again, Chicanos must investigate what cultural traits and side-by-side economic and political realities can be converted into specific programs for rehabilitation of the pueblo, which is both the Chicano people and where they live. Take the issue of housing. Mexican American people tend to exist in substandard housing five or seven times more often than Anglos. Somehow our people survive in living conditions that are as bad as any in the country. There is no competition as to who lives in the worst conditions—it's a fact of Chicano life. One of the cultural traits that has been adulterated by gringo social mores (suburbanismo) is la raza's propensity for communal living as a survival technique and a social function. The 1968 Housing Act provides for the purchase by tenants of public housing. Suppose a barrio community organization working with a public housing tenants group were to effect such a purchase; the tenants would become owners of their own units and would be bound together in community ownership of the whole project. Responsibility for upkeep and maintenance, for payments on the loan, and for management would be in the hands of the tenant-owners. In effect, rents would be loan payments, and if the project were handled as a shareholding operation, the tenant-owners might expect a dividend at the end of the year or some return on their investment, should they move. The co-operative and communal nature of such a housing project corresponds to the interdependence for survival among Mexican American families which we have experienced throughout our entire history.

The phrase "black capitalism" was in vogue as an answer to the problems of the black ghetto until blacks realized that very few black businessmen would actually benefit and that by and large, ghetto enterprise would remain an extension of the white corporations, another form of Anglo colonialism. Because the Chicano's predicament is set within the barrio, often an isolated community, it follows that in order to rehabilitate the barrio, entrepreneurship must be established barrio-wide. Chicanos have to engage in co-operative enterprises that benefit as many people as possible.

A situation might develop thus: a barrio organization scratches up the financing for a wholesale produce outlet. An adjunct of the outlet would be an open-air market, a typical raza form of commerce. Stores in the barrio could buy from the outlet at reduced prices, or a block group could form a buying co-operative. Perhaps a few aspiring entrepreneurs might be encouraged to set up their own tiendas. Meanwhile, small farmers in the area, attracted to the produce outlet, would organize themselves into a farmers' co-operative so that they could get the best price. The Chicano outlet can still offer the lowest possible prices to the barrio consumer, while larger produce houses will be forced to compete on retail prices but maintain the farmers' level of payments. In various barrios of the Southwest, Chicano organizations are developing co-operative ventures of this kind. An organization need only observe what serv-

ices are brought into the barrio and controlled by
Anglos to know what services they can begin to offer,
thereby undercutting the Anglo's influence in the barrio. These are the kinds of enterprises that should be
high priority in the plotting for economic turnovers by
Chicano organizations. Restaurants are being opened
by Chicano groups. Home delivery of Mexican foods, a
mattress factory, and a publishing house are other efforts
that have developed out of barrio unification and barrio
needs. The Tierra Amarilla farming co-op is only the
first of many more to come. The people's clinic in Tierra
Amarilla, bombed out once already but reopened, is an
example in the health field. Churches, foundations, or
unions could well afford to supplement these most relevant efforts, not to dictate how they are to be run or
how the funds are to be allocated, but to support what
is one of the most fundamental developments in Chicano action.

For some time, I've had the idea that a barrio union
might be a concept worth exploring for implementation
in certain areas. The idea might not be feasible in some
barrios, but might be quite practical in others. Basically, the barrio union would develop out of already
existing organizations or simply from barrio people
coming together to pool their resources. Much like a
labor union, barrio members would pay dues; they
would meet regularly, once a week or once a month, or
whenever necessity demanded, and elect officers and
bargaining representatives. They would have basically
the same weapons that labor unions have (except for
the Taft-Hartley Act): the strike, walkout, boycott,
picketing, threats of any of these, plus withholding of
taxes and the vote. The barrio union's representatives
would bargain collectively with city, county, or state
authorities to remedy barrio citizens' possible complaints, such as: street lighting, paving of streets, sewer
improvements, improved police and fire protection, as
well as controversies over police misconduct, court in-

justices, increased representation in government, zoning laws, and the distribution of job resources in businesses or industries relocating near the barrio. The barrio union could also establish its own community agencies, such as a crime-prevention unit, which would maintain surveillance of the neighborhoods to hold down all crime but also to keep down chota crimes. Such a union might advise that taxes be withheld until street lights or sewers were allocated for the barrio, for, in the event of complete cutoff of services by the city or county, the notoriety that would befall such a city administration would be highly undesirable. Besides, in some barrios, the difference between services rendered and complete cutoff is very slight.

Such an approach could work, I believe, because some of the fundamental features required to carry it out are deeply ingrained in the Chicano experience. The concept of union dues is well known, if not a common experience, among Chicano communities. The necessity for the people to pool their resources to help each other is well grounded in the Beneficencia societies which still operate in a few barrios. The concept also depends on cultural bonds that are being more strongly and openly asserted in the barrios; a barrio union falls right into the raza cultural mode. Membership in the barrio union could have immediate benefits for joining. A small dues payment per month would entitle a member immediately, for example, to membership in a buying co-operative, free medical and dental services, a subscription to a barrio newspaper published by the union, and, most importantly, to a voice and a vote in the determination of barrio union programs and policies.

An urban project that seems on the threshold of realizing the barrio union concept is The East Los Angeles Community Union (TELACU), a multifunded operation in East Los Angeles. Its director is Esteban "Ed" Torres, an organizer for the United Auto Workers. "Essentially, TELACU is directed toward a membership form of organization, dues paying or share holding," says Torres. TELACU is an urban version of the rural model for organizing the Chicano that the United Farm Workers Organizing Committee demonstrates in Delano, more than a hundred miles north of Los Angeles. Each is involved in a credit union, economic development, job improvements, housing, and health. TELACU, Torres suggests, is a kind of reception center for the workers displaced by farm automation: "Someone has to meet the problem of the increased influx of unemployed from the farms and rural areas."

TELACU is also interested in developing a business-industrial complex in the East Los Angeles area that would include already established Chicano entrepreneurs, the creation of new firms, and the recruiting of non-Chicano firms on a lease basis to a central, barrio-controlled corporation. Along with provisions for training and hiring of Chicano barrio residents by outside firms, a business-industrial complex would also be geared to include health facilities, child care, schools, and motels. While the basic framework and rationale of the union organism could undergird the barrio union, I do not suggest that unions attempt to establish barrio locals, as it were.

Delano represents the nearest thing to a barrio union among Chicanos, or in the nation, for that matter, because the barrio community and union members are in large part the same. However, because of its affiliation with AFL-CIO, the barrio-community element has lost a degree of autonomy that it had until the original Filipino-Chicano UFWOC affiliated with AFL-CIO in 1966. The barrio union, at its best, would establish a self-sufficient organism, as independent as possible from outside controls and resources but attuned to the techniques for utilizing consultant and technical assistance. The achievement of self-sufficiency is all-important to the fulfillment of the Chicano nation. The barrio union is a potential method for rehabilitating the barrio from within. Only the Chicano himself can accomplish this. The economic and political barriers to implementing this concept are unquestionably enormous; they are also unknown, and this may be the greatest barrier, a fear of trying something that hasn't been tried before.

An imperative to establishing the barrio union or any form of barrio organization that utilizes the cultural and psychological strengths of the Chicano pueblo is political activism. One might lead to the other, but certainly where a barrio is isolated by the encroachment of Anglo domination, the only recourse is to organize the barrio totally. The organizational effort for this to be accomplished must be ingenious and prolonged, but unless Chicanos act to revitalize the barrio—the most immediate resource we have for a land base—internally and soon, the more difficult it will be to enkindle the sense of peoplehood and protect the political advances we may achieve.

The stress in barrio organization must be on cooperative action, whether it is in social action or in business enterprise. When profit-producing businesses of one kind or another are established in the barrio—that is, businesses which are essentially outgrowths of barrio entrepreneurial and barrio manpower resources—the structure under which they are incorporated should be on a profit-sharing basis for the employees. The workers should have an opportunity to become partners in the enterprise, in this way gaining a greater share of the barrio profits from the development of businesses or industries, rather than having all profits go to a few entrepreneurs. The idea of employee ownership of companies is a relatively new concept, but one that is being tried in several places. One of the few companies totally independent of major corporation boards of directors for its profits and direction is a black manufacturing firm in Portland, Oregon's Albina ghetto. Blacks manage the company, type on the typewriters, work the lathes, push the brooms; and each is building up a share

ownership in the business. The blacks who spearheaded
the development of the corporation intend to implement a new form of corporate structure—a radical departure from the usual top-heavy profiteers of the major
corporations—to motivate workers by providing the opportunity to share in owning and guiding the future
of the company, and to establish a second-income
source based on a form of stock investment in the company. The Second Income Plan—as it is called by its
most prominent promoter, Louis Kelso, a San Francisco
corporation lawyer—develops as follows:

A deferred-compensation trust (essentially a retire-
ment plan until the company achieves a profit margin,
in which case it could pay dividends) is established in
behalf of employees. The trust program is administered
by both the trust and the corporation, both of which are
comprised of a board of directors, as broadly representative of the company and the community as possible. The individual employee, at the end of each year of
employment, is vested or assigned 15 percent of his
total income in shares; his regular income has not been
touched. The 15 percent is predicated on the expected
corporate growth of the company. After the first three
years of employment, the worker will own outright 30
percent of the number of shares he has built up. Gaining an added 10 percent each year, by the end of ten
years he will have complete ownership of his shares. He
can sell his shares at any time, of course, according to
the percentage of value they represent.

The Portland ghetto corporation is a complex inter-
relation of many factors: hard-core job trainees, hard-
nosed and experienced black specialists in contracting,
managing, and product development; community involvement; white consultants; and government (SBA
and OEO) subsidization. It is not a proposition which
can be easily capsulized; but because of its most notable
features of employee ownership, capital-sharing, and
community involvement, it falls right into line with the

strengths and needs of the barrio. Capital investment is considered a luxury for the more affluent to indulge in. As long as it remains the fundamental means of the production of wealth, minority people should also be in on the receiving end of the profits which they help produce. And there is "progressively more of it each year," according to Kelso, who asserts that equality of economic opportunity should also connote "opportunity to produce affluence." Even Chavez stresses this point of view in regard to farm workers sharing in the benefits that automation brings to the farmer. Barrio organizations should investigate the potential of this second-income plan approach; it may become a prerequisite to permitting companies to set up in the barrio or to utilize barrio manpower.

Kelso's theories, which go beyond the basic income-investment proposal, are spelled out in his book, *The Two-Factor Theory.* In this slender volume, which must be read with due caution by the noneconomist, Kelso points out that less than 1 percent of American households are capitalist, that is, make at least half their income from capital investments. A concomitant fact is that in the past eleven years, U.S. corporations generated new capital internally rather than from newly issued stock. This was done in such a way that ownership of these corporations was more concentrated rather than broadened. These facts refer to the corporations that produce most of the goods and services of the U.S. economy.

While capital investment has far outdistanced land as a source of wealth in the United States, land still has a permanence and productivity beyond stock-market quotations that appeals to many Chicanos. Land has been the life of northern New Mexicans. Land held in common for many years formed the economic and social buttresses of life. Historians, law analysts, and the Alianza alike can prove that fraud and violence robbed the Spanish, the Mexican, and the mestizo forebears of the Chicano people of the life-giving foundation of the land. We maintain that there exist blood bonds and cultural bonds to the land of the Southwest; we do not deny the Indian peoples' claims to the land. We believe we have had at least a share in its perpetuation through the hands of those who originally worked the land and who have historical claims to it. This issue of land and its relationship to the Chicano should be discussed with Indian tribesmen. An understanding must be reached on the viability of pursuing a land strategy aimed at recovering lands once held by the Indians or the Spanish. Chicanos have a blood relationship to our Indian forebears. Descendants of early Spanish colonists who reject such an alliance with the Indian natives of the Americas also reject the most obvious claim to retribution for the misdeeds committed by the Anglos who stole the land, the United States Government in particular. The only feasible program is to demand retribution; the land itself will simply not be returned. We Chicanos can assume control politically over an area—whether it is a section of a city, the city itself, a county, or a state, but we cannot completely reclaim the land that was taken from our ancestors.

The Treaty of Guadalupe Hidalgo, of course, is the ethical and legal basis for the retribution demands that Chicanos will make. But the United States Government should not be the only target; the churches, the foundations, the corporations, and the unions should be reminded that they, too, have a debt to repay. The churches, especially the Catholic Church, have helped the Anglo American to rob us of our pride. They have told us, "Have patience, mi hijo" (and don't forget to put something in the collection basket); and we have learned to bide our time.

Catholic bishops have sided with the growers in California in their efforts to break the farm labor strike. They have remained silent lest the growers withhold their annual pledges. The bishops have silenced young priests who have attempted to implement the teachings of Pope Leo XIII and Pope John XXIII. Catolicos por

La Raza, a new group which sprang up in Los Angeles, vigorously protested the million-dollar expenditure for a cathedral by the former Los Angeles archbishop and cardinal, James McIntyre. Money that dioceses or archdioceses spend for buildings these days, whether in Los Angeles or in Washington, D.C., is tainted by racist attitudes when it is spent to house the glittering ceremonies for the middle-class and upper-class Roman Catholics. The poor, the blacks, and the Chicanos invariably wind up with the financially failing parish plants, ill-financed schools, shabby churches, and mediocre pastors who can't finagle anything better for themselves.

The Catholic Church has been criticized for ignoring the black people of the United States, or for segregating them when they do convert. What does the church owe to Chicanos who are traditionally the mass base for the church's erection of edifices and the unpaid or underpaid manpower for their construction as well? How would the Catholic Church like to make up for the repression of our people it has caused by its concentrating on patience and penance rather than justice and freedom? We do not need preachers among the pueblos of la raza; we need a Hidalgo and a Camilo Torres.

Chicanos have to liberate themselves from guilt feelings or fears about telling the church where it stands now. When Chicanos deliberate about taking over institutions, they should not forget the churches. The churches belong to us, the people; so do the school buildings and the diocesan newspapers. The church bureaucrats can no longer operate their fiefs without regard for the needs of the poor.

It does appear that churches were planned to serve the rich. Recently, when Bishop Fulton Sheen tried to turn ownership of a parish plant in Rochester over to the black community, to fill its particular needs, church officials, clergy, and rank-and-file Christians criticized the move so strongly that the former television homilist was forced to withdraw the offer. Never have I known a rich parish to freely share its resources with a poorer parish. Every diocese in the country should have a pool of money to be shared with less affluent parishes; on the national level, more affluent dioceses should willingly combine funds to assist poorer dioceses.

Chicanos have given much to make the Catholic Church a living presence in the Western Hemisphere. Our forefathers absorbed the Christian doctrine—it was similar to theirs in many respects—and eventually Catholicism became the pervasive top layer of Mexican-Indian religiosity. It was the Mexican Indians who made the expeditions of the adelantados and padres possible; it was the Indians who built the missions; it was the Chicanos who labored and sacrificed to build the churches of the Southwest. Thus it should not be a matter of debate as to whether the Chicano and Indian peoples deserve outright financial support from the churches; the only question is how much and how fast will the churches invest in helping the people whom they have spiritually enslaved for generations.

The churches trespass on our land and our lives; so, too, the corporations with their tax loopholes, the foundations, and the unions owe their wealth and influence to the Chicano's work-bent back and straining muscles. In March 1969, the Inter-Agency Committee invited 36 foundations to meet with its staff to ascertain how these resources of program and research funds could aid Mexican Americans. Only two of the smaller foundations demonstrated interest, the rest, including the major ones in the United States, were too busy or did not believe that their funding interests related to Mexican American needs.

To recoup land losses, especially for those raza who believe they have legal claims to the land, and to exact retribution from the United States Government, which may be more desirable and more feasible than actually reclaiming the land, la raza must establish a new relationship with Anglo America. La raza must make the concept of nationhood a living reality. We can look toward someday convening a national congress of Chicanos that would deliberate and arrive at a consensus as to the forms of retribution that must be made to our people. Why could we not elect representatives to such a congress from the various pueblos in the nation? Why could we not establish a framework of autonomous, democratic pueblos which would not relate to political parties or class distinctions? Why could we not petition as a nation for at least an elected, nonvoting delegate in both the House and Senate? Puerto Rico has such a representative, Jorge Cordova, for its 2.7 million puertorriqueños. We deserve at least one, if not two, who could represent the Chicano. Obviously, I doubt that the Spanish surnames in Congress adequately represent the Chicano. We could lead the way through such a procedure to unify (not absorb or lead) the Third World forces which at present are at the threshold between life and death. We must do something as a people to change the United States, to change the Americas. Perhaps such a conversion could take place in the seventies; perhaps it is an impossible dream. But regardless, Chicanos must create for themselves, if we are to survive as a people, a new form of existence. It can come from the barrios, from the colleges, from the colonias, from the fields, from everywhere Chicanos live. We have a very personal stake in altering the attitudes and conduct of the Anglo-American and the black American. These two can destroy themselves and with them us and the raza of Latin America. Yet, we have not begun to speak out against the atrocities that the United States is committing in Bolivia, in Santo Domingo, in Cuba, in Mexico, as well as in East Los Angeles, Denver, San Francisco, Delano, Phoenix, Albuquerque, Tierra Amarilla, San Antonio, Chicago, and Rio Grande City. Where are the Chicano legislators and leaders to speak out against the murders of Chicanos by gringo chotas, against the deaths of Chicanos in a gringo war against another oppressed people, and against the assassinations of raza in Mexico, Santo Domingo, Bolivia, and Colombia through counterinsurgence meddling by the United States?

Increasingly, the Chicano will discover that the social and economic revolution in which he is involved in the United States is a part of the revolution that is developing in Latin America. Senator J. William Fulbright addresses the issue of U.S. attitudes toward Latin America in *The Arrogance of Power* (1966) as if North American foreign policy affected raza only beyond the U.S. borders. The Arkansas senator need only have observed U.S. "foreign" policy toward the Chicano to understand somewhat more rudimentarily why the United States is a counterrevolutionary force in the Americas as well as in the world. "America forced on Spain a war," ostensibly to liberate the Cuban people, "that [Spain] was willing to pay almost any price short of complete humiliation to avoid," Fulbright says. But 50 years before the war with Spain, Anglo America had liberated a huge expanse of land from Mexico through a war which would never have occurred except for the gringo government's disdain for the Mexican people. Fulbright adds, "The movement of the future of Latin America is social revolution. . . . Paternalism is no longer a workable basis for our relations with Latin America." That is obviously correct, but he is far from correct when he asserts that the United States "has already come to terms with one great social revolution in Latin America," meaning Mexico. The United States has yet to comply fully with an agreement made 123 years ago with Mexico, and with the Mexican American (as a silent, third party). The United States has meddled in some way with Latin America's social and political development ever since it could turn its attention away from its own revolution of 1776. In April 1965, to cite a recent instance, the United States violated the Charter of the Organization of American States when Marines were sent into the Dominican Republic. The history of

North American impertinence and impudence toward Latin America is astounding. Chicanos should have something particularly insightful to say about U.S. policy because we are as much victims of the U.S. attitude as la raza in South America. We are treated as foreigners; Spanish is taught as a foreign language although it predates English in the Americas. Revolutionary forces in South American countries, from the Mexican students to Brazilian insurgents, consider the United States —this includes the Chicano people—the worst enemy of their people. I wonder how many Chicanos have been trained as special forces or are used as instructors for CIA-sponsored counterinsurgent military units which infiltrate and combat revolucionarios. Do peoples of Latin America realize that a distinct Chicano community exists in the United States? Have Chicanos done anything to make our Latin American brothers aware of our existence? Chicanos can fulfill in part the desire for freedom of raza all over the Americas by making ourselves more aware of their history and struggle, of which we are so much a part.

One of the important means by which Chicanos will make known their collaboration with the peoples of Latin America is for more and more Chicanos to turn their minds and talents to an expression of their feelings and their ideas through the arts—writing, music, painting, sculpture, dance, and drama. Generations of Chicanos have come and gone and we are only now beginning to form a body of literature or fine arts that are distinctively Chicano. We have to create these works from our own hands and minds. Men and women of la raza, from Spain to South America, Central America and the Caribbean have contributed some of the greatest manifestations of literary and artistic talent, and philosophic and interpretative thought, in the world. Not many Chicanos know this reservoir of inspiration exists; or worse, through unfounded fears and timidity, they hold themselves back from emulating it and, I believe, surpassing it. Chicanos have told me that they want to paint, to carve and mold, to write novels, essays, and poetry; the esthetic swells within our people. As Abelardo Delgado, a 39-year-old Chicano poet has said in a 1969 poem,

"stupid america":

stupid america, see that chicano
with a big knife
on his steady hand
he doesn't want to knife you
he wants to sit on a bench
and carve christfigures
but you won't let him.
stupid america, hear that chicano
shouting curses on the street
he is a poet
without paper and pencil
and since he cannot write
he will explode.
stupid america, remember that chicanito
flunking math and english
he is the picasso
of your western states
but he will die
with one thousand masterpieces
hanging only from his mind.

We are striving to formulate a new body of writings and art that will tell our story our way, that will preserve the Chicano esthetic for sight and sound and movement. The Chicano press newspapers, barrio publications that have paralleled the movement's pace and vigor, are a basic outlet for young and old writers of history, culture, poetry, and the graphic arts. Individuals have published slim volumes of poetry—including Rodolfo Gonzales of Denver and Delgado of El Paso. Quinto Sol Publications in Berkeley, California, is a young publishing house that prints *El Grito,* a literary magazine, and volumes such as *El Espejo,* a compilation of various Chicano writers' works. A handful of books by Chicano authors are in the works or just recently published by major companies. But efforts for more Chi-

cano publishing firms are increasing, notably Barrio Press
in Denver, Mictla Publications in El Paso, and Chicano
Features Syndicate in Washington, D.C.

Teatros, small mobile drama-comedy troupes presenting satires and Actos (commentaries on Chicano
life and experience) are quickly becoming a living art
form of Chicanismo. First promoted by Luis Valdez in
Delano with El Teatro Campesino (the Farm Workers'
Theater), teatros have multiplied and become one of
the freshest forms of expression for Chicanos. Lupe
Saavedra and Augustin Lira are other prominent proponents of the barrio theater. Since literature, theater,
and the other arts distill the essence of a people, the
Chicano is on the verge of a renaissance.

Our own artistic creativity should be stimulated, but
it is important also that Chicanos should themselves
control the channels of communication that pipe information *into* the barrio, as well as direct the barrio
media that informs the outside world about the barrio.
Chicano newspapers and magazines must proliferate.
Opportunities need to be provided for Chicano youth to
learn basic skills, from writing to film-making. We need
to take over local newspapers, radio and television stations, where possible; establishing publishing houses
and our own news service—all such ventures are greatly
needed by the Chicano community. But when certain
institutions in or related to the barrio cannot be expro-
priated by the people, compliance with the demands of
the barrio will have to be forced through some means. A
newspaper, a radio or television station should publish
or program Chicano activities and interests; certain
federal regulations require community-wide program-
ing of the electronic media. The key, of course, to such
direct action is the foundation of a political and economic power base, either through fully organizing the
barrio or through exerting a strong influence in the political sector.

Stemming from these avenues of action, which are
but an overview of the kinds of things Chicanos will be

doing in the next few years, the effects of the Chicano uprising on the international level can be limitless. In the past couple of years, I have known of only one interpretative article about Mexican Americans to appear in a foreign country—England, of all places. While the article itself contained several inaccuracies based on a limited understanding of the Chicano, it may have given the first inkling to other peoples of the world that something else besides the black movement was happening in America. The international branching-out of the table grape boycott also added weight to the emergence on a global scale of Chicano aspirations. The boycott, however, may be easily misconstrued as only a management-labor dispute while the cultural overtones go unnoticed. I believe that the Chicano does have an international origin, for he was a party, a silent third party, to an international agreement, the Treaty of Guadalupe Hidalgo. Therefore, he should be accorded certain international rights, such as the right to present, before such bodies as the United Nations or a world court, his cause in relation to lands stolen from him in violation of the treaty. He has the right to retribution owed him for the injustices of 120 years of peonage to the gringo. In this way, we might startle the world, and particularly the United States, if we were able to demonstrate that Chicanos must seek justice through world institutions, since we have been denied a hearing from our own government.

Until now, the Chicano has been forced to play the white man's game on the defensive side; the Anglo encourages and perpetuates division among minority peoples to maintain control over them. We Chicanos are now making this isolation work for us. In the future we should not undertake activities that would only divide us or separate us from other peoples in the United States. Incidents and words are used today that create artificial barriers and misunderstanding. However, Chicanos also realize that the character of our revolt against gringoismo will prevail through our being more positive

and unified in our words and actions. We must not under-
mine, by seeking wholly separatist avenues of action, the
distinctive role we can play in the future of the Americas.
There is an overwhelming need for the Chicano to find
himself and for Chicanos to find each other. He needs to
fortify himself with tradition, language, history, and culture. The events of the past decade suggest the Chicano's
sense of history, his longing to establish a modern tradition, and his hunger for dates of beginnings and culmi-
nations that are his to cherish. A parallel realization of
these aspirations is the understanding of our duality of
culture and insight that may very well be the most important factor in our relations with the non-Chicano
world tomorrow.

We can look for Chicanismo to influence more mexicanos—that is, more of those persons of Mexican-Indian
origins—including the return of many who previously
disavowed their heritage. Chicanismo has that kind of
redemptive force.

The essence of Chicanismo will become more deeply
internalized through an ever-increasing identification
by raza with each other. Also, through the Chicanos'
expression of Chicanismo in almost every art form, the
peoplehood we seek will clearly manifest itself.

The quest for Aztlán will never be fulfilled, for
Aztlán is not just a thing or a place to the Chicano.
Land and power will come into the Chicanos' hands,
but Aztlán will remain an inspirational ideal and a goal
ever drawing us forward.

Because Chicanismo is part of the raza revolution
that encompasses the Americas, Chicanos should strive
to influence international thought and action, particularly between the United States and Latin America. The
Chicano is of key importance to future relations in the
Americas; he is that latent bond between the peoples of
the Western Hemisphere, because already he embodies
the two worlds of the North and South American continents.

15

THE CHICANO OF THE AMERICAS

RELYING on the past as the basis for pride in one's self and in one's people is insufficient to build a truly viable identity as Mexican Americans, as Chicanos, both distinct and inseparable from the total American society. The Chicano himself is obligated to determine and mold his own future in order to achieve his new presence in the Americas. By investing his whole personality in the design of that role for the years ahead, the Chicano will more readily aspire to fulfill the promise that is in him. Striving for a personal future completes the balance that the Chicano must achieve with his past and his present situation.

It would be very easy for me or other Chicanos to become self-serving in assessing the kinds of contributions we, as a people, could make to the evolvement of a North American culture and character far different from the paranoid supernation that foreign observers must now perceive. The Chicano considers himself an asset to this country rather than a liability. The black man and the red man feel the same way, too. Chicanos have yet to hear a single plausible reason for denying any longer their differences from the Anglo American or for severing certain links that do exist with the Anglo mentality and experience.

As a matter of history, the Chicano has already done his part, along with the other ethnic groups that have come to the North American continent, in creating the world's most affluent and diverse nation. Chicano genius, skills, talents, labor—and lives—have added to the material development of the greater part of this nation. Yet, the Chicano has benefited the least of any of the national groups, for all his numbers and length of involvement. When we have been accorded our rights, it has always been with leftovers; leftover funds, leftover programs, and leftover recognition. Until the Chicanos revolted against indifference and oppression, we had not been shown the slightest concern, less even than the Indians and Negroes had enjoyed in a number of ways. The Chicano revolt is partly directed at this insensibility toward his predicament.

But, an intangible, psychological deprivation has been eating away at the inner Chicano. He has been denied the free expression of his ideas and the unhindered perfecting of his innermost self through the arts. He strikes out against this insidious form of suppression by forcing the entire nation to become aware of him and to accept a diversity of peoples that includes not just the white man, but the brown man, the black man, and the red man. Each identity—Negro, Indian, Chicano—tends to break down the white monolith concept gringos hold to; and each identity leads every American to a realization of a broader national view and a saner world perspective as well.

As people with a distinct culture, we can begin to focus the attention of the American Government on the needs and ambitions of brown people in the Western Hemisphere. Anglo Americans may be shocked to realize someday soon that the most imminent, yet the most positive, threat to North America (aside from the ominous threat the United States represents to itself) is not

from the Soviet Union or Red China but from Latin
America. In terms of numbers, untapped resources, and
aspirations on the brink of fulfillment, Latin America
could engulf the United States, perhaps not economically but certainly as the overwhelming voice of political or international policy in the Western Hemisphere.
America is not a leader in world politics; it is a coercive
force. There is an important difference between exerting
moral and intellectual influence in the world and gaining influence by force of arms or "deterrent" strength.

The Chicano is part of that revolution of la raza.
That revolution began when the United States committed an international crime and its first imperialist act
against the Spanish-speaking countries by overrunning
Mexico and then nearly destroying the people it captured within the new boundary lines. Consequently, the
United States should also recognize the Chicano revolt
for what it is—part of something bigger, but, assuredly,
itself worthy of acceptance and significance as an important development within the national sphere.

Through the Chicano, the United States has much
to learn about the peoples to the south. The United
States may even come to terms with the whole Latin
American world, if it will recognize the Chicano as a
unique phenomenon of the Americas and assure him the
rights and status that are his due. That will be a major
step by Anglo America to move beyond itself into a
communion with the world nations, free of paranoia or
the delusions of being policeman for the world.

While the Chicano revolt unfolds in the Southwest
and lengthens into the rest of the country, the United
States will experience some rather unique changes in its
composition—economically, socially, and politically.
We may even affect the deeper psychological under-
pinnings of this miasma called America. In every area of
present need—housing, education, employment, and
barrio rehabilitation—the Chicano himself is attempting to rescue something of what is left of the past in

order to rebuild, or to prepare for the future. He will review his strengths, culture, tradition, customs, and language. He will go beyond relying on these factors merely for survival, and expand them. For example, rather than relying solely on internal family resources, he will forge an interdependence on the internal resources of the broad Chicano community. The Chicano can demonstrate that self-reliance and self-determination are still a natural and responsible means, not only of enduring but of achieving independence. But the basis for his liberation must be an awareness of the interior relationship in the bond of Chicanismo.

The proliferation of human problems at this moment in history supports the development of nationalistic identity; many of the underdeveloped countries have achieved, or are achieving, autonomy by a relentless pursuit of a national character secure from foreign controls and ideology. Although on a global scale, this movement also affects individual nations; within the United States it is occurring group by group. The Mexican American population of the United States alone exceeds the populations of many sovereign countries in the world. The Spanish-speaking community itself far surpasses the populations of other, far stronger and larger nations.

With the sense of nationhood expanding from the colonia to the big-city barrio, with gringo repressive tactics, with more unfulfilled promises from the political parties, and with more leche de polvo (powdered milk) from the government, the trend toward separatism will become stronger (and to some Chicanos more feasible) as political liberation of cities and counties takes place. A Chicano who is not usually given to radical comment has suggested that Texas be split in half, the southern half reverting to Chicano control. Whether such a development would occur and how it would come about is highly debatable, but the tendency should be kept in mind in the light of the Chi-

cano mystique. The concept of Aztlán is undergirded by
a desire for restitution of the land of Aztlán. The Chicano does not wish to have merely an empty dream.
Just as for other displaced peoples in the world's history, the cry of the land is keen in our ears; we, too,
have had title to the land which was violently taken
from us. Geography and culture make the vision of a
new state for the Chicano not quite so wild an idea; the
direct roots we have sunk into the land can burgeon
once more.

If we seek an irredentist solution—a Chicano state
between the United States and Mexico—would that be
the best means of liberating ourselves? Or will we be
unwilling and without the resources to fulfill the potential of such a scheme? Would a separate state be viable?
My guess is that the United States Government would
act very quickly to suppress Chicano efforts toward this
end. In fact, police overkill can be expected at any time
now in the Rio Grande Valley, in northern New Mexico,
in Denver, in the Central Valley of California, in San
Antonio, in El Paso, and in Chicago as Chicanos begin
to threaten or actually take over the gringo institutions.
Our barrios and new city-states will appear like other
Cubas to the Department of State that sees only red in
every revolution, and we will be put down in the name
of national defense or in the name of law and order.

The United States cannot accept the idea that other
countries, let alone peoples within the United States,
might not want U.S. paternalism anymore. The Nixon
Administration is so blind that it even sends one of the
grandest of the patrónes grandes, Nelson Rockefeller, to
study and report on Latin America—and, on the way,
check into his plants and land holdings scattered all
over South America. What an insult to the latino intelligence and dignity.

It is not self-serving, I believe, to forecast that the
Mexican American will alter the character of American
society; but, it cannot be stated often enough, that he

can accomplish this only by maintaining his own identity and personality as a Chicano. There is so much about Anglo American society that cuts across the grain of Chicanismo. The obsession with consumption and the pollution of the environment are interrelated Anglo American proclivities which together can destroy the atmosphere, the land, and the people. The United States, which comprises 6 percent of the world's population, annually consumes 35 percent of the world's raw materials. By the end of this century, scientific speculators estimate, the United States will use up annually about 80 percent of the world's raw materials. But the inordinate consumption of resources unleashes itself in another form—pollution. It seems incredible that the Anglo American society requires more than a third of the resources of the world. This is nothing less than gluttony; and just as the glutton will vomit to consume yet more, the gringo public does the same. The result is waste, despoliation of the earth's plants and animals, and poisoning of the air and waters. Somehow, the advocates of environmental self-preservation by-pass the origin of so much of what they fear. To eliminate certain sources of pollution will necessitate changing gringo attitudes toward consumption and their reevaluation of luxuries and necessities. Altering priorities for national spending must also be made concomitant with changing the public's penchant for using up goods. Billions of dollars are spent from the nation's treasury— for war, for defense, for space travel, and for supersonic planes—without the people's acquiescence. One administration after another has decided what is best for the people with regard to the Vietnam War, defense spending, and space exploration. President Nixon devoted a third of his "State of the Union" message of January 22, 1970, to the environmental crisis; but not long before that he had approved the development of the SST, the supersonic airliner. That costly error would fly in the relatively stable layer called the stratosphere. Scientists suggest that the pollution of that layer of the earth's atmosphere will result in a smog screen that will produce a "greenhouse effect," that is, a warming of the insulated air between the earth and the stratosphere. Eventually the warming trend would melt the polar icecaps, raising the oceans as much as 300 feet—people would have to live on what are now the tops of mountains! So much for the commitment of the present administration to rescuing the environment.

My Chicano brothers and I have been susceptible to this gringo trait, Veblen's still irrefutable description of conspicuous consumption, gone middle class and nationwide. Yet excessive use of goods and indifference to the effects on our environment should be concepts alien and even obscene to Chicanismo. Respect for the land, as for another's rights, is integral to peace. Chicanos, as well as the American tribesmen, are still strongly attuned to the sacredness of our physical surroundings; it is an understanding inherited in culture and tradition and borne out in our history. The issue of what the gringo world is doing to nature, therefore, is linked to the Chicano's view of Anglo society as the functional and most critical part of the ambiente, the environment in which he lives and which he must contend with and change. Chicanos must attack the onslaught that man is making against the natural world. He can enhance his own identity if he seeks reasons for his attack not merely on the grounds of economics or self-preservation but on the basis of centuries of Chicano, Mexican, and Indian respect for the land. We have to make it clear to the nation, especially to the youths who seem to be mounting the strongest offensive against political and economic interests, that the environment is more than physically threatened. Basically, the environment has a rational, or nonmaterial, aspect that is withering, and unless this element of the environment can be redeemed, all efforts to preserve the material world will be worthless.

Having nearly succumbed to the effluvia of the Anglo environment as a youth, I perceive that now (conscious of my origins and aware of the failure of the Anglo society) I, like any individual Chicano, have an obligation to assist my raza in some way. As every other American, I can make a contribution or cause harm to the national society. An individual may alter the course of history; many individuals together can assure that history will not merely happen. Whether an individual effort, mine or another Chicano's, will be beneficial to la raza is for la raza to decide; whether it is of consequence to the larger American society will at best be difficult to ascertain. But every effort must be made to end the war, to reclaim the forests and rivers, and to assure equality of rights. The Chicano has to be cognizant of his role in these crises, but he has the added duty of striving to liberate his people in any way he can.

This obligation resolved the quandary in my mind as to whether I should undertake the writing of this book: Would it serve the Chicano people? That question would never be answered if the book were not written and, after all, it is time for Chicanos to begin writing for ourselves. As it has turned out, for me the work has been like looking at a glass that at once reflects my own image and at the same time permits a view beyond. Introspection has led me to make certain evaluations and conclusions about the Chicanos, and contemplation on Chicanos has brought me to understand many things about myself. Clearly my role is not as a leader or spokesman but as a communicator of thought and inspiration.

Chicanos generally are undergoing the same kind of process. We are trying to achieve an equilibrium about ourselves as individuals and as members of a unique form of fraternity, living in a society that in many ways is alien but whose broad principles and modes of conduct we accept. But we do more than accept; we absorb and fuse into ourselves some features of the Anglo, the Mexican, the Spanish, the Indian, and the Negro, who for us are the other dominant factors of the American equation. Neither the Anglo, nor the Negro, nor the Indian does this. What does this kind of multicultural intuition promise for the future of the Chicano, of the United States, or of the world?

Fundamentally, I see the Chicano as the prototype of the citizen of the Americas a century from now. The Chicano is striving to assert a consciousness which will be the prerequisite for the thought and conduct of the fully civilized man of the next century. We are a people of prophecy. Like any prototype, the Chicano is not without flaws, but he does embody the process of acculturation that will have to take place throughout the Americas from Tierra del Fuego to the northernmost settlement. This is what the peoples of the Americas must come to—not that everyone will be poured into a single mold but that a balance of understanding and acceptance of other peoples and other cultures, and the assimilation or distillation of the best features of them all, will occur.

Walt Whitman wrote, prophetically, a century ago:

The seething materialistic and business vortices of the United States, in their present devouring relations, controlling and belittling everything else, are in my opinion but a vast and indispensable stage in the new world's development. Character, literature, a society worthy the name, are yet to be established. To that composite American identity of the future, Spanish character will supply some of the most needed parts. No stock shows a grander historic retrospect, grander in religiousness and loyalty, or for patriotism, courage, decorum, gravity and honor.

Whitman's "future" is still far off, but the character of which he took note still undergirds "that composite American identity" and will bring the future much closer, much sooner.

Someone once accused me of avarice for wanting

the best of two worlds—my psychological independence as a Chicano and the freedom as well to take the best of what the United States had to offer. I agreed, but I also pointed out that the United States steadily has less and less to offer. Besides, cultural isolationism or strict ethnocentrism are virtually impossible anywhere in the world. Hardly anyone remains untouched by modern technology and communications, or undefiled by the Anglo Americans' intrusiveness. In some way or other, the United States affects every nation in the world; yet, in the Latin American countries, its influence characteristically has been oppressive, colonialist, very often stupid, and sometimes fatal. In essence, Anglo American policy has been based on the conviction of racial or cultural supremacy—simply, that the United States is better than any other country or any other people. It is trying its best to imitate the colonial powers of previous centuries—England, France, Spain; it should not be surprised that its colonial victims are reacting as the United States itself did nearly two hundred years ago.

Anglo America's insensitivity to the aspirations of Latin American countries is usually clouded over by charges of "Communist influence," "red satellite," and "Castroite guerrillas." Such is the case in respect to the Latin nations' first insurgent action against the United States paternalismo in the twentieth century: Augusto Sandino of Nicaragua. His story is illustrative of North America's attitude and conduct toward Latin America in this century.

A revolt broke out in Nicaragua in 1909 against the dictator, José Santos Zelaya, involving U.S. intervention. Adolfo Díaz was chosen provisional president in 1910 and ruled until 1916. The Díaz regime itself came under public criticism, which led to a counterrevolution in 1912; some one thousand U.S. Marines, at Díaz' invitation, intervened to squelch the revolt. National elections in 1924 led to civil conflicts which threatened U.S.

interests. So, in 1925, U.S. Marines, which had only recently been withdrawn, were brought back to restore order. In 1928, U.S. Secretary of State Henry L. Stimson negotiated a peace between opposition leaders and the government (led again by Díaz, who had been installed as president by U.S. intervention the year before).

The peace provided for national elections in October 1928, but Sandino, an army general, refused to submit to the agreement. He resisted as a guerrilla fighter for five years, until early in 1933, when, following the general elections of 1932, he agreed to stop warring against government forces. All his followers, except one hundred, surrendered their arms, and all were given amnesty and land. In 1934, troops of the National Guard, which had been trained by U.S. Marines, executed Sandino in an ambush.

Historian Samuel Eliot Morison, in *The Oxford History of the American People*, describes Sandino:

A troublemaker from school days, he had escaped justice for murder and lived for several years in Mexico, where he made useful contacts with Communists and other left-wing elements. . . . The Communist party played him up as a hero of liberation . . . fooled gullible liberals in the United States and Europe into supporting Sandino as the savior of his country from the imperialists.

He concludes his report by noting cynically that Colonel Anastacio Somoza, who led the squad which shot Sandino down, "assumed the presidency and became a dictator. But Nicaragua was at peace."

Associated with communism, Sandino becomes a dupe rather than a savior. His troublemaker days as a youth seem to have had something to do with his actions as a rebel: he was a murderer and a fugitive, but his greatest sin was resisting the intrusion of the United States Government and its Marines. However, Morison admits that Sandino was "a precursor of Fidel Castro," although his only basis for the statement is Sandino's and Castro's relationship with Communist ideology, rather than their similarity of purpose and commitment to their countries. Sandino was this century's first national liberator of la raza. Castro had as many "gullible liberals" (including government officials) supporting his revolution; but it was not until he told the United States to go to hell and not until he irrevocably allied with the Soviet Union against "yanqui imperialismo" that the Anglo American government and press disavowed his national movement.

Gringo insensitivity, which sent Nixon to South America in 1956 and Governor Rockefeller there two years ago, must be dispelled by the Chicano. The United States will persist for a time in its arms deals, counterinsurgent forces, foreign aid, and outright exploitation by private corporations in league either with the Anglo government or with the dictators of Latin countries. North America persists in exporting its version of necessities and culture in order to corrupt other peoples. U.S. intent, of course, is to improve the material lot of the raza nations; in effect it merely advances U.S. entrepreneurs while adding to the moral decay of the raza countries. The Chicano, being part of both, can stand between these two worlds and exert a moral and humanistic influence on their conduct. Our leaders, writers, and artists must interpret the Chicano point of view and attempt to undo the harm of U.S. interventions, insolent secretaries of state, and stupid presidents who manage to perpetuate the crimes of the past. In so doing, Chicanos can awaken the concern and camarada of Latin American peoples to our common problems and simpatía. Perhaps we can establish a true alliance for progress.

We Chicanos have to project ourselves into the future if we are to move beyond today. We can inject into the seventies a new meaning of la raza as an international people; otherwise, the spiritual corruption of the peoples of the Americas will continue unabated, the persistent exploitation will go unchecked, and the indifference to the inhuman conditions of oppressed pueblos will inevitably lead to violent insurrection. Perhaps the Chicano can restore sanity to the American peoples.

The role that history seems to project for the Chicano involves the achievement within la raza Chicana, in the next few decades and certainly in the seventies, of a deeper understanding of our own personality and potential. We certainly have much to learn from the thinking of Latin Americans engaged in gaining independence from Anglo American economic and diplomatic control. We wish to have the same things on a national basis—not a severance of relations but a mutual understanding and interdependence. Just as the U.S. Department of State insists that South American countries must establish "responsible" economic structure, meaning just like North America's, which is impossible, the Anglo American society pressures everyone in America to become Anglo if they are to be true Americans—and that is also impossible.

Until now, Chicanos have had little influence in the development of a foreign policy toward Latin America or in regard to the U.S. foreign posture in general. For a while in 1968 we had a Chicano as an alternate delegate in the delegation to the United Nations, Dr. Hector P. Garcia. A few persons of Mexican American origin have held ambassadorships or high foreign service posts, but our presence in the Foreign Service or the Department of State is negligible. We've had many Peace Corps officials, particularly in administrative positions of national programs or orientation schools, but few Peace Corpsmen. We should in the near future attain positions as full delegates to the United Nations or ranking posts with Chicano legations, not only in Latin America but throughout the world. We should have a special post in the Department of State as an Assistant Secretary of State to Latin America, and later on, a cabinet post for a Secretary of Latin American Affairs.

As the Chicano revolt intensifies and becomes more definite in its goals, American society will be greatly affected by our new presence. We are now directing ourselves toward an irreversible impact with an as-yet-unsuspecting Anglo America. In doing so, we will force changes in political and economic structures, and we will arouse social turbulence as well. We may also prompt new barriers to be thrown up against the Chicano. In a few years, through this concerted effort, Latin America will become aware of the presence of an ally in its relations with the United States. The Chicano will imbue the whole society with an openness to other cultures, especially the Spanish-Indian, by making Anglo America aware of him and of the link, through him, with the peoples of Mexico, the Caribbean, Central and South America. Undoubtedly the United States will maintain its ugly Anglo American attitudes for some time to come. But hopefully, the Chicano will see to it that never again will we offer only gringoismo to the brother nations of the Western Hemisphere.

16

A PERSONAL MANIFESTO

I AM a Chicano. What that means to me may be entirely different from what meaning the word has for you. To be Chicano is to find out something about one's self which has lain dormant, subverted, and nearly destroyed.

I am a Chicano because of a unique fusion of bloods and history and culture. I am a Chicano because I sense a rising awareness among others like myself of a fresh rebirth of self and self-in-others.

I am a Chicano because from this revived and newly created personality I draw vitality and motivation more forceful and tangible than I ever did or could have from the gringo world.

I am a Chicano in spite of scorn or derision, in spite of opposition even from my own people, many of whom do not understand and may never fathom what Chicano means.

I am a Chicano, hopeful that my acceptance and assertion of Chicanismo will mean a better life for all my people, that it will move others into making the same act of will to accept and develop a new-found identity and power.

I am a Chicano, confident that through my efforts,

joined with other Chicanos, the Mexican American community will share fully in the benefits and responsibilities which are our birthright in the United States.

I am a Chicano, and I will resist any attacks against me or anyone else who is Chicano. We who call ourselves Chicanos recognize in that word something that is ours, a name that we have given to ourselves, not one that has been forced upon us by the Anglo.

Chicanos encompass a new way of looking at life, of interpreting history, of defending our social role, of rejecting an alien and degrading concept which the gringo would rather have us accept.

There is a mystique among us Chicanos, something that we have searched for and now have found. It draws us together, welds from insecure, disparate groups and viewpoints a common focal thought, experience, and power. For so many years we have disclaimed or claimed this or that label, sought leadership even from the Anglo, founded any number of organizations, worried over internal issues, fought for prestige and position within our little groups; and all the while the Anglo kept us in subjugation.

To be Chicano is nothing new; it is as old as our people. But it is a new way of knowing your brown brother and of understanding our brown race. To be Chicano means that a person has looked deeper into his being and sought unique ties to his brothers in la raza.

I nearly fell victim to the Anglo. My childhood was spent in the West Side barrio of San Antonio. I lived in my grandmother's house on Ruiz Street just below Zarzamora Creek. I did well in the elementary grades and learned English quickly.

Spanish was off-limits in school anyway, and teachers and relatives taught me early that my mother tongue would be of no help in making good grades and becoming a success. Yet Spanish was the language I used in playing and arguing with friends. Spanish was

the language I spoke with my abuelita, my dear grandmother, as I ate atole on those cold mornings when I
used to wake at dawn to her clattering dishes in the tiny
kitchen; or when I would cringe in mock horror at old
folk tales she would tell me late at night.

But the lesson took effect anyway. When at the age
of ten I went with my mother to California, to the San
Francisco Bay Area where she found work during the
war years, I had my first real opportunity to strip myself
completely of my heritage. In California the schools I
attended were all Anglo except for this little mexicanito.
At least, I never knew anyone who admitted he was
Mexican and I certainly never thought to ask. When my
name was accented incorrectly, Réndon instead of
Rendón, that was all right; finally I must have gotten
tired of correcting people or just didn't bother.

I remember a summertime visit home a few years
after living on the West Coast. At an evening gathering
of almost the whole family—uncles, aunts, nephews,
nieces, my abuelita—we sat outdoors through the dusk
until the dark had fully settled. Then the lights were
turned on; someone brought out a Mexican card game,
the Lotería El Diablito, similar to bingo. But instead of
rows of numbers on a pasteboard, there were figures of
persons, animals, and objects on cards corresponding to
figures set in rows on a pasteboard. We used frijoles
(pinto beans) to mark each figure on our card as the
leader went through the deck one by one. The word for
tree was called: Árbol! It completed a row; I had won.
Then to check my card I had to name each figure again.
When I said the word for tree, it didn't come at all as I
wanted it to: AR-BOWL with the accent on the last
syllable and sounding like an Anglo tourist. There was
some all-around kidding of me and good-natured laugh-
ter over the incident, and it passed.

But if I had not been speaking much Spanish up
until then, I spoke even less afterward. Even when my
mother, who speaks both Spanish and English fluently,

spoke to me in Spanish, I would respond in English. By the time I graduated from high school and prepared to enter college, the break was nearly complete. Seldom during college did I admit to being a Mexican American. Only when Latin American students pressed me about my surname did I admit my Spanish descent, or when it proved an asset in meeting coeds from Latin American countries.

My ancestry had become a shadow, fainter and fainter about me. I felt no particular allegiance to it, drew no inspiration from it, and elected generally to let it fade away. I clicked with the Anglo mind-set in college, mastered it, you might say. I even became editor of the campus biweekly newspaper as a junior, and editor of the literary magazine as a senior—not bad, now that I look back, for a tortillas-and-beans Chicano upbringing to beat the Anglo at his own game.

The point of my "success," of course, was that I had been assimilated; I had bought the white man's world. After getting my diploma I was set to launch out into a career in newspaper reporting and writing. There was no thought in my mind of serving my people, telling their story, or making anything right for anybody but myself. Instead I had dreams of Pulitzer Prizes, syndicated columns, foreign correspondent assignments, front page stories—that was for me. Then something happened.

A Catholic weekly newspaper in Sacramento offered me a position as a reporter and feature writer. I had a job on a Bay Area daily as a copyboy at the time, with the opportunity to become a reporter. But I'd just been married, and there were a number of other reasons to consider: there'd be a variety of assignments, Sacramento was the state capital, it was a good town in which to raise a family, and the other job lacked promise for upward mobility. I decided to take the offer.

My wife and I moved to Sacramento in the fall of 1961, and in a few weeks the radicalization of this Chi-

cano began. It wasn't a book I read or a great leader
awakening me, for we had no Chavezes or Tijerinas or
Gonzaleses at the time; and it was no revelation from
above. It was my own people who rescued me. There is
a large Chicano population in Sacramento, today one of
the most activist in northern California, but at the time
factionalized and still dependent on the social and
church organizations for identity. But together we
found each other.

My job soon brought me into contact with many
Chicanos as well as with the recently immigrated Mexicans, located in the barrios that Sacramento had allocated to the "Mexicans." I found my people striving to
survive in an alien environment among foreign people.
One of the first stories I covered concerned a phenomenon called Cursillos de Cristiandad (Little Courses in
Christianity), intense, three-day group-sensitivity sessions whose chief objective is the re-Christianization of
Catholics. To cover the story properly I talked my editor into letting me make a Cursillo.

Not only was much revealed to me about the phony
gilt lining of religion which I had grown up believing
was the Church, but there was an added and highly
significant side effect—cultural shock! I rediscovered
my own people, or perhaps they redeemed me. Within
the social dimension of the Cursillo, for the first time in
many years I became reimmersed in a tough, macho
ambiente (an entirely Mexican male environment).
Only Spanish was spoken. The effect was shattering. It
was as if my tongue, after being struck dumb as a child,
had been loosened.

Because we were located in cramped quarters, with
limited facilities, and the cooks, lecturers, priests, and
participants were men only, the old sense of machismo
and camarada was revived and given new perspective. I
was cast in a spiritual setting which was a perfect background for reviving my Chicano soul. Reborn but im-
perfectly, I still had a lot to learn about myself and

my people. But my understanding deepened and renewed itself as the years went by. I visited bracero
camps with teams of Chicanos; sometimes with priests
taking the Sacraments; sometimes only Chicanos, offering advice or assistance with badly needed food and
clothing, distributed through a bingo-game technique;
and on occasion, music for group singing provided by a
phonograph or a guitar. Then there were barrio organization work; migrant worker programs; a rural self-
help community development project; and confrontation with antipoverty agencies, with the churches, with
government officials, and with cautious Chicanos, too.

In a little San Francisco magazine called *Way*, I
wrote in a March 1966 article discussing *The Other
Mexican American:*

The Mexican American must answer at the same time: Who
am I? and, Who are we? This is to pose then, not merely a
dilemma of self-identity, but of self-in-group-identity. . . .
Perhaps the answer to developing a total Mexican American
concept must be left in the hands of the artist, the painter, the
writer, and the poet, who can abstract the essence of what it
is to be Mexican in America. . . . When that understanding
comes . . . the Mexican American will not only have acculturized himself, but he will have acculturized America to
him.

If anyone knew what he was talking about when he
spoke of the dilemma of who he was and where he belonged, it was this Chicano. I very nearly dropped out,
as so many other Mexican Americans have, under the
dragging pressure to be someone else, what most of
society wants you to be before it hands out its chrome-
plated trophies.

And that mystique—I didn't quite have it at the
time, or the right word for it. But no one did until just
the last few years when so many of us stopped trying to
be someone else and decided that what we want to be
and to be called is Chicano.

I owe my life to my Chicano people. They rescued

me from the Anglo kiss of death, the monolingual, monocultural, and colorless gringo society. I no longer face a dilemma of identity or direction. That identity and direction have been charted for me by the Chicano—but to think I came that close to being sucked into the vacuum of the dominant society.

Chicano is a beautiful word. Chicano describes a beautiful people. Chicano has a power of its own. Chicano is a unique confluence of histories, cultures, languages, and traditions.

Chicano is the one unique word of the Mexican American people. Its derivation is strictly internal; it owes nothing to the Anglo penchant for categorizing ethnic groups. In a way, Chicano is indefinable, more a word to be understood and felt and lived than placed in a dictionary or analyzed by Anglo anthropologists, sociologists, and apologists.

Chicano has the ring of pachuco slang, of shortening a word, which is typical of our Mexican American experience. It also echoes the harsher sounds of our native ancestors of the Mexican Valley, but is softened by the rounded-vowel endings of our Spanish forebears. It is the perfect word to characterize the mezcla that is la raza. It portrays the fact that we have come to psychological terms with circumstances which might otherwise cause emotional and social breakdowns among our people if we only straddle cultures and do not absorb them.

Chicano is a very special word. Chicano is a unique people. Chicano is a prophecy of a new day and a new world.

APPENDIX:
FOUR DECLARATIONS OF
INDEPENDENCE

These are four plans, or manifestos, which have been written by Chicanos and which evolved out of specific and significant events in the past five years.

EL PLAN DE DELANO

Plan for the liberation of the Farm Workers associated with the Delano Grape Strike in the State of California, seeking social justice in farm labor with those reforms that they believe necessary for their well-being as workers in these United States.

We, the undersigned, gathered in Pilgrimage to the capital of the State in Sacramento, in penance for all the failings of Farm Workers as free and sovereign men, do solemnly declare before the civilized world which judges our actions, and before the nation to which we belong, the propositions we have formulated to end the injustice that oppresses us.

We are conscious of the historical significance of our Pilgrimage. It is clearly evident that our path travels through a valley well known to all Mexican farm workers. We know all of these towns of Delano, Fresno, Madera, Modesto, Stockton, and Sacramento, because along this very same road, in this very same valley the Mexican race has sacrificed itself for the last hundred years. Our sweat and our blood have fallen on this land to make other men rich. Our wages and working conditions have been determined from above, because irresponsible legislators who could have helped us have supported the rancher's argument that the plight of the Farm Worker was a "special case." They saw the obvious effects of an unjust system, starvation wages, contractors, day hauls, forced migration, sickness, and sub-human conditions.

The farm worker has been abandoned to his own fate—without representation, without power—subject to the mercy and caprice of the rancher.

We are suffering. We have suffered unnumbered ills and crimes in the name of the Law of the land. Our men, women and children have suffered not only the basic brutality of stoop labor, and the most obvious injustices of the system; they have also suffered the desperation of knowing that that system caters to the greed of callous men and not to our needs.

Now we will suffer for the purpose of ending the poverty, the misery, and the injustice, with the hope that our children will not be exploited as we have been. They have imposed hungers on us, and now we hunger for justice. We draw strength from the very despair in which we have been forced to live. WE SHALL ENDURE!

This Pilgrimage is a witness to the suffering we have seen for generations. The Penance we accept symbolizes the suffering we shall have in order to bring justice to these same towns, to this same valley. This is the beginning of a social movement in fact and not in pronouncements.

We seek our basic God-given rights as human beings. Because we have suffered—and are not afraid to suffer—in order to survive, we are ready to give up everything, even our lives, in our fight for social justice. We shall do it without violence because that is our destiny.

To the ranchers and to all those who oppose us we say, in the words of Benito Juarez, "Respect for another's rights is the meaning of Peace."

We seek the support of all political groups, and the protection of the government, which is also our government. But we are tired of words, of betrayals, of indifference. To the politicians we say that the years are gone when the farm worker said nothing and did nothing to help himself. From this movement shall spring leaders who shall understand us, lead us, be faithful to us, and we shall elect them to represent us. We shall be heard!

We seek, and have, the support of the Church in what we do. At the head of the Pilgrimage we carry the Virgin of Guadalupe because she is ours, all ours, Patroness of the Mexican people. We also carry the Sacred Cross and the Star of David because we are not sectarians, and because we ask the help and prayers of all religions. All men are brothers, sons of the same God; that is why we say to all men of good will, in the words of Pope Leo XIII, "Everyone's first duty is to protect the workers from the greed of speculators who use human beings as instruments to provide themselves with money. It is neither just nor human to oppress with excessive work to the point where their minds become enfeebled and their bodies worn out." God shall not abandon us!

We shall unite. We have learned the meaning of unity. We know why these United States are just that— united. The strength of the poor is also in union. We know that the poverty of the Mexican or Filipino worker in California is the same as that of all farm workers across the country, the Negroes and poor whites, the Puerto Ricans, Japanese and Arabians; in short, all of the races that comprise the oppressed minorities of the United States. The majority of the people on our Pilgrimage are of Mexican descent, but the triumph of our race depends on a national association of farm workers. We must get together and bargain collectively. We must use the only strength that we have, the force of our numbers; the ranchers are few, we are many. United we shall stand!

We shall pursue the Revolution we have proposed. We are sons of the Mexican Revolution, a revolution of the poor seeking bread and justice. Our revolution shall not be an armed one, but we want the order which now exists to be undone, and that a new social order replace it.

We are poor, we are humble, and our only choice is to Strike in those ranches where we are not treated with the respect we deserve as working men, where our rights as free and sovereign men are not recognized. We do not want the paternalism of the ranchers; we do not want the contractor; we do not want charity at the price of our dignity. We want to be equal with all the working men in the nation; we want a just wage, better working conditions, a decent future for our children. To those who oppose us, be they ranchers, police, politicians, or speculators, we say that we are going to continue fighting until we die, or we win. We shall overcome!

Across the San Joaquin Valley, across California, across the entire Southwest of the United States, wherever there are Mexican people, wherever there are farm workers, our movement is spreading like flames across a dry plain. Our Pilgrimage is the match that will light our cause for all farm workers to see what is happening here, so that they may do as we have done.

The time has come for the liberation of the poor farm worker. History is on our side. May the Strike go on! Viva la causa!

March 1966

PLAN DE LA RAZA UNIDA
PREAMBLE

On this historic day, October 28, 1967, La Raza Unida organized in El Paso, Texas, proclaims the time of subjugation, exploitation and abuse of human rights of La Raza in the United States is hereby ended forever.

La Raza Unida affirms the magnificence of La Raza, the greatness of our heritage, our history, our language, our traditions, our contributions to humanity and our culture. We have demonstrated and proven and again affirm our loyalty to the Constitutional Democracy of the United States of America and to the religious and cultural traditions we all share.

We accept the framework of constitutional democracy and freedom within which to establish our own independent organizations among our own people in pursuit of justice and equality and redress of grievances. La Raza Unida pledges to join with all our courageous people organizing in the fields and in the barrios. We commit ourselves to La Raza, at whatever cost.

With this commitment we pledge our support in:

1. The right to organize community and labor groups in our own style.
2. The guarantee of training and placement in employment in all levels.
3. The guarantee of special emphasis on education at all levels geared to our people with strong financial grants to individuals.
4. The guarantee of decent, safe, and sanitary housing without relocation from one's community.
5. We demand equal representation at all levels of appointive boards and agencies, and the end to exploitative gerrymandering.

6. We demand the strong enforcement of all sections of the Treaty of Guadalupe Hidalgo particularly the sections dealing with land grants, and bilingual guarantees.

7. We are outraged by and demand an end to police harassment, discrimination and brutality inflicted on La Raza, and an end to the kangaroo court system known as juvenile hall. We demand constitutional protection and guarantees in all courts of the United States.

8. We reaffirm a dedication to our heritage, a bilingual culture and assert our right to be members of La Raza Unida anywhere, anytime and in any job.

THE DEL RIO MEXICAN AMERICAN MANIFESTO TO THE NATION

(Original Version as Read to an Audience of More than Two Thousand)

On this historic day, March 30, 1969, the Mexican American community of the United States of America stands in solidarity with the Mexican American poor of Del Rio, Texas. The infamy recently perpetrated upon them by local and state authorities has exhausted our patience. From throughout the country and all walks of life, we have come to join our voices with theirs in denouncing the forces that oppress them and us, and in demanding redress of their grievances and ours. We believe that both our denunciation and our demand are firmly in keeping with a country made up of minorities and committed to abide by democratic ideals.

Recent events in this city have made it amply clear that our minority continues to be oppressed by men and institutions using the language of democracy while resorting to totalitarian methods. A highly regarded OEO project of self-determination, the Val Verde County

VISTA Minority Mobilization program, has been arbi-
trarily cancelled by Governor Preston Smith at the request of three Anglo county commissioners representing
less than five percent of the population. The fourth
commissioner, a Mexican American representing the
rest of the citizens, while originally abstaining, joined
his vote to that of the other three following the Governor's decree. The charges were pathetic—a reflection of
nervous power-wielders who saw the growing assertiveness of the poor served by VISTA Mexican Americans
as a threat to their traditional supremacy. A collusion
was alleged between the VISTA volunteers and the
Mexican American Youth Organization (MAYO), a local
group of youngsters, mostly high schoolers, who frequently assail the injustices of what they call the "gringo
system." Without bothering to consult with the local
Community Action Program Board, or the Austin
Regional OEO office, both of which continue to endorse
the Del Rio VISTAs, the Governor sent wires to the
National VISTA office and to all Texas judges in whose
counties other VISTA programs are operating, informing them of the cancellation of the Val Verde County
program, and adding, "the abdication of respect for law
and order, disruption of the democratic process, and
provocation of disunity among our citizens shall not be
tolerated by this office."

A dispassionate analysis of this appalling misuse of
power by both the Val Verde Commissioners and the
Governor reveals it is they, not the poor, the VISTAs, or
MAYOs who are guilty of "abdication of respect for law
and order, disruption of the democratic process, and
provocation of disunity among our citizens." Del Rio
was no paradise of unity, before VISTAs and MAYOs
arrived. Except for minor differences of detail, the list of
local grievances they have dramatized parallel the experience of countless other communities where Mexican
Americans are still treated as conquered people. We see
our own conditions elsewhere as we review the sorry

catalogue that ᵀ ur destitute Del Rio brothers have shared with us in describing the Anglo-controlled establishment:

1. It is they who built a multi-million dollar school for their children, then built barracks for ours.
2. It is they who stole our land, then sold it back to us, bit by bit, crumb by crumb.
3. It is they who speak one language and resent us for speaking two.
4. It is they who preach brotherhood and practice racism.
5. It is they who make ado about equal opportunity but reserve it to themselves or their replicas.
6. It is they who proclaim concern for the poor through a welfare system calculated to keep our people in perpetual dependency.
7. It is their police system that harasses and over-polices our sons and daughters.
8. It is their educational system that violates the innocence of our children with required literature like *The Texas Story*, a book that caricatures our ancestors.
9. It is their double standard of justice—minimum penalty for gringo and maximum for Chicano—that makes criminals of our young men.
10. It is they who denounce our militancy but think nothing of the legal violence they inflict on us mentally, culturally, spiritually and physically.

There must be something invincible in our people that has kept alive our humanity in spite of a system bent on suppressing our difference and rewarding our conformity. It is such an experience of cultural survival that has led us to the recovery of the magnificence of LA RAZA. However we define it, it is a treasure house of spirituality, decency, and sanity. LA RAZA is the affirmation of the most basic ingredient of our personality, the brownhood of our Indian ancestors wedded to all the other skin colors of mankind. Brown is the common denominator of the largest number among us—a glorious reminder of our Aztec and Mayan heritage. But in a color-mad society, the sin of our coloration can be expiated only by exceptional achievement and successful imitation of the white man who controls every institution of society. LA RAZA condemns such a system as racist, pagan, and ultimately self-destructive. We can neither tolerate it nor be a part of it. As children of LA RAZA, we are heirs of a spiritual and biological miracle where in one family blood ties unite the darkest and the fairest. It is no accident that the objects of our veneration include the black Peruvian Saint Martin de Porres, the brown Indian Virgin of Guadalupe, the blond European madonnas, and a Jewish Christ of Indian and Spanish features.

We cannot explain our survival and our strength apart from this heritage—a heritage inseparably linked to Spanish, the soul language of LA RAZA. On this day we serve notice on Del Rio and the nation that for their sake and ours we are willing to lay down our lives to preserve the culture and language of our ancestors, to blend them with that which is best in these United States of America, our beloved country. Let no one forget that thousands of our Mexican American brothers have gallantly fought and died in defense of American freedoms enjoyed by us more in hope than reality. We shall escalate the defense of such freedoms here at home to honor those who fell for them yesterday, and to sustain those who live for their fulfillment tomorrow. We are committed to non-violence, even while living in the midst of officially tolerated violence. We are prepared, however, to be as aggressive as it may be necessary, until every one of our Mexican American brothers enjoys the liberty of shaping his own future.

We feel compelled to warn the Val Verde Commissioners and Governor Preston Smith that they are inviting serious social unrest if they do not immediately rescind their VISTA cancellation action. Likewise, we feel compelled to warn the United States Congress that unless legislation is enacted to protect the VISTA principle of self-determination from arbitrary termination by local and state officials, the entire concept of volunteer service, whether at home or abroad, will be prostituted in the eyes of those idealistic fellow-Americans who participate in it. Lastly, we feel compelled to warn the whole nation that unless the ideal of self-determination is upheld with our poor at home, the entire world will judge us hypocritical in our attempt to assist the poor abroad.

On this day, Mexican Americans commit themselves to struggle ceaselessly until the promise of this country is realized for us and our fellow-Americans: *one* nation, under God, *indivisible*, with liberty and justice for *all*.

THE SPIRITUAL PLAN OF AZTLÁN

(Crusade for Justice Youth Conference, Denver, Colorado)

In the spirit of a new people that is conscious not only of its proud heritage, but also of the brutal "gringo" invasion of our territories, *we*, the Chicano, inhabitants and civilizers of the northern land of Aztlán, from whence came our forefathers, reclaiming the land of their birth and consecrating the determination of our people of the sun, *declare* that the call of our blood is our power, our responsibility, and our inevitable destiny.

We are free and sovereign to determine those tasks which are justly called for by our house, our land, the sweat of our brows, and by our hearts. Aztlán belongs to those that plant the seeds, water the fields, and gather the crops, and not to the foreign Europeans. We do not recognize capricious frontiers on the Bronze Continent.

Brotherhood unites us, love for our brothers makes us a people whose time has come and who struggles against the foreigner "gabacho" who exploits our riches and destroys our culture. With our heart in our hand and our hands in the soil, we declare the independence of our mestizo Nation. We are a bronze people with a bronze culture. Before the world, before all of North America, before all our brothers in the Bronze Continent, we are a Nation. We are a union of free pueblos. We are *Aztlán.*

To hell with the nothing race.

All power for our people.
March 31, 1969

050685